NUMBER ONE

The Clayton Wheat Williams

TEXAS ★ LIFE ★ SERIES

Major funding for this series was provided by
CLAYTON W. WILLIAMS, JR.
Director, Texas Mercantile Corporation

PLANTATION LIFE IN TEXAS

Plantation

Life IN TEXAS

BY ELIZABETH SILVERTHORNE

ILLUSTRATED BY *Charles Shaw*

TEXAS A&M UNIVERSITY PRESS : COLLEGE STATION

Library of Congress Catloging-in-Publication Data

Silverthorne, Elizabeth.
    Plantation life in Texas.

    (The Clayton Wheat Williams Texas life series; no. 1)
    Bibliography: p.
    Includes index.
    1. Plantation life—Texas—History—19th century.
2. Texas—Social life and customs.   I. Title.
II. Series.
F391.S57   1986   976.406   86-5810
ISBN 0-89096-288-X

TO MY SISTERS
Sissy, Marge, Pat, and Jenny
WITH LOVE AND APPRECIATION FOR SUPPORT
I CAN ALWAYS COUNT ON

CONTENTS

ILLUSTRATIONS

While I was growing up in Brazoria County, I was only dimly aware of the ghosts of its antebellum days. The names of the owners of once flourishing cotton and sugar plantations were familiar to me. Their descendants—Perrys, Munsons, Bryans, Sweenys, Mastersons—were family friends and even distant relatives through marriage. Picnicking under great oaks dripping Spanish moss, riding horseback over the prairies, fishing in Oyster Creek and swinging across it on grapevines, swimming in the bayous and in the Gulf of Mexico, I was much more aware of cattle than of cotton as a source of county pride.

When away from home, we were taught to reply to those who asked, "Where do you come from?" by saying, "I'm from Angleton, Texas, the county seat of Brazoria County, the largest cattle raising county in Texas!" If that didn't make enough of an impression, we'd boast about the sulfur and oil production of Brazoria County.

An uncle of mine owned a part of Bailey's Prairie, near Angleton, where a pioneer planter named Brit Bailey had lived. Uncle Steve ran his cattle on Bailey's Prairie, and on Sunday afternoons it was a great treat for us children to drive out there. The highlight of our visit was to see Hattie and Burrell, a black couple, both of whom were descendants of slaves. They lived on the place and took care of it and the cattle. Hattie always had spicy hot gingerbread and cold buttermilk for us, and no other gingerbread has ever tasted as good. When we were older, she gave us coffee mellowed with fresh, thick cream.

At Christmastime, we went deep into the woods to find holly, mistletoe, and yaupon for decorating and to pick little sour green grapes for our grandmother to make pies of. Some cattle owners in the area pulled down moss in winter for extra fodder, but we children used it to make huge nests and for hair, furs, and beards in our games.

A part of our ritual on visits to Bailey's Prairie was to visit eccentric Brit Bailey's grave, which was marked by a Cherokee rosebush. We heard and repeated the legends of his ghost, which appeared as a ball of light, as described later in chapter 5. About a century after his death, when a fire occurred in the West Columbia oil field only a few miles from Bailey's Prairie, the story was told that either the light of Bailey's lantern or a shot from his rifle had set off the explosion that started the fire, because Bailey resented having the field so close to his old plantation site.

My Uncle Steve was a trustee for the black school on Bailey's Prairie, and we attended the graduations with him. There were displays of handicraft and needlework and recitations. Knowing how much he enjoyed their music, the teachers always asked our uncle to request his favorite songs. These were mostly spirituals and included "Amazing Grace." "Swing Low, Sweet Chariot," always the last song, was drawn out to a plaintive sweetness in the little school in the woods.

On Juneteenths we went to the barbecue feasts on Bailey's Prairie as guests of the black school. Long before we reached the site, the aroma of the beef and pork, cooking in open pits all night and basted with a tangy sauce, made our mouths water. There was usually barbecued squirrel also. The climax of the meal was hand-cranked ice cream that melted with a delicious coolness on the tongue in the mid-June heat.

As I grew older, I acquired bits and pieces of knowledge about the "olden golden" age of the plantations in Brazoria County. There were school field trips to Peach Point to visit the site of the Perry-Austin plantation; visits to the Varner-Hogg plantation near West Columbia; a visit to the Bingham plantation, where one of my teachers, Miss Bettie Bingham, lived in the family home; and visits to the four state prison farms that had been built on the sites of at least a dozen plantations.

In spite of my casually acquired knowledge, I had no idea of the extent and the importance of the cotton and cane plantations that existed in Brazoria County before the Civil War. And I was even less aware of the large number of plantation domains that extended along a wide crescent running from the Gulf to the Red River.

Anyone who wants to learn about Texas plantations turns first to the fruits of Abigail Curlee Holbrook's lifelong exploration of the subject. In her master's thesis (1922), her doctoral dissertation (1932), and her articles in the *Southwestern Historical Quarterly* up to the 1970s, she has, with clarity and fairness, examined the operation and management of Texas plantations. Plantation researchers also owe a heavy debt of gratitude to Dr. Holbrook for her ability to persuade the owners of many documents and valuable correspondence relating to Texas plantations to donate this material to the archives of the University of Texas.

Two other writers have done in-depth research on individual plantations. Dorman Winfrey has given us a good picture of Julien Sidney Devereux's Monte Verdi plantation, and Marie Beth Jones has accurately traced the history of Peach Point plantation and the people who lived there.

In the 1930s the Works Progress Administration (WPA) sent interviewers throughout the South to find and talk with former slaves about their lives on plantations. This material has been skillfully collected and edited by George P. Rawick. After Rawick edited and published one series of interviews, he discovered that many of them had already been edited to omit some of the unpleasant facts about slavery. Using the original manuscripts that he found at the Barker Texas History Center at the University of Texas at Austin, he issued a new series which included the information that had been omitted from the first version. The original documents from the Texas interviews, which include a number of pictures taken by the interviewers, I have read in their entirety and compared with Rawick's first and second versions. For the sake of convenience, I have used Rawick's page numbers for reference as it is difficult to locate specific interviews in the original manuscripts, which are unnumbered and filed according to the region in which the interview took place. The originals of the Texas interviews and the photographs may be examined at the Barker Texas History Center.

The "slave narratives" must be used with a few cautions in mind. The former slaves' statements quoted in this book must be read with patience, recognizing that the persons who conducted the interviews and wrote down the former slaves' stories were not trained linguists. Thus, many of them tried to duplicate the slaves' speech on paper, some interviewers selecting spellings they recognized from contemporary written sources as being considered "black dialect." Other interviewers rendered all words in perfect grammar and spelling. In this book, all quotations from the slave narratives are given exactly as taken down by the WPA interviewers.

Also, the men and women interviewed were remembering back six, seven, or more decades. Many of them were still children when the Civil War ended, and quite a bit of what they relate was told to them. Some were on government pensions and fearful of losing them if they said things not pleasing to white "authorities" (and the interviewers actually were working for the government). As one interviewee put it, some blacks "closed the door" when talking to white people, refusing to relate their actual experiences as slaves. For some, time had erased and healed old hurts, while for others, bitterness and hatred had increased with the hard times in the thirties. Also, the most lurid stories of cruelty were those most apt to be frequently repeated and remembered among the slaves. Thus, one terrible incident, such as a pregnant woman being flogged while lying with her belly in a hole to save the baby, would be repeated until it was believed to have been a common event. Any generalizations I have drawn from these narratives have been arrived at after seeing facts repeated by a substantial number of interviewees.

The slave narratives can be (and have been) used by writers who extract from them only the information wanted to prove a certain viewpoint. But if they are used with fairness, the stories can be invaluable to show the black child's experiences on plantations, the interactions between owners and bondsmen, the slaves' day-to-day lives, their aggravations and pleasures as well as their dreams and fears. Details pertaining to shelter, food, and clothing as well as to religious experiences and recreations are revealed, as are the variety of working conditions on different plantations.

If this book comes close to fulfilling my purpose of cutting through myths about life on Texas plantations by giving an even-handed account of daily life, it is because I have received so much help in writing it.

My research has included visits to still-existing plantation homes and the homes of the descendants of plantation owners. I have found that the tradition of gracious hospitality is very much alive in these Texans. Many opened their homes to me, shared their family papers, toured me around their areas, and fed me delicious meals. I regret that space will only allow me to mention a few of the people who have kindly helped me in many different ways.

In San Augustine Mrs. C. T. Dorsey showed me through the expertly restored William Garrett plantation. At the Harrison County Historical Society Museum in the old courthouse in Marshall, I found much material on East Texas plantations, and I especially appreciate the assistance of Mrs. M. L. Scott Goldberg, Mrs. B. Scott, and Jim Caldwell, who took me to see Edgemont and other plantations.

At Karnack, Jerry E. Jones showed me through the plantation home of Lady Bird Johnson. In the charming Historical Museum in Jefferson I spent two pleasant days. And after touring the Freeman plantation, the present owner, Jesse DeWare IV, lent me his personal files and gave me a carton of fine East Texas preserves. On a beautiful fall morning, the curators of Monte Verdi gave me a tour and helpful information.

Pam Puryear of Navasota took me on a "plantation ramble," which included Washington, Anderson, and Grimes counties. She also shared with me her extensive personal files and her mother's grand cooking.

At Liendo plantation (now a ranch) I shared a delightful morning and lunch with Carl Detering, Sr., the present owner. And that afternoon I gathered much useful information on the Groce family in the Waller County Library in Hempstead.

In Angleton I visited with many descendants of plantation owners. I owe special thanks to Ruth Munson Smith for sharing her home and her personal files, to Dorothy Cotton for a tour of the Levi Jordan plantation, to John Bannister for showing me the Sweeny plantation and for information from his family file, and to Marie Beth Jones for sharing her files. Paul Strohm of the Brazoria County Central Library and Robert Stough of the Brazoria County Historical Museum gave me valuable assistance.

I owe thanks to Millie and Joe Bill Foster of Calvert, Texas, for a wonderful "plantation" lunch and tour and for sharing family papers. I am grateful for information furnished by Mrs. Sterling Robertson of Salado and by Mrs. Elisabeth Bates Nisbet of Houston.

My debt to librarians and curators in various towns and cities is great. As usual, the fine staff of the Barker Texas History Center, headed by Ralph Elder, have been of tremendous help as have the Texas State Library archivists. I particularly appreciate Dorman Winfrey's lending me material and taking time to discuss Monte Verdi with me. Curators Ellen N. Murry of The Star of the Republic Museum at Washington and Bettie A. Regester of the Parks and Recreation Department at Fort Worth gave me valuable assistance, as did Jane Kenamore of the Rosenberg Library at Galveston. I especially wish to thank Judy Kuykendall, Chris Boldt, and the staff of the Temple Public Library; Rose Anne Brasher of the Temple Junior College library; and Mary Pat McLaughlin of the Railroad and Pioneer Museum of Temple for their help.

Several people have graciously submitted to lengthy telephone interviews, including Inez Hughes of Marshall, Robert Strange of Gay Hill, Tom Scott of Bonham, and Mrs. Elisabeth Bates Nisbet of Houston.

Many people have furnished me with valuable leads. Among them are Bebe Ulrich of Crockett, Jane Judge Greer of Tyler, James L. Nichols of Nacogdoches, Richard Bauman of Austin, Mrs. Guy Adriance of Brenham, Cherry Brunson of Houston, Elmo Schwab of Galveston, Weldon Cannon of Temple, and John Wheat of Austin.

I owe special thanks to Thelma Fletcher of Salado, who shared with me her time, her knowledge of Texas history, her books, and her enthusiasm for my project. Lonnie Edwards, Mary Hill, and Carl and Mary Jane Taylor are other Salado friends who have generously lent me material from their personal libraries.

A number of people have been kind enough to suffer through the reading of a rough draft of some of the chapters to make sure I got them right. These include my brother-in-law Robert Merrill; my sisters, Patricia Merrill, Maxine Davidson, Margery Berndt, and Geneva Fulgham; and my friends, Ed and Glen Easterwood.

PLANTATION LIFE IN TEXAS

CHAPTER ONE

The Beginning

"Texas is the garden spot of the world."
—Davy Crockett

THE HERITAGE

The planters who made their way to Texas by covered wagon or on slow boats in the early nineteenth century brought with them bred-in-the-bone traditions and attitudes. Along with slaves and seeds, they carried ideas and ideals about the kind of life they wanted to create for themselves.

Although adaptations had to be made because of differences in soil and weather, the plantation system they established in Texas was essentially an extension of the plantation system of the southern United States. Their deep-rooted belief that slave labor was necessary to manage a large agricultural operation dated back to the establishment of plantations during the colonial days of America.

At first the American colonists thought they could supply their labor needs by using indentured servants from Europe. These laborers agreed to work a number of years for the employer, who had paid the servants' passage to the New World. Although twenty blacks were brought to Jamestown, Virginia, as indentured servants in 1619, chattel slavery was slow to develop in the American colonies. There is no specific date to mark its official sanctioning. Plantation owners began to take away the rights of their black servants as they came to realize gradually that a system of slavery had advantages over the indenture system of servitude. Custom predated law. However, by the end of the seventeenth century, Maryland and Virginia had passed statutes providing that: (1) blacks were to be slaves for life, (2) the child was to inherit the condition of the mother, and (3) Christian baptism did not change the slave's status. Over the years, additional laws defined the slaves as property and prohibited interracial marriages. As one historian pointed out: "The master class, for its own purposes, wrote chattel slavery, the caste system, and color prejudice into American custom and law."[1]

The demands of European tobacco addicts provided a great stimulus to the growth of the plantation system and its accompanying need for a large labor force. After Sir Walter Raleigh popularized tobacco smoking in England and Jean Nicot introduced it in France,[2] tobacco plantations multiplied in Maryland and Virginia. Dutch and German smokers also developed a craving for the American weed, and for many years tobacco was the chief product of the southern colonies. In Virginia, Maryland, and North Carolina, tobacco became a legal medium of exchange, and doctors, lawyers, and ministers were often paid with the golden leaves of tobacco instead of gold or silver coins.

American planters began to import African slaves by the shipload. When these planters found that tobacco rapidly exhausted the land on which it grew, they were not dismayed. The supply of land in America seemed endless and was easily obtained. There were also other crops with good marketing potential. After 1700, South Carolina sprouted plantations that raised rice and indigo, which was used in making blue or purple dye and in laundering. When Americans lost their British indigo markets during the Revolutionary War, the planters turned to raising cotton and became well known for the silky-fibered Sea Island cotton grown on the islands off the coasts of South Carolina and Georgia. Rice plantations were established in North Carolina and in Georgia. Many of the white indentured servants refused to work in the swampy, malaria-infested rice fields, and the rice plantations consequently developed a huge appetite for black slave labor.

As provincial America began to depend less on subsistence agriculture and more on the cultivation and manufacture of products to sell in world markets at the beginning of the eighteenth century, land became the capital needed to supply revenue, and the desire for more laborers to work the land increased accordingly. For the next one hundred years, American slave ships joined those of European nations in exploiting the human resources of Africa. Northern as well as southern families made fortunes in the slave-trading business. And across the ocean, African kings waged war on each other in order to capture enemy tribesmen to sell or exchange with the traders for guns, rum, cloth, and other items. Hundreds of thousands of Africans were carried to North and South America in the dark, stinking, filthy holds of slave ships. Many of the captives died en route from brutality, from disease, or by suicide.[3]

By the mid-eighteenth century, the number of slaves in the colonies had increased dramatically. In Virginia the slave population leaped from 2,000 in 1670 to 23,000 in 1715, and rose to 150,000 by the eve of the American

1. Kenneth M. Stampp, *The Peculiar Institution: Slavery in the Antebellum South,* pp. 22–23.

2. The genus *Nicotiana tabacum*, to which tobacco belongs, is derived from his name.

3. *Encyclopaedia Britannica*, 1977 ed., XVIII, 952.

Revolution. In South Carolina in 1700 there were about 2,500 blacks in the population. By 1765, there were 80,000 to 90,000, with the blacks outnumbering the whites by 2 to 1.[4]

There were many in the colonies who opposed slavery from the beginning. Following the Revolutionary War, the U.S. Congress passed legislation prohibiting the importation of African slaves after January 1, 1808, but the law was poorly enforced, and slave merchants continued to practice their highly lucrative trade of bringing in human cargoes. Nevertheless, in addition to the Quakers, who were always strongly against the institution of slavery, others began to speak out against the evils of the system. A strong movement arose to abolish slavery entirely in America. For a brief moment it seemed that peaceful emancipation might really be possible.

But on a Georgia plantation a clever Yankee inventor was working on an invention that would destroy that possibility. As a boy of twelve, Eli

4. Ibid.

Whitney had made a violin, and during the Revolutionary War while still in his teens, he had run his own business, making hand-wrought nails. Now he was working on a machine that would clean the seed from cotton as fast as fifty men working by hand could do it. After 1793, Whitney's cotton gin made it practical to grow cotton at a profit, and cotton cultivation was well suited to the gang labor of slaves. The timing was perfect. In England, newly perfected spinning and weaving machines were hungry for cheap cotton to use in producing textiles. With the new market and the new ability to remove the seed from the fiber economically, cotton growers increased their acreage, and the demand for slave labor was greater than ever. The chance for peaceful emancipation vanished—never to come again. And slave smuggling flourished.

After Louisiana joined the Union in 1812, the sugarcane planters there became good customers for slaves. It took a large work force to run a sugar plantation. The cane had to be ground within a few hours after it was harvested, and the production of syrup and sugar required the time and attention of many men. The demand for slaves also grew when the large cotton-growing states of Mississippi and Alabama joined the United States in 1817 and 1819.

On the tobacco, rice, indigo, sugar, and cotton plantations, the planters developed similar life-styles. They used their slaves to plant, weed, and harvest crops. Those slaves who showed quickness and tractableness were trained as blacksmiths, tanners, coopers, weavers, carpenters, and bricklayers. The most presentable and trustworthy slaves were used as house servants and carriage drivers.

The large plantation owners formed a squirearchy with considerable political power. Many of them sent their children to England to be educated, and most of them belonged to the Anglican church. Amid tall pines, moss-hung oaks, and fragrant magnolia trees they built their stately mansions with spacious galleries and verandas supported by graceful, soaring pillars.

These planters did none of the actual physical labor, but worked at planning, hiring overseers, trading slaves and horses, and selling their crops to London merchants. On the return trip to America, the ships that had taken their product to market sailed into their private ports bringing Dutch linens, French cambrics, gold and silver lace, damask tablecloths, almonds, chocolate, fine tea, and large quantities of Madeira wine. The ships also brought the planters furniture, the styles and makers' names of which would become classics—Chippendale, Hepplewhite, Sheraton, and the Adam Brothers. The plantation owners lived like English country squires, delighting in their fine horses and hounds. Their leisure was spent reading, attending horse races, hunting, drinking, gambling, entertaining, and being entertained by their peers. They prided themselves on their chivalry toward women and were quick to defend their own "honor" and that of their female kinfolk. Dueling was one method of accomplishing this.

French officers who had come to the aid of the American colonists during the Revolutionary War introduced them to the French version of the code of honor known as dueling. In America, dueling almost immediately became more deadly than it was in France, where swords were the common weapon and where a wound in which blood was drawn was considered satisfactory. The American duel was more likely to be fought with pistols (the choice of weapons belonging to the challenged) and often ended in the death of one of the contestants.[5]

Many famous Americans such as Aaron Burr, Alexander Hamilton, Andrew Jackson, Commodore Stephen Decatur, Henry Clay, and John Randolph fought duels. Only gentlemen fought duels, and it was not necessary for a man to accept the challenge of a person below his social level who might be pretentious enough to challenge him. Aristocratic planters, who were likely candidates for duels, frequently owned an elaborate set of matched dueling pistols, engraved or etched on the metal parts and inlaid with mother-of-pearl, carved stag's horn, and rare wood.

ON THE WAY TO TEXAS

By the end of the Revolutionary War much of the land in the old settlements was worn out by wasteful and careless farming methods. Explorers, trappers, and hunters were leading the way across the Appalachians through the Cumberland Gap to the fertile, virgin lands beyond. Along with the "cabin and corn patch" farmers, debt evaders like Daniel Boone, and land speculators, the large planters looked westward toward the vast "promised land" on the other side of the mountains.

One of these early pioneer planters was Col. David Meade, who sent his slaves ahead from Old Virginia to the bluegrass country near Lexington to prepare a plantation there. Then he and his family followed and in time developed Chaumière du Prairie, one of the most famous Kentucky plantations.[6]

The large planters, who could afford the best transportation available, traveled in the top-of-the-line wagons—the Conestogas. Developed by German settlers in Pennsylvania, these "camels of the prairies" had curved wagon beds that kept the cargo from rolling and spilling out as they went up and down hill. There were also brakes and skids to aid in going downhill. The Conestogas were usually red, white, and blue, with dark blue underbodies, bright red upper woodwork, and white Osnaburg (heavy canvas) tops. The large, broad wheels were helpful in getting through mud, and the construction of the wagons was so tight that they could be floated across

5. Robert Baldick, "Duel," *The Complete Encyclopedia of Arms and Weapons*, p. 456.
6. Clement Eaton, *A History of the Old South*, p. 128.

water. Weighing about three thousand pounds, they could carry from three to four tons. Their speed was about two or three miles per hour, depending on whether they were being pulled by teams of horses or oxen, the latter more often the case on long trips. For safety and company, the settlers usually traveled in caravans of dozens of wagons.

Barrels of flour, dried fruits, dried beef, and corn were carried for meals along the way. Chickens, hogs, and cows also provided eggs, meat, milk, and butter. These supplies were supplemented with buffalo meat and other wild game and with berries and whatever wild fruits the land yielded.[7]

Adventurous planters from Kentucky and Tennessee followed the Natchez Trace to Natchez, Mississippi, which was the extreme western edge of the frontier in 1800. They planted their cotton in the rich soil along the Mississippi and built their mansions on the bluffs overlooking the river, giving the estates romantic names that testify to the owners' longing for an aristocratic way of life.

Near Natchez, a young man named Jim Bowie fought a duel in which he almost lost his life as the knife he held twisted from his grip. Legend has it that he complained to his brother, Rezin Bowie, who then designed and gave to him a knife that had a long blade with a cutting edge and a false cutting edge, a short hilt with arms, and a grip with wooden or horn sidepieces. This well-balanced knife was 10 to 15 inches long and 1¾ inches wide. It became one of the most important weapons of the American pioneers, who used it for everything from hunting, skinning animals, and eating to fighting duels.[8]

The strange interlude that was the War of 1812 checked the westward movement only briefly, and between 1815 and 1836 the Great Migration flowed inexorably on. One of the events that gave the movement impetus was Maj. Gen. Andrew Jackson's crushing defeat of the Creek Indians at Horseshoe Bend in 1814 and the treaty by which he extorted from them more than twenty million acres of desirable farming land in Georgia and Alabama.

Early in the westward movement, the U.S. government sold land to the emigrating settlers of the new southern states on easy credit, and even a poor planter could acquire land and set up his own small estate. But in 1820, the federal government abolished the credit system and set a minimum price of $1.25 an acre, in cash. Land speculation was no longer the great bonanza it had been in the new states, and some of the more adventurous planters began to look with interest still farther west to Texas, then a province of Spain.

Moses Austin, an aging but still adventurous Connecticut Yankee who had made and lost a fortune in lead mining in Missouri, obtained per-

7. Clarence P. Hornung, *Wheels across America*, pp. 21–23.
8. The Bowie knife was refined by various blacksmiths. It was popular with Texas Rangers and with pirates on the Mississippi River. A form of this knife was used by British and American commandos in World War II. "Bowie Knife," *The Complete Encyclopedia of Arms and Weapons*, pp. 100–101; *Handbook of Texas* I, 197–98.

mission from the Spanish government to bring three hundred American settlers into Texas. When Austin died before he could complete plans to lead this expedition, his twenty-seven-year-old son Stephen undertook to carry out his father's plans. The first settlers he introduced into Texas included a number of pioneers, but they were by no means the first planters or farmers in Texas.

Indian tribes from the Big Bend to the piney woods grew corn and vegetables, and in the early 1700s, Spanish missions were established in Texas to Christianize the Indians and teach them agricultural and domestic skills. The crops planted and animals raised were vital to the missions because importing food and clothing was so difficult. Corn, vegetables, cotton, and tobacco were raised successfully by the mission dwellers, but the failure to convert Indians to Christianity and European ways led to the decline of the mission system by 1800.

A few Anglo-Americans straggled into Texas between 1800 and 1820, but these were mostly traders and filibusters more interested in making deals for furs and hides or in stirring up trouble between Mexico and Spain than in cultivating the land. However, up in the extreme northeast corner of Texas, in what would become Red River County, there were about eighty families in several small communities by 1821. When Stephen F. Austin opened up his colony that year, a few of these families came down to join it.

While the pioneer Anglo-American planters were cutting trees to build their log dwellings and clearing land to plant their first crops, Mexico was fighting for its independence from Spain. In 1821 Spain acknowledged Mexico's independence, but the government of Mexico remained unstable for many years as various leaders fought among themselves for control of the country.

The Mexican Constitution of 1824 united the provinces of Coahuila and Texas as one state and offered generous quantities of free land to settlers. Many men rushed to become empresarios, or agents, to bring in families to settle the land, but only a few were successful. Among the most capable of the empresarios were Austin, Sterling C. Robertson, and Green DeWitt, who settled several thousand families in the lush prairie lands and along the rich river bottoms of south central Texas during the Colonial Period.

The land of the towering pines and moss-hung cypress in East Texas also attracted farmers. In April of 1825, an empresario named Hayden Edwards received a grant allowing him to settle the land between the Sabine and the Navasota rivers with a total of eight hundred families.

Advertisements, placed in U.S. newspapers by Austin and the other empresarios, promised a planter's paradise of virgin soil with abundant timber and water. The ads also implied that the Mexican government was kindly and liberal toward Anglo-American settlers. For planters struggling to raise crops on worn-out, eroded farmland, and given the high price of land in the

States (which had to be paid for in cash), the offer of fertile land for the small fee of 12½ cents an acre to cover the costs of surveying and paperwork was enticing.

In addition to exhausted soil, there were other motives that led the early planters to uproot themselves and their families to start over in a land that, in spite of all its inducements, held many dangers, such as Indians and wild animals as well as all the other difficulties of a pioneer existence. Undoubtedly some came to Texas to escape problems in their private lives. The very difficulty of traveling dissuaded the likes of debt collectors or other pursuers, making it easier to run away from debts, pending court trials, unhappy environments, and broken love affairs. Merchants who were stuck with unpaid accounts regretfully initialed them "G.T.T." to indicate that the debtors had "gone to Texas" without settling their bills.

Others came for a more adventurous existence, responding to the challenge of the questing spirit that has always led some men and women to leave the old and known for the excitement of the new and unknown. Business and professional men came to speculate in land or to practice a profession and became converts to agriculture. A few planters came with visions of building an empire—with cotton as its king.

They had to learn to measure their land in *varas* (32 to 43 inches) instead of yards and their holdings in *leagues* (4,428 acres) and *labors* (177 acres). And they had to go through a curious ceremony to take formal possession of their land. On July 6, 1824, the "commissioners," Baron de Bastrop and Stephen Austin together with three witnesses and a surveyor, went with William Kincheloe to the land he proposed to take over. The survey of the land was carefully recorded and included such markers as a red oak two feet in diameter, a pecan, a cottonwood, an ash tree, and the Colorado River. Then Austin reported to the Mexican government: "We put the said William Kincheloe in possession of said tract of land taking him by the hand and causing him to walk over them, telling him in loud and audible words that by virtue of the Commission and powers in us vested and in the name of the government of the Mexican Nation we put him in possession of said tracts of land. . . ." Then Kincheloe, to show that he was in possession of the land, "cried out, pulled weeds, threw stones, drove stakes and performed the other necessary solemn acts. . . ."[9]

Abigail Curlee noted that historians and economists generally defined a planter as "one whose family had ceased to labor in the field beside his slaves and who himself either directed agricultural operations or delegated the management to another."[10] Small farmers with little land and few slaves but large aspirations sometimes called themselves planters. On the other hand, some sugarcane growers listed themselves on census rolls as "sugar manufacturers." T. R. Fehrenbach defines a planter as a farmer with at

9. Annie Lee Williams, *A History of Wharton County*, pp. 7–9.
10. Abigail Curlee, "A Study of Texas Slave Plantations, 1822–1865," p. 28.

least twenty slaves.[11] Obviously, it is necessary to be somewhat arbitrary in distinguishing between a planter and a farmer.

The colonists who came to Texas to take advantage of its agricultural potential can be divided into three groups: (1) yeoman farmers who managed small crops with only the help of their families and, perhaps, fewer than ten slaves, whom they owned or hired by the season; (2) small planters who owned from ten to fifty slaves and who often acted as their own overseers; and (3) large plantation owners who owned more than fifty slaves, employed one or more overseers, and who sometimes owned more than one plantation.[12]

Although farmers of the first group were by far the most numerous and were the backbone of Texas society, this book is concerned with the other two groups, whose farms (with at least twenty slaves) will be classified as plantations. They soon owned a disproportionate amount of the best land in Texas, and they had an influence on Texas affairs far out of proportion to their numbers. Their time on the stage of Texas history was brief, less than fifty years, but the impression they made lives on in institutions and in ways of thinking and doing handed down through generations of their own descendants and those of their slaves.

GONE TO TEXAS

A number of the planters in Austin's first colony, called the Old Three Hundred, were would-be empire builders. Jared E. Groce was one of the most successful of these. Born on a Virginia plantation, Groce had been moving west all of his life, observing and managing plantations in Georgia and in Alabama before setting out for Texas. The forty-year-old widower came to his new home as well prepared as any man could be to face the hazards of life on the frontier.

In January of 1822, mounted on fine thoroughbred horses, he and his oldest son, Leonard W. Groce, and an overseer led a caravan of fifty covered wagons into Texas. An experienced traveler, Groce carried along pontoons with which he ferried his wagons across rivers. The caravan included the women and children of his family, more than ninety slaves, furniture, spinning wheels, looms, clothing, farming equipment for a large operation, and food to feed this entourage along the way. A train of livestock, including mules, cows, sheep, hogs, and extra horses, followed the wagons.

Groce chose the site of a high bluff by the Brazos River, four miles south of the present town of Hempstead, for his home. Dividing his work force, he set some of them to building a small log cabin for immediate shelter

11. T. R. Fehrenbach, *Seven Keys to Texas*, p. 5.
12. Francis Butler Simkins and Charles Pierce Roland, *A History of the Old South*, p. 132.

and the rest to clearing the ground to plant the seed corn and the cottonseed he had brought along. He named his plantation Bernardo.

The severe drought of 1822 had no respect for empire builders, and when his corn crop failed, Groce and his family and slaves had no bread until a crop was raised successfully in 1823. Like the other colonists, the Groce household became dependent on wild game for subsistence. They found that the deer were lean and the turkeys fleet. However, fat mustangs were plentiful and easily captured, and the flesh could be made into jerky of any degree of dryness. Perhaps to fool their appetites, they considered the driest jerky their bread and the less dry their meat. Another great trial during the first year was living without salt.

Although the first corn crop failed, the dry weather and rich, virgin soil produced cotton more abundantly than even an experienced planter like Groce had expected. But getting the cotton to market was difficult. The first crops were taken to Mexico on pack mules. Colonel Groce always led the party himself, accompanied by his body servant, Edom. Because his arms were crippled, Groce was dependent on Edom for many services.

One slave could manage ten or twelve pack mules, walking or riding behind them, urging them on by loud yells. The small bales of cotton, weighing seventy-five or eighty pounds each, were strapped to each side of a mule, and a sack of feed tied on top of its back. The drove of mules walked in single file along Indian trails, which were the only roads, and did well to make eighteen to twenty miles per day.

At night the caravan camped around a fire, and the mules, relieved of their burdens, were hobbled nearby. The travelers felt secure from Indian attacks because they believed the Indians were too afraid of black men to attack them. Nevertheless, they went heavily armed. In Mexico, Groce exchanged his cotton for coffee, tea, and clothing, which he needed badly, and for sacks of Mexican silver dollars, for which he had little use.[13]

Eventually Groce built a landing near his plantation. This enabled him to float his cotton on homemade flatboats down the Brazos River to Velasco and put it aboard schooners for shipment to New Orleans, where it would be sold by agents. Other plantation owners as well as many travelers made use of this landing, which was called Groce's Ferry.

Groce's oldest son, Leonard, returned to Georgia to complete his studies, which he had interrupted in order to help his family move to Texas. When he came back to Texas, he took over much of the responsibility of running his father's business, which was constantly expanding. In 1825 Leonard brought the first cotton gin to that part of Texas.

13. Some of the Mexican silver was made into plates and tableware. Leonard Waller Groce, "Personal Recollection of Leonard Waller Groce, as Related to His Son, William Wharton Groce," transcript, Barker Texas History Center. Rosa Groce Bertleth, "Jared Ellison Groce," *Southwestern Historical Quarterly* 20 (Apr. 1917): 358–68.

The Groce family's plantation empire continued to grow until the time of the Civil War. After a few years Jared Groce built himself another plantation in present-day Grimes County in order to escape the malaria of the Brazos River bottoms. Appropriately, this home was called Groce's Retreat. In 1853, Leonard Groce built for himself and his growing family a mansion, also near Hempstead. He called his new home Liendo—the musical name of the original landowner, Justo Liendo. When Colonel Groce's only daughter, Sarah Ann, married William H. Wharton, the couple went to live in Nashville, Tennessee. But Groce, who wanted his family nearby, enlisted the help of Stephen F. Austin to persuade them to return to Texas. As an added incentive, Groce promised to build them a plantation of their own. They did return, and he built for them the beautiful Eagle Island plantation on Oyster Creek. There Sarah Groce Wharton became a famous hostess and a political help-mate to her husband.[14]

Many of the earliest settlers in Texas were family groups like the Groces. John McNeel and his sons and a grandson established five plantations along the Brazos and Bernard rivers, and the two McNeel daughters married plantation owners. At China Grove, named for the chinaberry trees surrounding the house, the patriarch of the McNeel clan established a working plantation and ranch. Like other planters, John McNeel hired an Indian to hunt game for the family table. Such hunters were also clever at getting the honey from bee trees and the eggs from birds' nests. McNeel set about raising cotton and cattle so successfully that in 1830 he made five thousand dollars on his cotton crop and had eight hundred head of cattle. He and his sons built a landing on the San Bernard River, and they also built a cotton gin, which they shared.[15]

Another large family group was that led by John Sweeny. With his wife, seven sons, and two daughters he plodded overland from Tennessee, bringing a long train of wagons, slaves, and work animals. He established a plantation in Brazoria County and acquired so much land that each of his five surviving sons was given a good plantation of his own upon reaching maturity.[16]

The Mills brothers—David, Robert, and Andrew—came from Kentucky bursting with energy and business know-how. At Lowood they developed the largest sugar plantation in Texas and had three successful cotton plantations. They were also highly successful in the shipping, merchandising, and banking businesses. Between $25,000 and $500,000 in notes of the defunct Northern Bank of Mississippi, countersigned by the Mills brothers, circulated as gold in Texas and New Orleans. These notes were called "Mill's

14. Leonard Waller Groce, "Personal Recollections"; Bertleth, "Jared Ellison Groce"; W. P. Zuber, "Biography and Life Work of a Prominent Immigrant of 1822," *Houston Post*, 1904, in Groce file, Barker Texas History Center; *Handbook of Texas* I, 738–39.
15. Abner J. Strobel, *The Old Plantations and Their Owners of Brazoria County, Texas*; *Handbook of Texas* II, 124–25.
16. Sweeny Family Papers, privately held, John Bannister, Old Ocean, Texas.

money." By the time of the Civil War they had eight hundred slaves and were reputed to be worth between $3 million and $5 million.[17]

Another pair of merchants who branched out into the plantation business were Col. Morgan L. Smith and John Adriance. They were joint owners of Waldeck, another fine sugar plantation, which was later sold to Hamblin Bass.

Many of the immigrant planters were accustomed to being leaders in their communities. So although setting up a new plantation demanded considerable time and energy, most of the substantial planters managed to become involved in local and national affairs. Such a leader was Josiah H. Bell, who came to Texas after living in Tennessee, Missouri, and Louisiana. When Stephen F. Austin had to go to Mexico City in 1822 to straighten out the affairs of his colonists with the new Mexican government, he asked his good friend Josiah Bell to take over for him as director of the scattered settlers. Austin's stay in Mexico was extended to a year, and he gave Bell credit for having kept the colony together during his absence.

At the site of his plantation on the Brazos near Columbia, Bell built a landing and expanded it to include docks, sheds, and storage rooms for freight. Bell's Landing became an important inland river port and a depot for the cotton and sugar plantations that soon sprang up around it. Bell's plantation home, a double log cabin with attached sheds, was headquarters for Sam Houston and other government officials of the Republic of Texas during the time in 1836 when Columbia was the capital. Bell, who had established the town of Columbia, also lent Houston his separate office to use for official business.[18]

Stephen F. Austin, who was responsible for persuading so many planters to move to Texas, never had a plantation of his own. But he talked his sister and her husband, Emily and James Perry, into making the move from Missouri and chose for them a spot of great beauty near the Gulf of Mexico, where thousands of wild peach trees grew and where the land was very fertile. He named it Peach Point and drew up elaborate plans for the house and garden he wanted them to establish there. The east wing of the house was to be his, a place for him to keep his books and other valuables, conduct his business between trips, and above all to call home. Planning the details of the house, outbuildings, and gardens at Peach Point gave him pleasure and no doubt welcome relief from his constant struggle with the problems of his colonists. James Perry, who had been trained in the mercantile business, applied sound business practices to running the plantation and taught his son, Stephen S. Perry, to do the same.[19]

Two doctors, Anson Jones, originally from Massachusetts, and Ashbel Smith, originally from Connecticut, eventually made their way to Texas,

17. *Handbook of Texas* II, 200, Supplement, p. 601.
18. Andrew Phelps McCormick, *Scotch-Irish in Ireland and in America*, pp. 115–17.
19. Austin (Moses and Stephen F.) Papers, Barker Texas History Center.

expecting to practice their profession and perhaps to make money in land speculation. Each served in the Texas Army, each held important positions in the Texas government, and each acquired a small plantation. Another doctor, James Aeneas E. Phelps, moved to Texas from Mississippi at the urging of Stephen F. Austin. He arrived on the *Lively*, a thirty-two-ton schooner that operated between New Orleans and Galveston, and established Orozimbo, a successful cotton plantation in Brazoria County. Like Jones and Smith he served in the Texas Army and held government positions.

Financial problems motivated several planters to move to Texas. The Devereux family, who had lived on plantations in Georgia and Alabama, were among these. Like many affluent men in the United States, Julien Devereux had lived too much on credit and speculated too much in land. After the general panic of 1837, he was hounded by creditors and threatened with court action. Texas looked like a good place to start over. Julien's aging father came reluctantly, but father and son learned to plant successfully in Texas. Monte Verdi, the impressive mansion Julien Devereux built high on a hill in Rusk County, still commands a magnificent view of many of the thousands of acres that were once planted in cotton.[20]

Financial problems also prompted William Pinkney Rose to leave Mississippi with his two sons and his son-in-law, William T. Scott, to settle in Harrison County. Rose, who had helped frame the second Mississippi constitution, was a successful planter, but he became much better known for his determined efforts to bring law and order to East Texas. According to whether the speaker was friend or foe, Rose was referred to as "a patriot and statesman," "The Lion of the Lakes," and "Hell-roarin' Rose."[21]

Rose's son-in-law William T. Scott became the empire builder of East Texas. He acquired five plantations and was the largest slaveholder in Harrison County. He founded the town of Scottsville and built the first school and the first church in the community. He served a total of eight times in the congresses of the Republic and the state, and he was influential in bringing the railroad to Texas.[22]

Albert Sidney Johnston, a West Point graduate, had farming experience near Saint Louis before he came to Texas. In 1836 he enlisted in the Texas Army as a private and was quickly promoted to senior brigadier general and given command of the army. The officer he replaced, Felix Huston, promptly challenged Johnston to a duel. In the contest, Huston shot Johnston through the hip, wounding him seriously. In 1839, Johnston, under President Lamar's orders, led an expedition against the Cherokee Indians, which helped to drive them from East Texas. He bought a plantation in Brazoria County,

20. Dorman H. Winfrey, *Julien Sidney Devereux and His Monte Verdi Plantation*, pp. 27–30.
21. *Handbook of Texas* II, 503–504. For an interesting fictionalized account of the Regulator-Moderator War in which Rose was involved, read *Love Is a Wild Assault*, by Elithe Hamilton Kirkland.
22. Scott (William T.) Papers, Harrison County Museum.

where he planted chinaberry trees and Cherokee rose hedges, which still thrive in the fourth quarter of the twentieth century. But he could not raise the money necessary to buy the slaves and develop the land to make a financial success of the plantation, and he gave it up to continue his career in the army. Nevertheless, he said that the happiest time of his life was spent on his Texas plantation.[23]

Martin Varner, one of the early settlers on the Red River, moved down to the Brazos to become one of the Old Three Hundred of Austin's first colony. He grew sugarcane on the banks of Varner Creek and was the first person to manufacture rum in Texas.

As news of the cheap land spread in the United States, Texas began to seem more and more a land of opportunity. Each family who planned to engage in farming was offered one *labor* (177 acres) of land, and each family who planned to raise stock was granted one *sitio* or square *league* (4,428 acres). Naturally, most of the planters classified themselves as stock raisers, and in reality most of them did raise large numbers of hogs and cattle and keep a good supply of mules and horses on hand.

The cavalcade of small and large farmers kept rolling in to claim the best agricultural lands, which lay in a wide band extending inland from the Gulf Coast to the "Red Lands" in East Texas and beyond to the northeastern section along the upper Red River and Caddo Lake.

The newcomers found that Texas did have the fertile, cheap land advertised. (The price of 4,428 acres in Texas was the same as that of 80 acres in the States). And there was abundant timber, water, and wild game. But there were also a number of problems the settlers had not anticipated.

PESTILENCE AND WAR

The troubles of the new Texans were small and large, natural and man-made. They were as tiny as the clouds of mosquitoes that plagued them in the wet months. The question: Was it better to pull the shutters to and stifle in the summer heat in hopes of shutting out the tiny pests, or to throw open doors and windows and endure their torment? During "mosquito storms" houses were kept dark at night and fires were built outside in an attempt to thwart the nuisances. Mosquito bars or nets were a necessity for a peaceful night's sleep. More serious was the malaria transmitted by some of the mosquitoes, although the settlers did not know its cause. Other fevers, dysentery (commonly called "summer complaint"), diphtheria, scarlet fever, whooping cough, and pneumonia attacked with terrible frequency. With little or no understanding of the causes of these diseases, no known cures for

23. Strobel, "China Grove Plantation," *Old Plantations and Their Owners*, n.p.; *Handbook of Texas* I, 919–20.

most of them, and with practically no professional medical help available, many of the sick died from their disease—or from the harsh treatments, which usually included heroic purging and bleeding.

Other natural plagues included droughts, floods, and occasional hurricanes that had devastating effects on the crops. At times, even in South Texas, there were prolonged periods of damaging cold weather. And if the crops managed to survive despite all these threats, there were also a number of crop-eating pests that could destroy in a matter of days a planter's hopes for a profitable crop.

Man-made difficulties stemmed from the settlers' relationships with the Indians and the Mexicans. The incoming planters naturally chose the best and richest land for their crops and stock raising. The Indians just as naturally resented the intrusion of the newcomers on sites they had considered theirs from time immemorial. The white men brought with them prejudices against Indians and the attitude that the red man had no rights. Clashes occurred, and when there were deaths, the codes of both the white and the red man required that revenge must be taken, to the extent that the vendettas became a way of life for both races. The large planters did not fear raids by the Indians as much as the smaller farmers did, but they too had to keep their stock protected at night, make sure their families were guarded at all times, and take precautions against surprise attacks when traveling.

As the Mexican government changed hands during the power struggles there, so did the rules and regulations governing its colonies. At first most of the planters in Texas followed Stephen F. Austin's policy of supporting the Mexican authorities in power. However, this did not mean that they complied with every rule. Although most of the settlers had Protestant backgrounds, it was easy for them to say they were Roman Catholics in order to comply with Mexican law that citizens be Roman Catholic. Their attendance at mass could hardly be required because priests were rarely sent to Texas. And, as far as the law against importing slaves to Texas was concerned, they could get around that by calling their slaves "indentured servants" and making out work contracts for them. The pioneer planters felt much more oppressed by the provisions of the Law of April 6, 1830, which prohibited further immigration of Americans into Mexico and canceled all empresario contracts. This law cut them off from their friends and relatives in the United States and ended a favorite pastime of enticing their kindred to join them in Texas. Another provision of this law that greatly displeased the Texans was that it called for construction of military garrisons in Texas. The frightening talk was that these posts were to be manned by convict soldiers, who would be allowed to settle in Texas when they had served their terms.[24]

In opposition to Austin and the conservative planters who supported him was a group called the "War Dogs." Two of the leaders of this group were William H. Wharton, Jared Groce's son-in-law, and John A. Wharton,

24. Seymour V. Connor, *Texas: A History*, pp. 88–90.

William's brother. Ill feelings between the Whartons and Austin grew until they culminated in a duel between William T. Austin (a distant relative of Stephen's) and John A. Wharton. Austin was coached for the duel by another planter, Warren Hall, who warned his pupil to get in the first shot because Wharton was a skillful shooter. Austin did fire the first bullet, which struck Wharton in his right arm just below the elbow and caused him to drop his pistol. Wharton's arm was so stiff following the duel that he had to learn to write with his left hand.[25]

Before long, however, the Whartons and Austin were brought together by common grievances against Mexico. Differences in culture, customs, religion, and interpretation of the law all continued to widen the split between the Mexicans and the Anglo-Americans. There was a serious clash

25. Strobel, "China Grove Plantation," *Old Plantations and Their Owners*, n.p.; William P. Hogan, *The Texas Republic; A Social and Economic History*, p. 275.

as early as 1826 in the Edwards Colony over the rights of the newcomers to settle on lands on which there were already some Mexican settlers. Some of these settlers were there legally, and some were not. Hayden Edwards's brother Benjamin took an opportunity while Hayden was away to stir up the colonists to revolt against Mexico. The plan was to divide Texas in two: one part for the Indians in return for their help, and the other part for a republic, to be called Fredonia. Many of Austin's colonists did not approve of the uprising, and Jared Groce even offered the Mexicans the use of his ferry, his wagons, and his teams to aid in quashing the rebellion. Although the Fredonia rebellion was quickly put down, the restlessness under Mexican rule increased.

A decree that import duties must be paid on goods brought into Texas hit planters particularly hard, as they were the ones who did the most importing of foreign goods. This duty, plus other grievances, led to disturbances at Anahuac and at Velasco, in which many of the planters were involved. Both were heady victories for the Texans. The fight at Anahuac was relatively bloodless, but the battle of Velasco resulted in casualties on both sides. Capt. Brit Bailey participated in the fight, as did his two sons, Smith Bailey and Gaines Bailey, both of whom were listed as wounded. Other planters involved in the fighting at Velasco were John and Sterling McNeel, Robert and Andrew Mills, Benjamin Mims, Henry W. Munson, Thomas Jamison, William H. Wharton, Edwin Waller, and Andrew and James Westall. Austin assured Mexican officials that these disturbances were not indications of general insurrection by Texans.[26]

As the outbreaks of violence became more numerous, more planters became convinced that the War Dogs were right in insisting that Texas and Coahuila be separate states. Stephen F. Austin was chosen to go to Mexico to present this proposal to the Mexican government. After six months of frustrated effort in trying to get the Mexican officials to see the viewpoint of the Texans, he wrote a letter that the Mexicans considered treasonous. Austin was arrested and imprisoned in Mexico City. By the time he was released, Austin and the majority of the Anglo-American planters had become convinced they would never be able to live in peace under Mexican rule.

The war for Texas' independence from Mexico had a definite beginning, from which there could be no turning back, at the town of Gonzales on October 2, 1835. A plantation owner named John Henry Moore led the Texans there in refusing to surrender a cannon that the Mexican government had given to the Texans four years earlier for protection against Indian attacks. Tradition has it that Moore designed the flag of defiance that challenged the Mexicans to "Come and Take It."[27]

Meanwhile, back in Tennessee, empresario Sterling C. Robertson was working to gather up colonists to bring to Texas. He published two long

26. James A. Creighton, *A Narrative History of Brazoria County*, pp. 62–68; *Handbook of Texas* I, 43; II, 836.
27. *Handbook of Texas* II, 229–30.

articles in the *Nashville Republican* of October 6, 1835. In the first one he reported that Santa Anna had sent word that he did not intend to invade Texas if the people remained quiet and peaceable. In the second, he encouraged capitalists to invest their money in Texas land, which he informed them "can now be got there for a trifling sum, that will in a few years sell as high as the lands do now in the southern lower country. . . . The present state of things cannot last long," he said, and he prophesied that Texas would carry her arms successfully and achieve independence "if no other alternative will do."[28]

His words proved true as Texans did take up arms. A number of plantation owners were casualities in the battles that followed. At the Alamo, at Goliad, and at San Jacinto, some were wounded and some gave their lives to win independence for the land they had chosen as their new home.

Jared Groce was unable to join the army because of his physical disabilities, but he did all that he could to help. During his preliminary maneuvering before the Battle of San Jacinto, Sam Houston camped with his men on the river opposite Bernardo for more than two weeks. Groce supplied to the army hundreds of free cattle and thousands of bushels of corn. He also supplied outfits for many of the men, and the women of the household sewed flannel bags for them to fill with sand and use as breastworks. The main house of the plantation was used as a hospital for sick and wounded soldiers, with the women helping to care for them.[29]

When Houston continued moving east, rumors of impending attack by the Mexican army led to panic. In the resulting pell-mell flight called the "Runaway Scrape," plantation families were swept along in the tide of retreating Texans. A letter from Sam Houston warning that he did not intend to fight between the Brazos and Colorado rivers and urging the settlers to move out before Mexican troops arrived convinced even the bravest pioneers that it was time to leave. Many of the wealthy planters took time to bury their silver and other valuables, to turn their stock loose to forage, and to pack food and provisions for their journey to they knew not where. Having horses and wagons made the trip more comfortable for them than it was for their fellow army of runaways, most of whom were slogging along on foot. But they still suffered from the drenching rain, from cold, from illnesses. And they endured the dangerous crossing of swollen creeks, the miserable nights when every shadow looked like a Mexican scout, and the terrible uncertainty of what the outcome of the fighting would be.

Emily Perry's son, Austin Bryan,[30] was with Sam Houston's army, so

28. Malcolm D. McLean, comp. and ed., *Papers Concerning Robertson's Colony in Texas* XI, 48–49.

29. Groce (Jared E. and Leonard W.) Family Papers, Waller County Public Library; *Telegraph and Texas Register* (San Felipe), Mar. 5, 1836.

30. Emily Perry had been married to James Bryan before she married James F. Perry. For a good account of the horrors of the Runaway Scrape, see Ann Raney Coleman's description in C. Richard King, ed., *Victorian Lady on the Texas Frontier: The Journal of Ann Raney Coleman*, pp. 82–92.

she felt doubly agitated when she and the other refugees in her group, camped on a soggy prairie, heard the guns at San Jacinto. After the joyful news of the victory, the weary travelers turned back to their deserted homes, fearful of what they would find there. At worst, the returnees found their homes looted and burned. At best, the planters found that chickens and wild birds and animals had raided their gardens and eaten the tender shoots of the new plants there; weeds had overgrown gardens; livestock and poultry had suffered from the lack of care or had been entirely lost. And, too, even though the defeat of the Mexicans had brought peace, it was an uneasy peace.

Texans argued hotly about how to deal with Santa Anna, the Mexican leader who had been captured after the Battle of San Jacinto. Threats were made against his life, and in July of 1836 he was moved to Orozimbo, the cotton plantation of Dr. James Aeneas E. Phelps, for safety. There, in a mood of depression, Santa Anna took poison in a suicide attempt. Dr. Phelps quickly pumped his stomach and saved his life. Santa Anna remained safely at Orozimbo plantation until November. Later he showed his appreciation for the kind treatment he had received from the Phelps family by saving the Phelpses' son, Orlando, from execution when he was condemned as a member of the Mier Expedition.[31]

In spite of forebodings and occasional alarms over renewed attacks from Mexico, the peace held. A new country was born, and for almost a decade the plantation owners in Texas would be living in a republic, which they would play a large role in running. Planters filled some of the highest governmental offices in the republic and served in its legislatures. They organized and supported schools, churches, professional groups, and cultural activities. They built and maintained roads and did everything in their power to have improvements made on rivers and bayous to aid shipping.

Many of the planters believed that annexation to the United States would be to their advantage in selling their produce and in realizing more profit. Most of them also had ties to the States through kin and friends there. So, along with the majority of Texans, they voted to give up their independence in order to receive the advantages of statehood.

During the war with Mexico that followed annexation, many of the plantation owners again became soldiers. For the younger ones, although they did not realize it, this war experience gave them training that they would put to use again in the Civil War, less than twenty years later.

The pioneer planters and their families who came to Texas were daring and courageous people, willing to take chances to try to reach their dreams. One of their outstanding characteristics was the ability to look to the future and see the potential of the land. One would-be empresario described what he saw and what he hoped for:

31. *Handbook of Texas* II, 371–72; Strobel, "The Phelps Plantation," *Old Plantations and Their Owners*, n.p.

I must say as to what I have seen of Texas it is the garden spot of the world, the best land & the best prospects for health I ever saw is here . . . expect to settle . . . no doubt the richest country in the world—good land & plenty of timber, best springs—good mill streams, good range, clear water & every appearance of health. Game a plenty . . . Buffalo pass from no. to so. & back twice a year & bees & honey plenty . . . Have great hopes of getting the agency to settle that country—[32]

It may have been the last letter the children of Davy Crockett received from their father. Although Crockett did not realize his dream, his death at the Alamo helped pave the way for cotton and cane empire builders who flocked to the "garden spot."

32. Davy Crockett to his children, n.d., quoted in A. W. Neville, *The Red River Valley Then and Now*, p. xi.

CHAPTER TWO

Black & White

"Marster and de Mistez tooks deys goodness by spells."
—Walter Rimm, Texas Slave Narratives

BUYING AND SELLING

That "peculiar institution," as antebellum southerners liked to call slavery, was indeed strange and full of contradictions. Many planters would refer to two "families" on their plantations—the white family occupying the "big house" and the black "family" occupying the quarters. The black "family" consisted of a number of small family groups plus some single slaves.

Despite Mexico's efforts to prevent Anglo-Americans from bringing slaves into Texas, a population report for 1834 lists twenty-one thousand whites and two thousand slaves.[1] Clearly, slave labor was extremely important in transforming Texas from a wilderness into a cotton kingdom.

The majority of the slaves were brought in under the quasi-legal ruse of calling them "indentured servants." But a number of them were smuggled in from Africa, usually by way of Cuba. James Bowie, along with his two brothers, smuggled slaves into Texas in collaboration with the pirate Jean Laffite. The Bowie brothers were reported to have made $65,000 between 1818 and 1820 from trafficking in slaves.[2] Col. James W. Fannin, who like Bowie would become a hero of the Texas Revolution, also engaged in the slave trade. In August, 1835, he wrote to a friend in the States: "My last voyage from the island of Cuba (with 152) succeeded admirably."[3] Among the Perry Family Papers is a promissory note that suggests a sale of slaves by Fannin to James F. Perry. The note, dated August 24, 1835, is for $1,973.34 and is marked "for value received."

1. Juan N. Almonte, "Statistical Report on Texas," trans. C. E. Castañeda, *Southwestern Historical Quarterly* 28 (Jan., 1925): 177–91.
2. Ben C. Stuart Papers, Rosenberg Library; *Handbook of Texas* I, 197.
3. Ben C. Stuart Papers; Eugene C. Barker, "The African Slave Trade in Texas," *Quarterly of the Texas State Historical Association* 6 (Oct., 1902): 145–58.

The most infamous slave trader in Texas was Monroe Edwards, owner of a sugar plantation at Chenango in Brazoria County. Fishing in the troubled waters caused by the Texas Revolution, Edwards and others increased their importation of Africans during 1835 and 1836. On March 2, 1836, William S. Fisher, collector of customs at Velasco, wrote to the provisional governor, Henry Smith, that Edwards had landed a cargo of 171 Africans along the Brazos River. The customs collector also reported to Governor Smith that plantation owner Sterling McNeel had landed an unknown number of slaves on the Brazos.

It was said that Edwards paid twenty-five dollars for the slaves he bought in Cuba and that he sold them for six hundred dollars. Edwards, a nephew of empresario Hayden Edwards, was also a talented forger and swindler. After duping high government officials in Europe with counterfeit letters from Daniel Webster and Martin Van Buren, he was finally brought to trial, and he spent the remainder of his life in Sing Sing prison.[4]

A few of the most prominent planters were actively engaged in slave smuggling or buying Africans from "blackbirders," as the smugglers were called. When Texas became a republic in 1836, the First Congress enacted a law that any person convicted of introducing Africans from any country except the United States should be put to death "without benefit of clergy."[5]

In 1837, President Sam Houston expressed the official stand of the nation: "It cannot be disbelieved that thousands of Africans have been lately imported to the islands of Cuba, with the design to transport a large portion of them into the Republic. This unholy and cruel traffic has called down the reprobation of the humane and just of all civilized nations. Our abhorrence to it is clearly expressed in our constitution and laws."[6]

For some two decades the African slave trade in Texas went underground and dwindled, only to revive in the late 1850s as the plantation system in Texas expanded and the demand for slaves mounted.

The majority of Texas planters, like Groce, brought some slaves with them, although few had as many as he did. Black parents in the nineteenth century, like white parents, had many babies, so there was a natural increase in the number of slaves. Also, there was forced breeding on some plantations. Some died from disease or from old age, and as the planters acquired more land, they needed more hands to work it. Although there were exceptions such as those noted above, most Texas plantation owners bought their slaves from each other or from trusted traders.

For the convenience of the buyers, the sellers might march the slaves to the county seat to be sold to planters. Here the slaves remained in bull pens at central locations where they could be inspected by buyers. Or they might be sold on auction blocks set up in front of courthouses.

4. Ben C. Stuart Papers; Barker, "African Slave Trade in Texas."
5. H. P. N. Gammel, comp., Act of December 21, 1836, *The Laws of Texas, 1822–1897* I, 1257–58.
6. Barker, "African Slave Trade in Texas," p. 155.

In New Orleans, Shreveport, Houston, and Galveston there were permanent slave marts and slave-auction companies that kept a continuous supply of blacks on hand. J. P. Sydnor, a mayor of Galveston, was also an auctioneer and commission merchant for slave traders. At 10 A.M. every Tuesday and Friday at his storerooms on the Strand he held an auction sale, charging his clients 2.5 percent commission on sales.[7]

If it was not convenient for the planter to go to market himself, he could have his factor or agent in these cities buy slaves for him. Slaves were bought and charged to the planter's account, the same as the other goods he purchased through his agents. In Houston one auction yard advertised that it handled "Negroes, horses, mules, and carriages."[8]

The New Orleans and Shreveport dealers supplied East Texas planters with slaves. Owners sometimes ran ads to sell individual slaves. In the *Texas Republican* (Marshall), G. J. Roberts offered to sell to the highest bidder ". . . a likely Negro man about 28 yrs. of age. Said boy is well-disposed, is a tolerably good hewer, and otherwise handy, and is accustomed to plantation service."[9]

At the auctions, the slaves and the livestock were sold in much the same manner—except the slaves were made to do their own grooming. Before being put on the block, they had to wash themselves and grease their faces and bodies with fat meat to give them a shiny, healthy appearance.

Being sold was horrifying enough for an adult, but it was doubly terrifying for a child. Emma Taylor remembers that when her master got old, he decided to reduce his operation and sell some of his slaves. An auctioneer was called in to handle the selling:

> He puts all de family up on a big platform, and when we had pulled off nearly all our clothes, so as he could tell how big we were, he began hollowing bout who gonna buy, who gonna buy. I wasn't very big, but I members being scared dat I was gonna have to leave my maw, and I began hollowing jist bout as loud as he was a hollowing. Den he turns around and he says, 'Shut up, you little coon you, I can't hear anything dats going on,' so I got scared sure nouf den, and I jist hid my face under my maw's appern and didn't know no more till we all was loaded in a wagon and started to our new home.[10]

Men and women alike were stripped half naked and made to "trot" in front of the buyers to show their agility. The buyers pinched skin to test for age. Young flesh sprang back quickly; older flesh took longer to return to normal. The bidders pried open the jaws of the blacks and examined their teeth, just as they looked at a horse's teeth to determine its age. They also

7. *Texas Almanac* (1857–1861), advertising sections.
8. *The Galvestonian* (Galveston, Tex.), Mar. 27, 1839.
9. *Texas Republican* (Marshall, Tex.), May 21, 1850.
10. George P. Rawick, ed., *The American Slave: A Composite Autobiography*, series 2, *Texas Narratives*, Emma Taylor, pp. 3762–63.

looked for scars from beatings, which the buyers believed might indicate a stubborn or lazy worker.

Sometimes members of a family were bought by different masters. Husbands and wives were separated; sisters and brothers parted, often never to see each other again. Young children were literally torn from their parents.

Decades after the Civil War, in their descriptions of the auctions and of the separating of their families and of their treatment, former slaves repeatedly referred to being thought of and being treated like animals by the whites. The holding places for the slaves before they were put on the block were called "bull pens." Former slave Susan Merritt recalled visiting a slave market and watching the buyers take their newly acquired bondsmen away chained together "like steers" and being driven along "like cattle."[11] Tom Holland was traded at auction for one hundred acres of land. He was not permitted to visit his former master and relatives who remained behind until he was "weaned" from his homesickness for them. "You have heard cattle bawl when you take their calves away from them?" he asked his interviewer. "That was the way with the slaves."[12] Green Cumby remembered seeing speculators driving bunches of slaves "jest like cattle through the country from one place to 'nother to auction 'em at de market places. De wimmen would be carrin' de little uns in dere arms. At night dey bed 'em down jest lak cattle right on de groun' 'side de road."[13] And Mollie Dawson summed up her attitudes and those of her fellow slaves:

> De slaves was about de same things as mules or cattle, dey was bought and sold and dey wasn't supposed ter be treated lak people anyway. We all knew dat we was only a race of people as our master was and dat we had a certain amount of rights but we was jest property and had ter be loyal ter our masers. It hurt us sometimes ter be treated de way some of us was treated but we couldn't help ourselves and had ter do de best we could which nearly all of us done.[14]

Some plantation owners went out of their way to keep slave families together, sometimes buying slaves they did not need. When Jared Groce's houscmaid Myra married Harry from another plantation, Groce purchased him even though he was crippled. When Groce's slaves grew too old to work, he would free them, but allow them to remain on the plantation with a younger slave assigned to take care of them. It would not have been safe for freedmen to travel in Texas, but they took pleasure in their new status nevertheless.[15]

11. Ibid., Susan Merritt, p. 2642.
12. Ibid., Tom Holland, pp. 1762–63.
13. Ibid., Green Cumby, pp. 1002–1003.
14. Ibid., Mollie Dawson, p. 1132.
15. "Plantation Life in Texas," Groce (Jared E. and Leonard W.) Family Papers, Waller County Public Library.

The prices of slaves depended on their sex, age, condition, skills, and strength. It also depended, of course, on how scarce or how plentiful the supply of slaves was. A Texas planter named W. S. Needham thought he had gotten an excellent bargain when he paid eighteen hundred dollars for a young black man named Bill, who could run a cotton gin, do blacksmithing, and make the plows and other iron implements for the plantation. In addition, Bill tanned all the leather for harnesses and made all the shoes.[16]

Apparently, prices paid for slaves varied from about one hundred to more than three thousand dollars, and there were slaves whose masters considered them too valuable to sell at any price. Prices for slaves rose steadily until the Civil War began. In 1859 the *Matagorda Gazette* reported the price for field hands ranged from twelve hundred to two thousand dollars and for plowboys, from one thousand to fifteen hundred dollars.[17]

Sometimes slaves were traded for land, and bankrupt planters sometimes were forced to hand them over to their creditors in lieu of money. When the sons and daughters of the planter married, he often gave them slaves as a wedding gift. Another way in which slaves might be uprooted and separated from families was when an owner would will them to various members of his family.

In 1838 Ashbel Smith was pleased with his purchase of three slaves in New Orleans for twenty-two hundred dollars. They were two young boys, ten and twelve, and Eliza, age seventeen, who was advertised as a good washerwoman. He expected to hire out all three for about ninety dollars a month.[18]

A master could hire out a slave for any kind of labor. An agreement between Stephen F. Austin and Jared Groce illustrates a typical arrangement:

> I have this day hired three negroes from Jared E. Groce towit a negro woman called Sally, a negro man called tame Jack and one called Kelly—the woman at eight dollars pr. month and the men at fifteen each. The hire to commence on the first day of November next, and continue for one year from that date, and I obligate myself to pay to said Groce the amt. of said hire at the expiration of the year. A boy called Fields is to be furnished to take care of Sally's child. The said negroes are to be well treated by me, and the said Groce is to cloathe them. Should they run away or die; the loss is to be Groces—sickness to my loss.
>
> Brazos River—October 19, 1823 Stephen F. Austin[19]

Some masters allowed slaves to hire themselves out during slack times. This practice of "hiring their own time" was limited to one day per week (except during Christmas holidays) by Texas law after 1846.[20]

16. Rawick, ed., *Texas Narratives*, W. S. Needham, p. 4361.
17. *The Gazette* (Matagorda, Tex.), Feb. 12, 1849.
18. Elizabeth Silverthorne, *Ashbel Smith of Texas*, p. 49.
19. Groce (Jared E. and Leonard W.) Family Papers, Waller County Public Library.
20. Gammel, comp., *Laws of Texas* II, 1501–1502.

Order and system were essential for making a plantation profitable, and the larger the plantation, the more important these were. Slaves were assigned tasks according to their abilities, but there were three main classifications on Texas plantations: house servants, craftsmen, and field workers. Each of these divisions had subdivisions in the "pecking order."

Carriage drivers and butlers occupied positions considered to be high among household workers. Body servants assigned to individual members of the white family were also considered important in position. Household workers also included the nimble-fingered maids, who brushed their mistresses' hair and mended, darned, and did fine needlework. In addition, there were parlormaids and nurserymaids, cooks and undercooks, waiters, butlers, and bootblacks.

A former slave named Ben Chambers, who had been a carriage driver, described himself to his interviewer as "kinder like the vice president" of the plantation. He took pride in keeping the buggy clean and shining. "Dat was one of de bestes' tasks on de plantation and some of dem other niggers was sorter jealous of me," he told his interviewer.[21] Another interviewee reported that his father was the shoemaker, "a fine job on de plantation."[22] In describing the different stations of the slaves, another former bondsman said: "De house servants wuz what de Master an' de Mistis called a different 'class,' dey wuz above de fiel'-hands, de house servants called dem 'corn-field niggers.'"[23]

Many slaves developed skill as gardeners, stockmen, brickmakers, carpenters, blacksmiths, weavers, nurses, seamstresses, cooks, gin operators, sugar makers, and other specialties. Field hands, who worked at various tasks according to seasonal needs, could win praise from their masters by being particularly good at their jobs. A man who could snatch more cotton, plow more rows, or manage oxen better than average was a source of pride to his owner, who sometimes managed to have unusual feats of skill by his slaves printed in newspapers.

The black drivers, or taskmasters, had more nebulous positions. Chosen by the overseer or master as leaders because of their strength and skill, they were often resented by the other slaves. If they were given the right to punish other slaves, they were sure to be hated and called "nigger traitors" behind their backs. But if the drivers were used only as pacesetters for getting a job done, and if the job and title rotated among the workers, there was much less resentment.

During the almost fifty years of slavery in Texas, slave insurrections were infrequent and widely scattered geographically. In 1835, some

21. Rawick, ed., *Texas Narratives*, Ben Chambers, pp. 670–72.
22. Ibid., Larnce Holt, p. 1780.
23. Ibid., George Glasker, p. 1503.

slaves along the Brazos River attempted a revolt. After the arrest of nearly a hundred slaves, many of them were whipped as punishment, and several were hanged. In 1841, planters in East Texas were alarmed by reports of a black uprising. Restrictions on allowing slaves to leave their plantations were tightened, and citizen patrols kept strict watch to prevent straying. In 1856, a slave in Colorado County revealed the details of a planned revolt to his master. According to reports, between two hundred and four hundred blacks had armed themselves with guns and homemade knives and were preparing to murder any whites who tried to stop them from fleeing to Mexico. A vigilance committee rounded up and whipped some two hundred slaves and hanged two or three of the ringleaders. A white abolitionist, William Mehrmann, was blamed for stirring the blacks to revolt, and he was ordered to leave the state. As arguments over slavery intensified in the United States in the late 1850s, patrol systems were strengthened and vagrancy laws stringently enforced.[24]

24. Abigail Curlee, "A Study of Texas Slave Plantations, 1822–1865," pp. 127–30; *Handbook of Texas* II, 618–19, III, 643.

African-born slaves had to learn the language of their masters. The teaching was done casually and haphazardly by overseers and native-born slaves. Younger blacks, and especially children, learned to converse in English with relative ease, while older Africans might take several years to acquire a degree of skill in the language. On large plantations where field workers had little contact with whites, many African-born slaves retained their native dialect and only used a patois as needed to communicate in English. The term "Gullah" was used to designate certain blacks living on the sea islands and tidewater coastline of South Carolina and Georgia and the dialect spoken by them, and some of these Gullah blacks were brought into Texas before the Civil War. Gullah is still spoken by some of their descendants in Washington and other Texas counties in the 1980s. The whites did, however, adopt some African words, including goober, yam, chimpanzee, and gumbo.[25]

OVERSEERS

White overseers occupied middle ground between slave and master: they had to please the owner by working the slaves hard enough to produce enough crops, yet they had to keep the slaves satisfied enough with their daily lives so they would not defy orders or run away. They also had to keep the plantation running smoothly and be responsible for the physical well-being of the workers and the livestock.

The pay for overseers varied greatly in Texas, ranging from less than $150 to $600 per year, depending on whether they got board and a percentage of the crops and livestock increase.[26]

Finding a satisfactory overseer was difficult in a country where most men preferred to have a farm of their own, no matter what size or how successful. In 1850, Julien Devereux wrote to an acquaintance about his need for an overseer for Monte Verdi. Devereux said that he had about twenty-five good hands, "all family negroes and easily governed." He added that he was contented with having "moderate work done" and that he would not have a severe or cruel overseer on any terms. He was willing to pay three hundred dollars cash and furnish the overseer's "bread corn for the year."[27]

Occasionally, slaves were used as overseers. To be given this responsibility, they had to be exceptionally capable and tactful. Ashbel Smith, who was so often frustrated in finding a competent white overseer, was delighted

25. John W. Blassingame, *The Slave Community: Plantation Life in the Antebellum South*, pp. 24–30; *Encyclopaedia Britannica*, 1977 ed., VI, 878–79; *The Compact Edition of the Oxford English Dictionary* II, 3981.

26. Curlee, "A Study of Texas Slave Plantations," pp. 89–105.

27. Julien S. Devereux to Mark Stroud, Nov. 4, 1850, Devereux (Julien Sidney) Papers, Barker Texas History Center.

to find when he returned from a long absence that his slave, "Old Peter," had produced one of the "best crops on the bay" at Evergreen.[28] Nearby in Brazoria County on the Bingham plantation, an old slave called "Uncle Billy" was the designated overseer.

The overseer who took his responsibilities seriously had a hard life. He was the first one up in the morning and the last one to bed at night. When the slaves worked outside in cold and wet weather, the overseer had to be there to watch them. He was responsible for ensuring that all physically able slaves were at work in the fields. He had to inspect the slave cabins to be sure they were clean. He had to assign tasks and keep records of weather, work done, crop yield, livestock information, and many other facts pertaining to the plantation operation. All day long he was making decisions and solving problems.

What did a reasonable plantation owner expect of an overseer? Charles William Tait, owner of the well-run Egypt plantation near Columbus, wrote out a long list of rules for his overseers to follow. Among them were these:

> Never punish a negro when in a passion. No one is capable of properly regulating the punishment for an offense when angry.

> Never require of a negro what is unreasonable. But when you give an order be sure to enforce it with firmness, yet mildly.

> Always attempt to govern by reason in the first instance, and resort to force only when reason fails, and then use no more force than is absolutely necessary to produce obedience.

> In giving orders always do it in a mild tone, and try to leave the impression on the mind of the negro that what you say is the result of reflection.

> In giving orders be sure that you are understood, and let the negro know that he can always ask for an explanation if he does not understand you.

> When you are under the necessity of punishing a negro, be sure to let him know for what offence he is punished.

> Never act in such a way as to leave the impression on the mind of the negro that you take pleasure in his punishment, your manner should indicate that his punishment is painful.

> Negroes lack the motive of self-interest to make them careful & diligent, hence the necessity of great patience in the management of them. Do not therefore notice too many small omissions of duty.[29]

Thomas Affleck, owner of Glenblythe plantation, near Brenham, outlined the duties of an overseer in his plantation record and account books.

28. Ashbel Smith to Marie Hudson, Jan. 12, 1845, Smith (Ashbel) Papers, 1823–1886, Barker Texas History Center.
29. "Plantation Rules," Tait (Charles William) Family Papers, Barker Texas History Center.

He reminded them that they had contracted with the plantation owner to carry out his orders "strictly, cheerfully, and to the best of your ability" and in all things to "study his interests." Affleck pointed out that much sickness among slaves was the result of carelessness and mismanagement by overseers. Overwork, unnecessary exposure to rain, insufficient clothing, improper or badly cooked food, and night rambles[30] all were causes of disease, he said. He gave the overseer practical hints on running the plantation efficiently and told him that he could feel he had had a good year if these six things had been accomplished: (1) The number, condition, and value of the Negroes increased; (2) the land and general condition of the plantation improved; (3) abundant provisions for man and beast produced and carefully stored; (4) summer and winter clothing made; shoes and harnesses made; (5) team and stock, farming implements, and buildings in good order; and (6) as heavy a crop of cotton or sugar as could possibly be made under the circumstances, sent to market in good season and of prime quality.[31]

Some overseers were unequal to Affleck's ideal overseer and resorted to controlling their charges through fear, threats, and frequent use of the whip. A slave called Uncle Richard Carruthers reported to his interviewer:

> My white people . . . treated me very well. The overseer, he rough . . . his temper born of the devil hisself. His name was Tom Hill, but us niggers call him "Devil Hill." At first when my missy find out the overseer's mean, she fire them out and turn them off, but when she git a new one, he jus' as mean . . . [Tom Hill] use to whup me and the other niggers . . . he stake us out like you stake out a hide and whup till we bleed. . . .[32]

Among the many interviews that Works Progress Administration workers held with former slaves, a few overseers received high marks, but on the whole, more would have rated a C or a D in the reports. Sarah Ford, a former slave, remembered Uncle Big Jake, a black overseer: "I 'spec Old Devil make him overseer down below long time ago." She acknowledged that her master treated his slaves well in other ways, but blamed him for letting Uncle Big Jake whip them so freely, concluding, "Even does your stomach be full, an' does you have plenty clothes too, dat bull whip on your bare hide make you forgit de good part. . . ."[33]

MASTERS

In nineteenth-century America the image of the gentleman planter carried with it connotations of a gracious life-style, which included courtly

---

30. A "night ramble" meant staying out all night to hold secret religious meetings or to socialize.
31. "The Duties of an Overseer," Thomas Affleck's plantation record and account book, Affleck (Thomas) Papers, Rosenberg Library.
32. Rawick, ed., *Texas Narratives*, Uncle Richard Carruthers, p. 628.
33. Ibid., Sarah Ford, pp. 1363–65.

manners, a proud (and touchy) sense of honor, a sense of obligation to participate in public affairs, and lavish hospitality. It also implied a manor house in a feudal setting complete with fine furnishings, thoroughbred horses and hounds, and vast amounts of land with enough slaves to manage the crops and stock so that the planter could enjoy such favorite pastimes as hunting, horse racing, and politicking.

The reality of the planters' lives on the Texas frontier often fell short of the stereotype of the aristocratic plantation owner derived from the gentry in the old southern states and originally from the gentry of England. However, even an abstemious bachelor like Ashbel Smith dreamed of the idealized life of the country gentleman. After Smith decided to make Texas his home, he told a cousin he intended "to have a house in the country with all the profusion, the hearty comforts and appliances for field sports that such a life affords." He added "This will be my *home*, here will be my negroes, my books, horses . . . my dogs and guns. Here I hope to see my friends. . . ."[34]

The small planter in Texas might have envied the life-style of the large landowner and even made fun of it at times, but he and his family imitated it nevertheless. They taught their children to act like little southern ladies and gentlemen and tried to promote their status through education and by acquiring land and slaves to hand on to them. They copied the manners and habits of the wealthy planters and aspired to be as well dressed, to own as many fine horses and carriages, and to show as much hospitality as they could manage.

Like George Washington and Thomas Jefferson, some slaveholders in Texas had ambivalent feelings about slavery. Stephen F. Austin wrote to his cousin Mary Austin Holley in July of 1831 that slavery was a "difficult and *dark* question."[35] A couple of years later he was more or less reconciled to it for Texas:

> I have been averse to the principle of slavery in Texas. I have now and for the last six months changed my views on that matter, though my ideas are the same as to the abstract principle. Texas *must be* a slave country. Circumstances and unavoidable necessity compel it. It is the wish of the people there, and it is my duty to do all I can, prudently, in favor of it. I will do so.[36]

Austin's attitude was the exception rather than the rule among Texas' planters, who felt themselves supported by the law (both U.S. and Texas penal codes) and the Bible. They pointed out that according to the Bible, slaves were acquired by capture in warfare, by purchase, or by being forced into servitude by poverty or debt. The slaves were exhorted by the scriptures to be obe-

34. Silverthorne, *Ashbel Smith*, p. 64.
35. Stephen F. Austin to Mary Austin Holley, July 19, 1831, Austin (Moses and Stephen F.) Papers, Barker Texas History Center.
36. Stephen F. Austin to Wily Martin, May 30, 1833, quoted in Eugene C. Barker, "The Influence of Slavery in the Colonization of Texas," *Southwestern Historical Quarterly* 28 (July, 1924): 28.

dient, faithful, trustworthy, considerate, and content. A favored quotation of the planters was from Paul's epistle to Titus: "*Exhort* servants to be obedient unto their own masters, *and* to please *them* well in all *things*; not answering again"[37]; abolitionists also quoted scripture, however.

Even such an idealist and humanitarian as Ashbel Smith believed that the institution of slavery was ordained by God. As a member of the Texas House of Representatives in 1855, he made speeches pointing out that the Bible "affirmed, nay commanded slavery," and declared, "That which is once right in the eyes of God is always right."[38]

In the end it was the owner whose personality and actions determined what life was like for the people and animals on a plantation. He could dismiss an overseer who was too cruel or too much of a "pusher" of men and beasts. He could also fire an overseer whom he considered too lenient. And he could use his overseer to do the "dirty work" of disciplining the slaves, reserving for himself the role of benevolent patriarch.

William Bollaert, a frequent traveler in Texas, gave his opinion about the treatment of slaves: "Generally speaking throughout the Republic the Negroes are well treated, and I can bear witness that they are not over-worked, or ill-used. In the eastern counties they are principally 'family Negros,' or brought up by their owners, and when they get old are kept upon the plantations and not sold to an indifferent master."[39]

Harsh masters who beat their slaves unmercifully, gave them short rations, and worked them to the point of collapse or death were considered foolish businessmen since they were destroying their own property. Most Texas planters subscribed to this thinking and were concerned for the welfare of their slaves for pragmatic if not for more humane reasons. Slaves might be punished, however, for any offense, from looking sullen to attempting to run away. The punishments ranged from a slap to fatal beatings. A few plantations had "jails" or a corncrib with a lock that was used as a jail, and some had stocks. The majority of owners depended on the whip to punish, although Thomas Affleck warned: "The indiscriminate constant and excessive use of the whip, is altogether unnecessary and inexcusable." He recommended that the planters return to the method of the early American colonists and use stocks. Affleck suggested that the offender be put in the stocks in a "lonely place" with no communication and be given only bread and water from Saturday noon to Sunday night (so that no working time would be lost). He promised that this method of punishment would prove much "more effectual in preventing a repetition of the offence, than any amount of whipping." Pragmatic planters agreed with Affleck's advice that "occasional

37. Ti. 2:9.
38. Elizabeth Silverthorne, "Once Right in the Eyes of God," *Civil War Times Illustrated* (Dec., 1980): 19.
39. William Bollaert, *William Bollaert's Texas*, ed. William Eugene Hollon and Ruth Lapham Butler, p. 270.

rewards have a much better effect than frequent punishments."[40]

Roving patrols kept slaves on the plantations they belonged to. The patrollers were white men, who sometimes took sadistic pleasure in catching and beating slaves who were away from their plantations. If they caught a slave who was off his plantation without a note of permission from his master, the standard punishment for a first offense was thirty-nine lashes with a rawhide whip that the slaves called the "black snake." The number of lashes increased with each additional offense. The slaves hated and feared these men, whom they called "paddyrollers" or "patter rollers." Most Texas slaves were familiar with at least one version of a song that, in part, went like this:

> Run nigger run, pattyroller catch you.
> Run nigger run, they give you 39.
> That nigger run, that nigger flew.
> That nigger lost his Sunday shoe.
>
> Up the hill and down the holler,
> White man caught that nigger by the collar.
> That nigger run, that nigger flew.
> That nigger tore his shirt in two.[41]

Eluding the patrollers was part of the price a slave paid for a few hours of freedom from the plantation to visit or just to roam for awhile. A common strategy was to tie vines across the trail to make the patroller's horse throw its rider.

In the days of colonization, a decree had ordered that each municipality supply to Mexico a list that included the name, sex, and age of each slave. But after independence there was no reliable system in Texas for identifying slaves and establishing title to them. They were not registered or numbered for the most part (although a few were branded), and they had no surnames. Advertisements for runaway slaves gave descriptions of clothing, appearance, and distinctions in speech or personality in an effort to identify them. In 1838, Edwin Waller ran an ad in the *Telegraph and Texas Register* (Houston):

> $200 Reward
> For the delivery of 2 African Negroes named Gumby and Zow, who absconded from my plantation, Oyster Creek, Brazoria Co. some time since. Slaves are about 30 yrs of age—one about 5 ft 10 ", the other 5 ft 8 "—the larger has a broad face, the other a wild look.
>
> Edwin Waller[42]

In 1840, William T. Austin advertised for a runaway slave named Anderson, about five feet, three inches, of a "down look, stout built, and yellow com-

40. Thomas Affleck's plantation record and account book, Affleck (Thomas) Papers.
41. Rawick, ed., *Texas Narratives*, pp. 4114, 4357.
42. *Telegraph and Texas Register* (Houston), Jan. 3, 1838.

plexion," and with one hand that had been injured in a cotton gin.[43] The *Brazos Courier* carried an ad promising a reward for the capture of a slave named Robert, who was "quick motioned, inclined to hold his head down when walking," could play the fiddle, and was "believed to be on the other side of the Brazos River."[44]

From 1836 until beyond the Civil War there were a number of lawsuits over the ownership of slaves. It was a felony offense to steal a slave or to entice a slave to run away.[45] Captured runaways were punished severely, and usually the other slaves on the plantation were required to witness the punishment, in the belief that it would keep them from trying the same thing. A few runaways from Texas plantations made it across the Rio Grande and found shelter with Mexicans until after the Civil War. Others hid in the woods and river bottoms for a few days or sometimes for months.

Most large plantations had dogs that were specially trained to track runaway slaves. But there were ways a slave could put the dogs off the scent. When he left the slave quarters, a clever individual would take some pepper with him. Taking off his shoes, he would put the pepper in his socks and thus leave a trail that soon discouraged the sneezing, teary-eyed dogs. Another tactic that was popularized by word of mouth was for the runaway to foil the bloodhounds by stepping repeatedly in fresh cow dung.[46]

It took courage for a slave to help a runaway, but when it was a family member, some braved their master's fury and slipped food and other comforts to the escapee. One way of getting supplies to the runaway was to send a young slave out to hunt or fish and have him take along a lunch and bread and an old blanket or two. The boy, acting on instructions, would become "scared" when he heard a prearranged sound, such as an owl's hoot. Dropping the food and blankets, he would run back to the quarters. With this plan, the boy could not be forced to admit to having seen or helped a runaway.

If a slave trader picked up a runaway, he might sell him on "chance." In the event that the original owner turned up and claimed the slave, he would have to be returned, but if not, the slave belonged to the one who had taken a chance on him.

The constitution of 1845 provided that slaves should be treated with "humanity." Slave owners who did not feed and clothe their slaves adequately were subject to fines. A slave who committed a crime was entitled to a trial according to Texas law. But in reality, if he was judged guilty by the white men who knew him, he was likely to be swiftly punished without benefit of any legal proceedings. Generally, the owner could, if he wished, get away with outrageous cruelty. Some forced slaves whom they considered untrustworthy to work chained together in the fields. And some fitted bells and iron

43. *Brazos Courier* (Brazoria), July 10, 1840.
44. Ibid., July 17, 1840.
45. Eugene W. Bowers and Evelyn Oppenheimer, *Red River Dust*, pp. 27ff.
46. Rawick, ed., *Texas Narratives*, Walter Rimm, p. 3315.

collars around their slaves' necks to keep them docile.[47] And there were instances of outright murder of slaves by masters. Noah Smithwick, a blacksmith who worked for the McNeels, told of a slave named Jim, who was working for Pleasant McNeel. One day Jim put his hoe down and said he was leaving. Pleasant McNeel ordered him to return to work or be shot, and when Jim ignored the warning, McNeel killed him with a rifle ball.[48]

Walter Rimm remembered seeing his father whipped. He didn't know the reason for the beating but told his interviewer that the slaves were whipped "ever' time de Marster feels cross," and added, " 'Twarn't nothin' Ise could does 'cept stand dere an' cry."[49]

Another former slave recalled seeing his mother's back so raw and bloody that she couldn't get her clothes off without help. She told him that the master had beaten her with a hand saw.[50]

The threat of whippings was always in the minds of the slaves even on plantations where they were seldom actually carried out. Jeff Calhoun said there was little whipping done on the plantation where he worked, but when one was carried out, it made a lasting impression on those who witnessed—as it was probably intended to do:

> I hab seed de slaves hands tied to a pole above der heads and de blood whipped outen dem, dey hab to be carried away. Den I seed dem tied hand and foot and a stick run under der nees and oveh der arms at de elbows and kicked oveh and whipped worsen a dog. Dey too had to be carried away.

These punishments, he added, were given to runaways.[51]

Even kind masters would not tolerate insubordination. Julien Devereux, who was careful that his slaves not work outside in bad weather, noted in his memorandum book that his overseer had given "July and Flora and Seven a good thrashing which they well deserved for impudence." And he mentioned having a fifteen-pound "clog made to put on negro man Ben."[52]

Slaves who survived the abuse of unkind masters learned to protect themselves. If the master was stingy with food, there were ways to sneak up on a chicken and kill it silently. With potato banks, watermelon patches, smokehouses, and cooks whose aprons had big pockets, there were always ways to get more to eat on a plantation.

If an overseer or master "pushed" too hard, there were ways to slow up the pace without risking punishment for being lazy. Field hands knew that if they picked a certain amount of cotton on a good day, they were apt to be

47. Rawick, ed., *Texas Narratives*, pp. 731, 881, 1690, 3315, 4289; *Houston Chronicle*, Apr. 19, 1936.
48. Noah Smithwick, *The Evolution of a State or Recollections of Old Texas Days*, p. 24.
49. Rawick, ed., *Texas Narratives*, Walter Rimm, pp. 3312–15.
50. Ibid., William Moore, p. 2767.
51. Ibid., Jeff Calhoun, p. 605.
52. Dorman H. Winfrey, *Julien Sidney Devereux and His Monte Verdi Plantation*, p. 73.

held to that amount the next, so they deliberately picked less. Since hard work brought slaves only the "reward" of more work, weavers and spinners also underproduced so that their tasks would be kept light. A plantation covered many acres, and the taskmasters could not be everywhere at once. The slaves used warning signals to alert a worker who might be taking a nap between corn rows to the approach of an overseer.

Forced breeding between the strongest and healthiest male and female slaves on some plantations was a grim fact of life. A robust young male would be designated a "stud" and expected to mate with women selected by the master.

Mollie Dawson said, "Dey would let you pick out a man or a man pick him out a woman and you was married and if de woman wouldn't has de man dat picks you, dey would takes you ter a big stout high husky nigger somewhere and leaves you a few days jest lak dey do stock now'days and you bettah begins raisin' chilluns too. If you didn' dey would works you ter death, dey say dat you no count and dey soon sells you.[53] Lewis Jones told his interviewer that his father was a "breedin' nigger," who had fathered at least fifty children on his master's plantation in Fayette County.[54] Katie Darling recalled that her master would pick out "a po'tly man and a po'tly gal and jist 'put 'em to-gether.' What they wanted was the stock."[55]

Jeptha Choice, whose master allowed him to attend the white children's school, reported that he was "much in demand for breedin'." He said, "The old Massa was mighty careful about the raisin' of healthy nigger families, and used us strong, healthy young bucks to 'stand' the healthy young gals."[56]

Rose Williams yielded to her master's demands to mate with a young, black male slave only after she was threatened with being whipped at the stake. She had two children by him, but separated from him after the Civil War.[57]

A strong belief that developed among women slaves was that chewing cotton roots would prevent pregnancies. Many young female slaves tried this method of contraception, rather than "breed" children for their masters. Women slaves also tried to terminate unwanted pregnancies by taking strong doses of turpentine and calomel.[58]

Another tragedy for young, attractive female slaves on some Texas plantations was that the white men—master, sons, or overseer—forced them to have sexual relations. Sometimes the result was what the slaves called "bright Negroes"—half-white children born to black mothers. Sometimes

53. Rawick, ed., *Texas Narratives*, Mollie Dawson, p. 1122.
54. Ibid., Lewis Jones, p. 2109.
55. Ibid., Katie Darling, p. 1050.
56. Ibid., Jeptha ("Doc") Choice, p. 709.
57. Ibid., Rose Williams, pp. 4117, 4121–23.
58. Rawick, ed., *Texas Narratives*, pp. 875, 1453, 2284, 2299.

these children were treated as favorites by their white fathers, and sometimes they were ignored. But they were never considered part of the white family by either race. Any person who was one-fourth black was "colored," but the formula never worked in reverse.[59]

Amanda Brice, who grew up in Bastrop County, never knew her father. "All dat I know is dat he was a white man," she told her interviewer.[60] Sarah remembered that "Marster Kit" Patton on his plantation near West Columbia had "a African woman from Kentucky for his wife." She was "uppity over the slaves," but Sarah admitted that she did try to teach the children manners. After "Marster Kit" died, his brother Charles took over the plantation and the woman, Rachel, was put to work in the field. However, she didn't stay out in the fields long but was put in a house of her own, and "she don't work no more," Sarah said.[61]

Stories of concubinage between white masters and black female slaves still exist. But as Abigail Curlee found in her research, these tales are subject to different interpretations. As an example, she tells of one aged planter who died in a "Negro cabin" on the banks of the Brazos River. One neighbor thought the event a "disgraceful example of miscegenation." But another neighbor saw it as the pathetic episode of a man, bereft of health and wealth, being loyally cared for and nursed by a former slave.[62]

Diametrically opposite the inhumane masters was Isaiah Day, whose plantation was near Dayton in Liberty County. He and his wife treated their slaves with affection, and the slaves called him "Papa Day," as he would not permit them to call him "Master." He gave them Saturdays and Sundays off, allowed no whipping of his slaves, and warned the patrollers never to touch them, even if a slave were caught off the plantation without a pass.[63]

Other planters were also lenient and paternalistic in the treatment of their slaves. "Aunt Sallie," who nursed all of Colonel Groce's children, continued to criticize their behavior after they were grown, but she enjoyed having her own four-poster bed with a feather mattress. Ashbel Smith's overseers complained bitterly that his slaves were spoiled. Steve Brown, who had been a slave on a plantation near Waco, recalled his former owner as "a kind and reason'ble man," who gave each slave family a cow so they would have their own milk and butter. "Marster Curley" also allowed Brown and the

---

59. The Texas legislature amended the law in 1863 to read: "All free white persons who have less than one-eighth African blood come within the meaning of the term 'free white persons'; and all free white persons who have that or a quarter portion of African blood come within the meaning of the term 'free persons of color.'" Gammel, comp., *Laws of Texas* V, 600.

60. Rawick, ed., *Texas Narratives*, Amanda Brice, p. 424.

61. Ibid., Sarah Ford, pp. 1360–61.

62. Abigail Curlee Holbrook, "A Glimpse of Life on Antebellum Slave Plantations in Texas," *Southwestern Historical Quarterly* 76 (Apr., 1973): 361–83.

63. Rawick, ed., *Texas Narratives*, pp. 937–43.

other slaves to make use of the smoked meat, vegetables, honey, and the wheat flour.[64]

Julien Devereux at Monte Verdi, the Perrys at Peach Point, and Ashbel Smith at Evergreen were typical of the masters who allowed their slaves to raise small cotton, corn, and vegetable crops for themselves and to sell the produce, using the money they received however they pleased.

The Perrys at Peach Point had close relationships with their slaves. When Henry Perry went off to school, he wrote back to his father, "Do not forget to remember me to all the negroes, for . . . I love our . . . blacks who I have known since childhood, particularly say howdy to mammy, Aunt Mary, Milly, Clearsy, Simon and all the house servants, for I know they all love me well." And when the slave Simon died, Guy Bryan wrote to his half-brother Stephen Perry: "You speak in your letter of the grief you feel at the loss of Simon I too felt & felt deeply his loss for a thousand associations clustered around his name. he was the favorit body servant of Uncle [Stephen F. Austin] & then of mother & afterward of your father & lastly of yourself; he bore his part well, he was a good member of society & you & I need not think it weakness to weep over his grave." On another occasion Stephen Perry wrote: "I have lost four negroe men and one child nine years old, a very serious loss to me. . . . I considered my pecuniary loss nothing compared with the feelings that I entertained for my negroes."[65]

Further evidence that some of the planters cared about their slaves is the fact that they are mentioned in wills. Josiah Bell specified that if a servant girl named Milindy outlived Mrs. Bell, then she should be allowed to choose which of the surviving children she wished to live with. The will also instructed that Moss, a slave, be freed after Bell's death, but be allowed to live with the family for the rest of his life if he chose to and that he was to have "a comfortable living" provided by them.[66] Julien Devereux requested in his will that none of his slaves be sold, as they were all "family negroes," and asked that they be humanely treated by whichever family member took over their ownership.[67]

Most Texas planters' treatment of their slaves, as revealed in the Slave Narratives, fell somewhere between the extremes of great cruelty or great kindness. The slaves were expected to work hard from dawn to dusk, first light to first dark, sunup to sundown, "can see" to "can't," five and a half days a week. They had food, shelter, and clothing, and if they became ill,

64. Rosa Groce Bertleth, "Jared Ellison Groce," *Southwestern Historical Quarterly* 20 (Apr., 1917): 363; Rawick, ed., *Texas Narratives*, Steve Brown, p. 491.

65. Henry Perry to James Perry, Mar. 22, 1850; Henry Perry to Stephen Perry, July 13, 1859; Stephen Perry to J. H. Brown & Co., Feb., 1858, all in Perry (James F. and Stephen S.) Papers, Barker Texas History Center.

66. Josiah H. Bell will, Brazoria County Courthouse.

67. Julien S. Devereux will, Devereux (Julien Sidney) Papers, Barker Texas History Center.

they received attention. Many masters allowed their slaves to have small gardens of their own to cultivate, allowed them to make baskets in their free time, and paid them for working on Sundays when the work was pressing. Most owners permitted their slaves to visit kin and friends on neighboring plantations and to have dances and parties on their home plantation.

Humane masters like Thomas E. Blackshear, owner of an inland plantation near Navasota, cared sincerely for their bondsmen. One July 4 Blackshear noted in his journal that his slave Edmund was "quite sick" and that he had sent for a doctor. But the doctor could not cure the illness, and on July 13, Blackshear wrote: "My good negro man Edmund died. He was an honest, truthful and industrious man and a faithful servant and I shall miss his services and influence a great deal." The next day he added: "Buried Edmund with a sad heart."[68]

MISTRESSES

Just as a good master kept close watch over his crops, livestock, and outdoor workers, a good mistress watched over her household. Her role was never simple or easy, and it was especially difficult during the pioneer days of Texas plantations and again during the Civil War. During these times there were hardly enough hours in the day to do all she needed to do. She had to train the household workers to her way of cooking, serving, sewing, spinning, and weaving as well as cleaning and laundering. She often had many children of her own for whose upbringing she was responsible; in addition to teaching them manners and morals, she had to teach them school lessons when teachers were not available. She often assumed the responsibility for religious instruction, too. Frequently, the mistress of the plantation was the one best trained to care for the sick, and she was often both doctor and nurse for both black and white families. Emily Perry at Peach Point found that overseeing the cooking and cleaning, raising a vegetable garden and an orchard, and preserving everything possible taxed her strength.[69]

Probably most mistresses of Texas plantations never achieved the leisurely social life enjoyed by their counterparts in other southern states. The closest they came to it was during the "golden" decade of Texas plantations between 1850 and 1860, when the political turmoil of the earlier years had subsided and agriculture was booming. Then there was leisure for visiting (and the visits were long ones) and traveling to "watering places" (resorts on the coast or on lakes), to New York for shopping, to New Orleans for the opera. And there was more time for music, dancing, games, horseback riding, and doing fine needlework, as well as reading and writing letters filled

68. Blackshear (Thomas Edward) Papers, Barker Texas History Center.
69. Marie Beth Jones, *Peach Point Plantation: The First 150 Years*, pp. 123–25.

with family news and often enclosing locks of hair. The mistresses of Texas plantations were frequently the daughters of planters, and they often had been to colleges or finishing schools in the eastern United States. They were as avid as their husbands for news and for reading material. Lizzie Neblett, living in Robertson County, regularly read five newspapers and four magazines. She organized a reading club to share reading experiences with other women of the area.

Lizzie expressed another deep concern of many wives in the nineteenth century—how to prevent pregnancy. The term "birth control" would not be coined until the time of the first world war, but it was a very serious concern of the women on plantations, both black and white. Apparently Lizzie used some of the crude devices (such as sponges) available during Victorian times, but in some of her letters to her husband she expressed a despair amounting to desperation over the fear of an endless succession of pregnancies.[70] A sad corollary to the many births was that medical science was still in its formative stages, and there were many infant deaths.

One woman, Rebecca McIntosh Hagerty, managed two plantations after she was widowed. Her cash crop on the Refuge plantation in Marion County and the Phoenix plantation in Harrison County was cotton. By the time of the Civil War she owned more than a hundred slaves. She allowed her slaves to have their own vegetable gardens and encouraged the women to grow flowers. A former slave of Mrs. Hagerty's told an interviewer that her mistress was "not mean but she *was* stern."[71]

Other former slaves remembered mistresses who were "angels" and some who were "she-devils." Katie Darling, a slave on a plantation in Harrison County, remembered that her mistress impressed on her that "niggers was made to work for white folks."[72] And Susan Merritt recalled a mistress who threatened her own daughter, Miss Bessie, with a cowhiding if she were caught trying to teach Susan to read and write. Susan also related that one day when she was helping to make soap, some little chickens got in the fire around the pot and burned to death. The mistress blamed Susan and made her walk barefooted through a bed of coals several times.[73]

Jacob Branch remembered the horror of wash day for his mother:

Eb'ry washday de ol' mistus give her a beatin'. She couldn' keep de flies from speckin' de clo's overnight. Ol' mistus git up soon in de mawnin', befo' mama have time to git de specks off. Den she snort and say, 'Renee, soo'n you git breakfas' and wash dem dishes I's gwineter teach you how to wash.' Den she beat her wid a cowhide. Look like she gwineter cut my po' mama in two. Many's de time I edge up and try to tek some dem licks off my mama.[74]

70. Neblett (Lizzie Scott) Papers, Barker Texas History Center.
71. Hagerty (Rebecca McIntosh Hawkins) Papers, Barker Texas History Center; Rawick, ed., *Texas Narratives*, Katie Darling, p. 1051.
72. Rawick, ed., *Texas Narratives*, Katie Darling, p. 280.
73. Ibid., Susan Merritt, pp. 2642–44.
74. Ibid., Jacob Branch, p. 410.

But Lucy Thomas, who grew up on the plantation of the Baldwins in Harrison County remembered that her mistress was so kind they called her "Love" instead of by her name.[75] And another former slave, Ann Ladly, recalled that the day freedom was announced, she and her mistress hugged each other and cried together.[76]

CHILDREN

Black children born to house servants had a special relationship with the white children they grew up with. Suckled by the same black mammies and taught manners and morals by the same white adults, they shared many of the same attitudes and prejudices. Children of both races referred to shiftless white people as "poor white trash," and both considered the house workers a cut above "cornfield niggers." Plantation slaves liked to consider their own white family as "quality folks" and brag about their master's house and possessions.

On many plantations the small black and white children at the big house shared the same games—the white children's games—of hide-and-seek, ring-around-a-rosy, drop-the-handkerchief, and puss-in-the-corner. They listened spellbound to their nurses' tales of Brer Rabbit and other animal stories that came originally from the slaves' African homeland.[77] From these tales the children absorbed, along with the humor and dialect, the shrewd philosophy they contained. The hero of the stories is usually Brer Rabbit, weak and harmless, but never helpless. He is tricky but not cruel, using his wits and cleverness to turn misfortune into triumph against the bear, the wolf, and the fox—all more powerful creatures than he.

As they grew older, the children played together—climbing trees, jumping on haystacks, fishing and wading in the creeks, swimming in the ponds, and riding the plow horses and mules. They also got into mischief together by chasing geese, teasing pigs, pinching frosting off cakes when the cook's back was turned, and dipping their fingers in the juice box in the sugarhouse. Sometimes when a black child had done something naughty, he would run and hide behind his indulgent white mistress for protection. In the same way, a white child who had done something he shouldn't might hide behind the skirts of his black mammy to escape his just deserts.

W. S. Needham, Jr., the son of a planter, remembered being protected from the wrath of his mother by two women slaves named Ca'line and Mary: "I wasn't mean, but was mischievous, and they knew it; so they tried to shield me from whippings. Ma would take out after me and I'd run to one

75. Ibid., Lucy Thomas, p. 3801.
76. Ibid., Ann Ladly, p. 2260.
77. Joel Chandler Harris collected these stories, which he had heard the plantation slaves tell, and published them as stories told by a fictional character called Uncle Remus.

of them. They were big women and I'd run under their dresses, and they'd beg off for me." He recalled one time when his mother was "madder than usual," and he hid under the covers in Mary's bunk in her cabin. When Mary discovered him, she carried him back to the big house, but persuaded his mother not to whip him until the morning, knowing that by that time her mistress would have cooled down and he would be out of danger.[78]

A former slave named Austin said that he had never seen a grown slave whipped on the plantation where he worked, but he told his interviewer it was different with children. "Dey got ter hab dere hide loosened iffen dey gwine grow up right. But Mammy and de odder servants whipped dem, white and cullud. You see, de sarvants dey had to look atter de w'ite one er grownin' up same as de cullud. An' effen dey didn't make 'em mind den dey grow up no 'count."[79]

In only a few years, however, the difference in their status became clear to the children of both races. In their pretend games, the children acted out the same roles as their parents, with the white children bossing the black. There were differences in their dress. The white children had store-bought clothes of fine materials, and the slave children, both boys and girls, usually wore only long homespun cotton shirts (called "duckings") until they were almost in their teens.

The toys, too, were different. Little black girls were likely to have corn-shuck or rag dolls, while the white girls had fine china ones with elaborate wardrobes. The little black boy played marbles with pecans or small dried mud balls and played ball with wadded-up socks, while the white boy had store-bought marbles and balls.

Besides having a black mammy, white children were taught to call some of the older slaves, who were favorites of the white family, "Uncle" and "Aunty." Since the slaves were never addressed as Mr. and Mrs., it was a way of showing them respect. Some of the "uncles" built swings and playhouses for the white children, and the "aunties" looked after them in the nurseries. Often a strong bond of affection existed between the young masters and mistresses and these favorites.

The children of slaves learned early that they were born to work. As soon as they were able, they were given such tasks as pulling weeds, picking up scrap cotton, or acting as moving scarecrows to keep the birds out of the corn and the hawks away from young turkeys. As soon as they were strong enough, they were assigned such tasks as hauling water barrels on wooden slides to the field workers and carrying their meals to them. By the time they reached ten, they might be doing field work such as hoeing and learning to plow. Female slaves were considered more skillful and careful hoers than the males. Young slaves who showed quickness and aptitude were informally ap-

78. Rawick, ed., *Texas Narratives*, W. S. Needham, Jr., pp. 4362–63.
79. Ibid., Lou Austin, p. 126.

prenticed to learn the skills of master cobblers, tanners, blacksmiths, and other craftsmen.

The black child who had been made a pet in the big house sometimes had a harder transition to make than the child in the quarters. Their favored status might end abruptly as they were put to picking up shuttles in the sewing room, bringing in kindling, hunting for eggs, and feeding the chickens and ducks. Older children learned to milk and were assigned to amuse and watch out for younger children, black and white. Young black girls worked in the nurseries or "depots," where new mothers left their children while they worked. The supervisor of these nurseries was usually an older black woman, who was called a "granny" or an "aunty." On large plantations there might be many black babies in cradles. A common way to quiet them between their mothers' visits for feedings was to tie a piece of fat bacon on a string around the babies' wrists to serve as a pacifier. Houseboys and housegirls learned to build fires, make beds, empty slops, run errands, make and use brooms of weeds and mops of rags, churn, shoo flies off tables and white adults with feather fans, and to wait on table. Sometimes the black playmate of a white child would be assigned to him or her as a companion and servant. Out of these relationships there might develop a deep and lifelong affection.

Victorian-era American workers of all kinds and all ages worked long hours in comparison with today's labor force. They also believed that sparing the rod spoils the child, and it was common practice to discipline children with blows from switches, rulers, and whips. White masters demanded the same long hours as well as obedience from their slaves.

The residents of Texas plantations, both slaves and masters, were fallible humans, neither angels nor devils. Masters could be solicitous or cruel, their slaves docile or rebellious. But even the most contented slave with the kindest of masters knew slavery was wrong and longed to be free. With tyrannical or sadistic owners and overseers, slavery was an unspeakable horror.

CHAPTER THREE

Necessities & Luxuries

"A stranger would be astonished to see, in this infant settlement, a taste & luxury displayed by females, in the articles of dress which would compare with that of the old settlements in our country."
—Mary Austin Holley

THE ELEMENTS

The Texas planter's wealth depended on the land he owned. One reason the settlers had so much trouble with the Indians was that they chose the same sites that the Indians preferred—and for the same reasons. Both groups needed to be near good, abundant timber and water. The relationship of the planter to nature was close and intimate. At times he must have felt hostage to it, when plagued by long periods of drought or flood, hailstorms, swarms of crop-eating insects, and epidemics that carried off numbers of his work force.

Others might ask how many acres he owned, how many slaves he had, or how much stock, but nobody asked how much money he had in the bank, for there were no banks as such to put money in. Even large planters lived on credit, paying their doctor only once or twice a year and reckoning up with their agents only after the crops were in. If the crops were good and he had cash left after he bought the basic necessities and whatever luxuries the family decided on, he almost invariably invested in more land and more slaves. If either master or slave had a little cash he did not intend to spend immediately, he was apt to bury it in the earth, near some landmark to help him remember where it was. He didn't hide it in his wooden house for fear it would be destroyed by another element—fire.

The Texas pioneers depended on fire to live comfortably. It was necessary to create light, cook food, provide warmth, heat water for washing, and provide heat for such craftsmen as blacksmiths and tinsmiths. Normally, fires were continuously burning for some reason on a plantation, and hot coals to start a new fire were always available. Copper boxes called "tinder boxes" were used to carry live coals from the fireplace to the slave quarters or wherever they were needed. Although friction matches were available by the time Texas became a republic, they were clumsy affairs that gave off poisonous gases, and it was safer to carry a piece of flint and metal to strike sparks to start a fire when traveling.

As much as he depended on the power of fire, the frontier dweller had great respect for it. When it got out of hand, there was little chance of stopping it until it had done great damage. Even with long lines of slaves participating, bucket brigades from the nearest source of water were not often effective. Since fires most often occurred in the kitchen, these rooms were built as separate structures, a little distance from the rest of the house. Prairie grass was tall and lush in Texas, but when it became dry, it caught fire easily and became a raging wall of flame and smoke, striking terror into man and beast. Julien Devereux, in Austin serving in the legislature, wrote back to his wife, "Next to the health of my family and my negroes the dread of fire gives me more uneasiness."[1] To form barriers to prairie fires, planters plowed around their wooden fences, and where they did not have fences, they plowed a few furrows as firebreaks. Another method used to stop prairie fires was to start a smaller fire ahead of the oncoming flames and hope that it burned back fast enough to meet the big fire and keep it from jumping over the burned grass and continuing on its way. Ahead of the fire would be rabbits, rats, opossums, skunks, and cattle fleeing toward the river, but only the fastest made it if the wind was blowing strongly.

Many of the early planters and their wives, especially those who had just settled on the Gulf Coast and in Central Texas, wrote back to friends in the States praising the delightful air of Texas. They changed their tunes sharply after their first experiences with "blue northers" that roared down upon them without warning, seemingly straight from the North Pole and sometimes dropping the temperature by forty degrees in minutes.

Farmers in Texas kept careful weather records, which reveal how time after time too much rain or an extended drought ruined their chances for good crops. Hurricanes and tornadoes were unwelcome surprises as there was no warning system except for the intuition of some weather-wise older person, who watched the skies and read the signs. Rings around the moon could mean rain, and the color of the sky and cloud formations could indicate wet or dry weather or the approach of storms.

The availability of water was of prime consideration in choosing the site for a plantation. Wood was important, but water was essential. Fortunately, Texas has many rivers and creeks and in most years an abundant (and sometimes overabundant) rainfall in the middle and eastern parts of Texas where the planters settled. Some fortunate settlers got pure water from plentiful springs on their land; others got good water by digging wells and by catching rainwater in big cisterns, above or below the ground. The cistern water was usually reserved for use by the white family and for sugar making.

Hauling water was not a favorite chore among the slaves. The

1. Dorman H. Winfrey, *Julien Sidney Devereux and His Monte Verdi Plantation*, p. 116.

wooden buckets or tubs were heavy, and the spring or well was often some distance from the house. The wooden buckets that sat on shelves outside each slave cabin had to be kept filled, and water had to be hauled to the field hands by the barrelful. Wash days were especially hard, for the water carriers had to haul many gallons to clean the clothes and linens for the large families and frequent guests in the big house.

SHELTER

Exterior   After choosing their plantation site, the pioneer family had immediate need for shelter for protection from Indians, wild animals, and weather. They were, naturally, anxious to begin living in something more substantial than the tents and wagons that were their temporary homes. A log cabin was the quickest kind of dwelling to erect.

The only absolutely necessary tool was an ax, which could be used to fell trees, trim them into logs, make saddle or dovetail notches, and fit the logs together. The builder could fill the chinks between the logs with clay mixed with straw, mud, rags, moss, or whatever was at hand. Then with his chopping, or felling, ax, he could make the necessary furniture and cut fuel for his fireplace.

Most new planters brought a number of carpentering tools with them in addition to their essential axes. With time, and if his laborers were more skillful, a planter might build a house of logs hewn flat with chisel-edged broadaxes and rived (split) with a froe (a knife-type wedge which was hit with a wooden mallet or "froe-club"). With a froe the carpenter could split a block of wood into shingles or clapboards. Drawing knives were used to shave the boards into smooth facings for windows and doors.

When available, saws were used in construction work. They varied from lightweight one-man saws to heavy two-man saws with a frame around them, to the long, ungainly pit saw used to cut logs into boards. To use the pit saw, a log was laid across an open pit. The man at the top of the pit straddled the log and held the top handle or metal tiller, while the man in the pit held the wooden "box" handle at the smaller end of the saw. It no doubt took some practice and considerable cooperation to make this awkward contraption work.

The log houses were more weatherproof and more permanent than the log cabins. Either log cabin or log house might have one or two rooms and an attic space that could be used as a sleeping room. Two-room log cabins or houses had an open hall, called a "dog run" or "dog trot," a long gallery or front porch, and a shed at the back to increase the living space. Another improvement was to join two cabins together to make a "double" log cabin. With a roof over the dog run, the area of the house was more than doubled.

Down Home

Except for fine cloth, furniture & staples like coffee, flour & salt, the typical plantations were self-sufficient.

The "Big House" Ⓐ, was home to the owner & his family.

The Kitchen Ⓑ was a separate, but attached building.

Vegetables, herbs & ornamentals were grown in a nearby garden Ⓒ.

The cash crop covered most of the land Ⓓ, & was worked by slave labor housed in "the quarters" Ⓔ.

Besides the field & house chores, slaves performed skilled jobs in the carriage house Ⓕ, blacksmith shop Ⓖ, & as animal caretakers around the barn & stock pens Ⓗ.

The cotton gin Ⓘ was set up as close to transportation as possible, in this case, the plantation's own riverboat dock Ⓙ.

Most plantations employed overseers who lived, with their families, close by the "Big House" Ⓚ.

Whites were laid to rest in the family cemetery Ⓛ.

Gone with the Wind

Most Texas plantations were untouched by the Civil War, with buildings & land intact. But freedom for slaves meant the end of cheap labor, and the end of the plantation. Many planters tried to keep going, offering to let former slaves share crop. Blacks wanted their own land though, & in a short time, packed their families & left.

A new wave of deposed southern farmers moved in & for a time, filled the share cropper role, but they, too, were looking for greener pastures.

By the start of the 20th century, outbuildings had fallen into disrepair or turned into silage storage.

Individual gins had shut down, bigger ones in nearby towns taking their place.

The once sprawling land holdings were divided up & sold for living expenses or taxes, the planter's children or grand-children holding on to the big house & grounds.

Chimneys could be built of stone or brick, but the simplest and quickest kind was the "mud-cat" chimney. Four tall posts were sunk into the ground for the four chimney corners. They were inclined slightly toward each other to make the chimney narrower at the top so it would draw the smoke upward. The crosspieces of wood were tied to the posts one above the other on all four sides. This framework was covered inside and out with clay mixed with dried grass or moss. The clay and grass or moss were mixed together into lumps called "cats and bats" before being thickly plastered onto the wooden frame.

At best these chimneys needed constant rebuilding, and at worst they frequently caught fire. When this happened at night, all the occupants of the cabin leaped out of their beds and joined together to push the chimney away from the rest of the building.

After the crops were established and he could spare the labor, the planter was ready to construct a more impressive residence. Usually he built a larger separate house and used the original cabin for other purposes, such as a "bachelor's hall" for the family's sons or a guesthouse for visitors, of whom there were many. Sometimes, however, he covered the original log building with clapboard and built onto and around it. The Varner-Hogg plantation, just south of present-day West Columbia, is said to incorporate the original log cabin built by Martin Varner inside its fourteen-inch-thick walls.[2]

David McCormick, who was trained in the building business, also used the principle of beginning with a log cabin and building around it. His nephew, Andrew McCormick, left us an excellent description of this dwelling:

> . . . the lumber in this house was gotten out of the woods by hand. The walls and the upper and lower joists were hewed logs; the floors window and door frames, facings and shutters, and the rafters, were whip-sawed hard ash lumber; the roof was of red cypress all heart split shingles; the sills were live oak, hewed to twelve inches square, the plates of Spanish oak hewed to ten inches square; the other logs were 22 feet long, twelve to fifteen inches in diameter, hewed down on two opposite sides so as to form a slab six inches thick; each end was so worked that in raising the walls, the ends of the logs or slabs would dove-tail together, forming a perfect joint and true perpendicular corner and reduce the space between the logs in the body of each wall, to a uniform size.
>
> These spaces were chinked with short thin split pieces of wood, worked in so as to set at an angle of forty-five degrees from the perpendicular. These chink pieces were from six to eight inches long, three to four inches wide and about one-half inch thick, and were so set in and driven that the lower edge of the lower end would jam hard against the log below it, and the upper edge of the upper end would jam hard against the log above it. . . .

2. "Tour Guide through Varner-Hogg Plantation Museum" (leaflet), Texas Parks and Wildlife Department, July, 1984.

These lines of chinked-in spaces were then plastered inside and out with good mortar of oyster-shell lime and sharp sand.

Andrew McCormick said that this log cabin was proof against all stress of weather, as well as being roomy, comfortable, and "sightly." Later on it had large additions made of "first-class mill-sawed cypress lumber," but McCormick maintained "the log room remained the best room in the larger dwelling house for twenty-five or thirty years."[3]

Noah Smithwick, an itinerant blacksmith, visited Thomas B. Bell, one of Austin's Old Three Hundred in the early days of settlement. He found the family living in a small cabin in the middle of a crop of corn. They were dressed in buckskins and ate sitting on stools around a clapboard table. The forks were made from joints of cane, and the knives ranged from butcher knives to pocketknives, while the cups were made from squash, scraped clean. The gracious host and hostess made no apologies for the simple food, which was served with fresh, sweet milk. Later, Smithwick reported, a handsome brick plantation house replaced the cabin, and the furnishings were the best "the country boasted."[4]

When they decided to build their manor houses, the pioneer planters relied on their memories of the mansions they had known in their old home states. The Greek Revival Style was the most popular, and many Texas plantations were characterized by spacious, high-ceilinged rooms, wide halls, and upper and lower verandas or galleries supported by tall columns. These homes were so well built that many lasted until they were swept away by fire or, in coastal areas, by the 1900 hurricane. And a few are still lived in today— a century and a half after their construction.

In the Gulf Coast area, a number of planters built mansions. As soon as Jared Groce was fairly settled at Bernardo, he put his slaves to work building a large, rambling story-and-a-half house of cottonwood logs. Hewn and counterhewn, these logs were as smooth as glass. Downstairs a large hall, fifteen feet wide with two large rooms on each side, and a gallery ran the length of the house. Six polished walnut columns supported the front gallery. The back gallery connected with a kitchen that had a huge fireplace across one end for cooking. Upstairs there were two rooms and a hall. The outbuildings included the overseer's house, a dairy, a doctor's house, quarters for the slaves, a day nursery for their children, and a separate kitchen and dining hall for their use. In his office building in the yard, Groce received his overseer each morning and conducted the business of the plantation. The original log building in which the family had lived became "bachelor's hall."[5]

For his daughter and son-in-law's Eagle Island plantation, Groce wrote to a friend in Mobile, Alabama, and asked him to have a house that he

3. Andrew Phelps McCormick, *Scotch-Irish in Ireland and in America*, pp. 52–54.
4. Noah Smithwick, *The Evolution of a State or Recollections of Old Texas Days*, p. 24.
5. Groce Family Papers, Barker Texas History Center.

admired copied. The friend obliged, and all of the lumber was pre-cut and numbered in Mobile. Then it was shipped across the Gulf of Mexico and up the Brazos River. The doors, window frames, and interior woodwork were solid mahogany. On the ground floor, four twenty-by-twenty-foot rooms were separated by a twenty-foot hall. The top floor had two large rooms and a hall. The walls were plastered. Later, two additional rooms were added, and the double office building and main house were able to accommodate thirty guests at a time. A large separate kitchen was kept busy providing meals for the family and a continuous parade of guests.[6] The separation of the kitchen from the main house not only safeguarded the big house in case of a kitchen fire but also kept the cooking odors, heat, and clatter isolated.

Stephen F. Austin's elaborate plans for Peach Point plantation had to be modified to suit his brother-in-law and sister's needs, but the development of the Perrys' plantation is a good example of how many Texas planters' estates grew over the years. At first there was a plain log house for the family. More rooms were added as time and finances permitted. Although Peach Point never boasted as grand a main house as some of the nearby plantations, it was planned for comfort. At Emily's insistence it included a number of closets, a feature rarely found in nineteenth-century homes.

A number of outbuildings served various purposes at Peach Point. One building was James Perry's office. Another was the washhouse, where the backbreaking work of keeping the family's clothes and linens clean was accomplished. The sewing room for spinning, weaving, mending, and making the slaves' clothes was in a separate building. Another cabin doubled as a schoolroom and as a place for Sunday services when a minister was available. A sugarhouse was added when sugarcane became an important crop at Peach Point. Also scattered around the grounds were cribs for storing corn and potatoes, plus two large brick cisterns for rainwater storage, and a privy. Emily Perry, anticipating a visit from her cousin Mary Austin Holley in 1837, wrote to her husband James, urging, "If you should have Carpenters imployed, I wish you to have a *Necessary House* built in the Back Yard, in the corner of the Fence by the Lane. . . . It can be set over a dich; these *City Dames* will think it Horrible to run into the Woods. . . ."[7]

Emily, who liked for everything to look nice, wanted both the fences and the house whitewashed "inside and out." One wagonload of seashells, she noted, would make enough lime to whitewash everything.

The Sweeny plantation on Chance's Prairie in Brazoria County was the center of a bustling community in the early days of Texas. In its confines were a brick kiln, a cotton gin, a commissary, a smithy, and a post office. When the mail boat docked at Columbia, a rider would carry the mail to Chance's Prairie. After spending the night at the Sweeny plantation, he went

6. Groce (Jared E. and Leonard W.) Family Papers, Waller County Public Library.
7. Perry (James F. and Stephen S.) Papers, Barker Texas History Center.

on to Matagorda to meet the boat there. He would then reverse the process.[8]

Maj. Abner Jackson planned and developed several plantations in Brazoria County, including one that became part of the Retrieve Penitentiary. Jackson's first residence in Texas was an elm-and-ash log cabin at Lake Jackson. As time passed, he built an impressive estate there, converting every cabin; the sugarhouse; and his twelve-room, two-story residence to brick, which he covered with stucco an inch thick, making all the buildings look as if they were made of solid rock. The main house was estimated to have cost more than twenty-five thousand dollars, not counting the slave labor used to build it.[9]

Generally, brick buildings were considered more fireproof and more durable than wooden ones, and even in their wooden houses, planters used brick foundations and fireplaces. In the early days of Texas plantation life, the bricks had to be made by hand. Any location that was considered suitable for planting usually had good red or yellow clay that could be used to make bricks. In the soft-mud process common in Texas before the Civil War, clay was mixed with water, poured into sanded wooden molds, and left to dry until the bricks shrank enough to be removed. Then they were set in a kiln or oven of brick or stone, and fired for days until they were hard. Metal molds gave sharper outlines to the brick, but they were harder to come by than wooden ones. The difference in the way bricks were used can be seen in Mimosa Hall, a plantation near Marshall. The face brick of the house front is made of precisely defined metal-molded bricks, while the bricks on the sides and back are more uneven and varied in size and obviously were made from wooden molds. These handmade bricks were often, but not always, larger and wider than modern bricks. Keystone-shaped bricks were molded for wells, cisterns, and the popular soaring columns that graced many plantations.

Because the bricks were made in fairly primitive kilns, they had a wide range of shapes and colors. Those bricks stacked nearest the flames were baked harder and darker than those on the outside of the kiln. These hard inside bricks were called "clinkers" or "iron" bricks. The bricks placed nearest the outside baked to a bright orange and were called "salmon" bricks, while those cooked in between the outside and the center bricks turned a reddish color and were called "cherry" bricks.[10]

Mortar to hold the bricks together was made by mixing sand with lime and water. Lime could be imported, but it was also made on the plantations by burning shells or natural limestone.

Several of the grander plantation houses were dubbed "castles." In Colorado County, "Robson's Castle" was a showplace. It covered fifty acres

8. Sweeny (John) Papers, Brazoria County Historical Museum.
9. Abner J. Strobel, *The Old Plantations and Their Owners of Brazoria County, Texas*; plantation file, Brazoria County Historical Museum.
10. Rebecca Fortson Fitch, "The Use of Native Materials in the Ante Bellum Buildings of Harrison County, Texas," M.A. thesis, North Texas State College, 1952.

and was built of gravel and homemade lime. Surrounded by a moat with a drawbridge, it was probably the first building in Texas to have a roof garden and running water.[11]

For more than sixty years a four-story mansion of huge proportions dominated the countryside near Coles Settlement (now Independence). Named Ingleside plantation, it was commonly called "Clay Castle." Nestor Clay, a relative of Henry Clay, began building the enormous, native-stone house, and his brother, Tacitus Clay, completed it in 1836 or 1837. Clay Castle was constructed in the popular plantation style with a long center hall flanked by two large rooms on either side. A graceful circular staircase led to the four large bedrooms on the second floor. The third floor was given over entirely to a huge ballroom. Atop this was the glassed-in "captain's walk" from which the owner could survey his extensive cotton fields and magnificent orchards.[12]

The German planters who settled in Central Texas for the most part disliked using slave labor and preferred to work small amounts of land with the help of family and hired workers. Their houses, well built and modest, reflected their philosophy of farming. An exception was Nassau plantation near La Grange, purchased by the Count von Boos-Waldeck, a leader in the organization of German noblemen that was founded to colonize Germans in Texas. Ferdinand Roemer, a German geologist, who was in Texas from 1845 to 1847, wrote a description of the manor house at Nassau:

> The whole house is built of rough hewn oak logs carefully grooved, lying horizontally over each other. It is separated in two parts, according to the custom of the country, forming in the center an open covered passage, which offers the inhabitants a cool, pleasant resort in summer. . . . On each end of the house is a fireplace built of ashlar stones reaching several feet above the top of the house which gives to the whole building a stately appearance. . . . Farm buildings of plantation lie about a gunshot distant from the manor house at the foot of a hill. Barns, storage houses, negro cabins and house for the overseer—all are rough log houses, made of roughly hewn logs covered with shingles.[13]

In Washington County, Thomas Affleck's plantation resembled a feudal settlement. The manor house included six bedrooms, two wide halls, a kitchen, laundry room, storeroom, dining room, parlor, and three enclosed galleries plus two open galleries that ran the length of the house. Near the big house were a lumber room, carriage house, stables, poultry yard, pigeonry, and a number of servants' houses. About two miles distant were the overseer's house, church, hospital, storehouse, and twenty frame slave houses. Close by

11. William Bollaert, *William Bollaert's Texas*, ed. William Eugene Hollon and Ruth Lapham Butler, p. 243; Colorado County scrapbook, Barker Texas History Center.
12. Betty Plummer, "The Clay House," *Historic Homes of Washington County, 1821–1860*, 45–52.
13. Ferdinand Roemer, *Texas: With Particular Reference to German Immigration*, trans. Oswald Mueller, p. 163; *Handbook of Texas* II, 259.

them were a sugar mill, flour mill, ginhouse, press, sawmill, blacksmith shop, and a house for the mill foreman.[14]

In Central Texas, near Salado, Elijah Sterling Clack Robertson, son of empresario Sterling C. Robertson, built a twenty-two-room mansion of cypress lumber. Off the front and back porches were rooms called "stranger's" guest rooms. These rooms, which did not open into the house, but only onto the porches, allowed the family to be hospitable to wayfarers and still maintain their privacy. Adjacent to the big house was a service area of native limestone, which included a laundry room, meat room, servants' dining room, kitchen, slave quarters, and stables. The burial grounds for white and black lay behind the house. Family and friends called the house "Sterling's Castle."[15] In 1986 this home is one of the most complete plantation complexes remaining in Texas, and it has been lived in by members of the same family for more than one hundred years.

Monte Verdi plantation in southeastern Rusk County was a showplace for that area. Located on a beautiful hill, it provided a splendid view of much of the 10,000 acres owned by Julien Sidney Devereux. With its long, columned front porch, fireplace in each spacious room, and kitchen some fifty feet from the house, it might have been lifted from some hillside in Virginia or Mississippi.[16]

In 1845 Holland Coffee, trader and planter, built Glen Eden plantation in North Texas. For ninety-seven years it was a showplace of Grayson County. Built like the typical stately homes of Texas planters, it had dog-trot halls upstairs and down, and walls and floors of split logs covered on the outside with clapboards. Great chimneys of native rock with huge fireplaces furnished heat. An unusual feature was a large wine cellar.[17]

In East Texas, planters also patterned their manor houses after the architecture of the grand mansions their owners had known in other southern states. Edgemont plantation just outside Marshall is a good example. The builder, Montraville J. Hall, was a prominent planter who was once nominated for governor of Texas. Edgemont was constructed by slaves using bricks made of clay dug on the grounds and lumber cut from trees growing there. The walls are three feet thick, and the rafters of heart pine are three inches thick and a foot wide. The twenty-acre yard is enhanced by hundreds of oaks. The seventy-foot-deep brick-lined well still yields pure water today. The barn of hewn logs could hold one hundred head of stock. A thirty-foot-long horse trough, hewn from a single pine log, watered the stock. Among the many outbuildings were a large log smokehouse and an icehouse.[18]

The William Thomas Scott home near Marshall represents another

14. *Handbook of Texas* I, 696.
15. Lucille (Mrs. Sterling C.) Robertson, interview with the author, Salado, Texas.
16. Devereux (Julien Sidney) Papers, Barker Texas History Center.
17. Mrs. J. W. Johnson, interview with Hazel B. Greene, Woodville, Tex., n.d., transcript, Barker Texas History Center.
18. Max S. Lale, "Edgemont" (July 6, 1981), typescript, Harrison County Museum.

kind of architecture that was popular in East Texas. Scott, who owned a total of five plantations, was the supreme empire builder in his section of Texas. For his manor house he chose a high spot surrounded by century-old oaks. This home, which became the nucleus for the community of Scottsville, is a raised cottage with clapboards of native timber. The boards are fitted to each other with wooden pegs. The glass and shutters for the windows were transported by steamboat from New Orleans to Jefferson by way of Caddo Lake and hauled by wagon to the plantation site.

Colonel Scott set aside land for a church site, cemeteries for the black and white families, and land for a camp meeting ground. Since he had business ties to New Orleans, he maintained an apartment on Dryad Street, where the family spent the winters.[19]

Another example of the raised cottage (combined with some Greek Revival details) in East Texas is the well-preserved Freeman plantation near Jefferson. The wood used in the foundation and frame was hand-sawed native pine and cypress joined together with wooden pegs. Stucco and white paint give the towering columns a smooth, striking finish. Both interior and exterior walls are made of brick manufactured by slaves from the red clay found on the grounds.[20]

Interior   As the number of cotton and sugar plantations in Texas grew, so did the ability of the planters to live more luxuriously. More boats coming to haul away the plantation produce meant that those boats could bring lumber, factory-made bricks, marble, carriages, furniture, and all sorts of material comforts. Stores began to cater to the life-styles that the planters' families were beginning to live. Among the specialized shops in Washington in 1849 were sign painters, tailors, daguerreotypists, wallpaper hangers, furniture makers, several bakers, piano teachers, and one music store, as well as a shoe- and bootmaker.[21] Planters near Independence could deal with Leander Cannon, who handled everything from groceries and medicine to hardware and books.[22]

Some merchants were also planters. In Columbia there was John Adriance, who was involved in extensive buying and selling with different partners from 1836 on. His caravans transported goods to and from Matamoros, and from there they were shipped to Cuba, New Orleans, and European ports. With his partner, Morgan R. Smith, he for a time owned and operated Waldeck plantation.[23] In East Texas Matthew Cartwright was a planter and a merchant. Not only did he provide a source of necessities and

19. Scott (William T.) Papers, Harrison County Museum.
20. Freeman Family Papers, privately held, Jesse M. DeWare IV, Jefferson, Tex.
21. Pamela Ashworth Puryear, private files, Navasota, Tex.
22. Washington County Probate Minutes, 1854, Washington County Courthouse.
23. Adriance (John) Papers, Barker Texas History Center.

luxury goods for the planters of that area, but by constructing a steam sawmill he supplied them with ready-cut boards for their houses.[24]

The grand houses of the plantations required equally grand furnishings, and the plain folk watched and gossiped about some of the extravagances they observed. It caused quite a stir when Martha Foster had her square rosewood piano shipped up the Brazos all the way to Port Sullivan. But Martha was making a lasting investment, for today the piano is still sitting in the living room of her nine-room log house, although the house and the piano have been moved.[25]

Many planters' mansions had handsome marble hearths and mantels and ornately decorated ceilings in the rooms and in the halls. Heavy, elegant furniture of mahogany, walnut, and rosewood was preferred by most plantation families. Silk and wool damask drapes and black hair upholstery like that at Bernardo were popular.

As early as 1838 Eagle Island was setting the pace for gracious living. When Mary Austin Holley visited there in the spring of that year, she commented humorously on the "elegance" of riding behind plow horses to get there. But she was impressed with the Whartons' beautiful furniture, damask curtains, silver, china, and books. There were velvet carpets on the floor at Eagle Island and brass chandeliers with crystal prisms that sparkled in the sunlight or in the romantic light of dozens of candles. Large gold-framed mirrors, reaching almost to the ceiling, hung in both the parlor and the dining room.[26]

The plantation establishments with their luxurious mansions created a demand for artisans and craftsmen to satisfy the owners' desire for beauty and elegance in decorating. Rudolph Melchoir was one of the family of artisans who emigrated from Prussia and came to Round Top in Fayette County in 1853. With his brother Richard he designed stencils, painted houses, hung wallpaper, and even bound books. The interior walls of the McGregor-Grimm House at Winedale, Texas, were probably the work of Richard Melchoir. They show nearly every technique known to the nineteenth-century decorative painter on wood: freehand painting, stenciling, graining, marbleizing, and pounce-pattern transfer (using transparent paper).[27]

Dining rooms had to have very long tables to accommodate the big families and many guests who dined there daily. Large, marble-topped sideboards were popular for storage and for helping with the serving of the extensive meals. In 1848, Emily Perry ordered for Peach Point four hundred

24. *Handbook of Texas* I, 304.

25. The Foster log cabin (of both logs and milled lumber) is the headquarters building in the Log Cabin Village in Fort Worth. Foster (Harry A.) Family Papers, privately held, J. W. Foster, Jr., Calvert, Tex.

26. Mary Austin Holley Papers, Barker Texas History Center.

27. Lonn Taylor, "The McGregor-Grimm House at Winedale, Texas," *The Magazine Antiques* 108 (Sept., 1975): 515–21.

dollars' worth of silverware to include pots for coffee, tea, and cream; a sugar bowl; a slop bowl; four ivory salt spoons; and one dozen each of teaspoons, dessert spoons, dining forks, and dessert forks.[28]

The furniture in the bedrooms was handsome and beautifully carved. Beds were usually four-posters with canopies and curtains that could be opened or closed according to the weather and were so high off the floor that a two- or three-step stool was necessary to climb into them. Trundle beds that were pushed under the big beds in the daytime were often used for small children. Bed warmers (metal pans with covers and long wooden handles) hung by the bedroom fireplaces, ready to be filled with hot coals and passed between the sheets to warm the bed when the weather was cold. Soft, plump feather beds also added to the sleeper's comfort. Each bedroom had a washstand with bowl and pitcher and soap dish on top and chamber pot with cover in the bottom compartment. These items were often of exquisitely painted china.

No matter how elaborate the mansion, it did not have indoor plumbing or a bathroom in the modern sense. Usually there was a tin bathtub called a hip bath, sitz bath, or slipper bath, according to its shape. After heating water in the fireplace oven, slaves hauled it to the tub, which was placed in front of the bedroom fireplace, and the bather stepped into the bath. More water had to be heated and hauled for rinsing and for keeping the temperature pleasant for as long as the tub occupant cared to linger.

Many people in the nineteenth century considered daily bathing to be dangerous to their health. However, others were beginning to think of it as a kind of medical treatment, and bathhouses along rivers, spring-fed creeks, and the Gulf of Mexico provided places for the wealthy to change into their cumbersome bathing costumes so they could enjoy splashing in the water. Some masters recognized the importance of cleanliness to the health of their slaves and required them to bathe regularly in nearby creeks or rivers. But a majority of people, rich and poor, white and black, satisfied themselves with sponge baths or with simply washing their hands and faces.

In addition to the fancy chamber pot in the bedrooms, each plantation had at least one "necessary house" for the white family's use; it was discreetly placed at the end of a garden path. This outside toilet facility had many names, including privy, outhouse, backhouse, biffie, loo, sanitary closet, willie, and johnnie.[29]

Some well-to-do planters refined their privies by adding shuttered ventilators and stone floors. A stack of the readily available corn shucks or corncobs served as toilet paper.

28. Perry (James F. and Stephen S.) Papers, Barker Texas History Center.
29. "Johnnie" or "john" comes from the name of the Reverend Edward Johns, the original owner of the firm that imported chamber pots to America from England.

Most planters reserved a large area around their houses as a yard, and they spent considerable thought and money on the beautification of this area. At Lake Jackson, Major Jackson spent $10,000 to have an artificial island built in the lake, which he kept stocked with fish and ducks for the pleasure of his guests.[30]

Stephen F. Austin and his sister Emily took great interest in growing trees, plants, shrubs, and different kinds of vegetables, such as asparagus, at Peach Point. Austin sent back from his travels seeds and plants for her to try, including roses, quinces, figs, plums, and radishes. Apparently she was successful, as her son, Guy M. Bryan, wrote to his friend Rutherford B. Hayes in 1843: "It has been perfectly green throughout the whole of the winter. It is pleasant to a *sore-eyed man* to wander in the *dead of winter* through walks embowered with roses & fragrant shrubs of every kind and colour; to meet at every turn, the orange and the vine, the fig and pomegranate, all of which abound in my mother's yard, the product of our genial clime & mother's care.[31]

The planting on Josiah H. Bell's plantation was extensive. Enclosed in a fence of split cedar pickets was a combination orchard, flower garden, and fancy vegetable garden. Here grew quince trees, pomegranates, several kinds of plums, grafted and budded peach trees, and fig trees. There was a great variety of flowers chosen for their colors and fragrance, as well as flowering shrubs such as crape myrtles and altheas. Bermuda grass covered the open part of the yard. A European gardener was employed to direct the slaves in tending the extensive planting.[32]

At Eagle Island, John Wharton also employed an immigrant landscape gardener—a Scotsman with a green thumb. Since the family did not want the large live-oak trees around the house disturbed, he placed shade-loving plants under them. He made rose beds in open places and lined the brick walks with amaryllis bulbs. Pink crape myrtle formed a hedge along the side fence, and yellow jasmine covered one end of the long gallery. There were bowers of snowy bridal wreath, and in the various beds, almost every flower that could be grown in the south bloomed at some time in the year.[33]

In East Texas, even before William T. Scott had the manor house built, Mrs. Scott was planting the flowers and shrubs she had brought from New Orleans. She planted eighteen different kinds of trees, including apple trees, willows, redbud, peach, cherry, cedars, and pecans.[34]

30. Strobel, *Old Plantations and Their Owners*, n.p.

31. E. W. Winkler, ed., "Bryan-Hayes Correspondence," *Southwestern Historical Quarterly* 25 (Oct., 1921): 104; Perry (James F. and Stephen S.) Papers, Barker Texas History Center.

32. McCormick, *Scotch-Irish*, pp. 114–15.

33. Sarah Wharton Groce Berlet, *Autobiography of a Spoon, 1828–1856*, p. 21.

34. Scott (William T.) Papers, Harrison County Museum.

Plants and seeds were much-appreciated gifts from visiting guests. At Glen Eden there was a giant magnolia that was supposed to have been planted by Sam Houston when he was a guest. And the catalpa trees there were grown by the mistress from seed brought to her from California by Gen. Albert Sidney Johnston. These trees eventually formed an archway over the path from the front gate to the steps of the front gallery.[35] On his own plantation in Brazoria County, Johnston took great pleasure in his roses, and his wife studied Texas wild flowers and made 101 watercolor illustrations of them.[36] At Monte Verdi, Julien Devereux took pride in his orchards of peaches, plums, figs, and apples. He and his friends enjoyed trading samples from their gardens. From Nacogdoches Adolphus Sterne sent cuttings, and Dr. James Harper Starr and Devereux exchanged fruit trees and sprouts and cutting of flowers.[37]

All of this planting and cultivation enhanced the natural beauty of the plantation settings, whether they were in the midst of huge oak trees dripping with Spanish moss or set among tall pines and cedars. Many plantations had towering magnolias that provided a different kind of beauty in every season. Two favorite hedges on plantations, the Cherokee rose and the Osage orange (or bois d'arc) had the added advantage of providing beauty as well as protection from wind, animals, horse thieves, and other invaders.

THE SLAVE QUARTERS

House servants might have rooms in wings of the "big house" as those at Ellersly and Waldeck did, or they might live in cabins in the quarters with the other slaves. Slave cabins, like planters' houses, varied in construction and in comfort. Typically they were clustered together about a quarter mile from the big house.

On large plantations the slave quarters resembled small villages. At Bernardo the cabins fronted on a lake. In East Texas, Stephen W. Blount, who was noted (and criticized) for his unusually considerate treatment of his slaves, furnished them with frame cabins, twenty by twenty feet, with brick chimneys. On the William T. Scott plantation each black family had two rooms with fireplaces. These cabins were built around an open square, which was a social gathering place.[38]

Occasionally the habitations were built like barracks, as on the Robertson plantation in Central Texas, but more often they were separate small log cabins.

35. Johnson, interview with Hazel B. Greene.
36. Allen Andrew Platter, "Educational, Social, and Economic Characteristics of the Plantation Culture of Brazoria County, Texas," Ed. D. diss., University of Houston, 1961.
37. Winfrey, *Julien Sidney Devereux*, p. 83.
38. Curlee, "A Study of Texas Slave Plantations, 1822–1865," pp. 237–38.

Usually one family occupied a cabin, and crowding depended upon how many children the family had and how generous the planter was in his building specifications. Typically, the cabins contained one small room, and if the family were very large, conditions were cramped at best, and at worst, dangerous for small children who got underfoot.

James W. Smith, who lived on a large plantation near Palestine, said that because his parents were house servants, their house was a little better than the regular cabins in the quarter, which he described:

> De cabins am cheap built. 'Twarnt any money spent on dem, only time fo' buildin' am de cost. 'Twarnt any nails used in de buildin'. De logs am held in place by dovetailin' dem at de corners. De space 'twix de logs am closed by wedges dat am driven in, an' covered wid mud mixed wid straw. De straw held de mud together. De frame wo'k fo' de dooah am held together by wooden pegs, an' so am de benches an' tables. De bunks, dat am de place fo' sleepin', am put together wid wooden pegs, too.[39]

39. George P. Rawick, ed., *The American Slave: A Composite Autobiography*, series 2, *Texas Narratives*, James W. Smith, pp. 3630–31.

On the Duvall plantation in Bastrop County, there were one-, two-, and three-room cabins for the slaves, depending on the size of the family. Most of these cabins had dirt floors, but some of them had floors made of split logs.[40]

Some of the quarters, like those at Ellersly, Waldeck, and the Robertson plantation, were built of brick or stone, but for the most part they were single-room log cabins. There might be a small front gallery and occasionally a lean-to in the rear. A door opened to the front; there were either no windows or one small window on each side, with shutters but no screens or glass. The rough hearths of the mud-and-stick chimneys served as the cooking area. In winter the fireplace provided heat for the drafty cabins. Frogs, lizards, snakes, mosquitoes, and flies frequently tried to move in with the inhabitants. Because bedbugs and cockroaches too were frequent visitors, it was the rule on many plantations that the slaves had to pour boiling water over the walls and floors of their cabins once a week. Cabins with puncheon (split-log) floors were hard enough to keep clean, but those with dirt floors were impossible, even though the dirt was swept to hardpan and covered with animal skins.

The most common kind of bed in the slave cabin was the "Georgia Hoss," a one-legged bed made by fastening two poles together, attaching them where they joined to a post, and poking the free ends of the poles through the walls in a corner of the cabin. For a foundation, slats were put across the poles or rope might be laced across them. Mattresses of ticking were filled with hay, corn shucks, moss, or scrap cotton. Few slaves ever knew what it was to sleep on feather beds, although they made many of them for the occupants of the big house. "Negro blankets" supplied to plantations by merchants were cheap, coarse, and undoubtedly very scratchy. The beds were often topped with colorful homemade patchwork quilts.

If the family were large, bunk beds could be made in the same manner by building a scaffold. Children slept in the upper bunks or on the pallets on the floor or sometimes in a rough loft made of a few boards.

Other furniture in the cabins depended on the skill of the black carpenters and the permissiveness of their master. Chairs and tables might be chunks and slabs of wood or nicely carved tables and straight-backed chairs with wooden pegs for nails and rawhide seats. Pegs on the walls held the few clothes the slaves owned, and a male slave might cut down a cedar tree to make a chest for storage of their few possessions.

Bathing facilities for the slaves were usually the nearest creeks or ponds. They were not permitted to use the white family's "necessary house" nor did their cabins contain painted chamber pots. They were expected to relieve themselves in designated outdoor areas, and were fortunate if their quarters contained a slop jar or pail for night use. With dirt floors, open-

40. Ibid., James Jackson, pp. 1896–97.

hearth cooking, and the difficulty of keeping enough water on hand, clean-liness was difficult.

Eating was a communal activity on plantations that had a common dining hall for the slaves. On others, where each family was given a weekly ration, cooking was done in the fireplaces in winter and outdoors in summer. The slaves' dishes and cutlery were of wood or tin.

On some plantations the slaves were encouraged to cultivate gardens around their quarters. Anthony Christopher, a slave of Charles Patton on a plantation near West Columbia, said that all the blacks had ground to "raise truck stuff, like 'taters and sech. . . . what you see at de store now we raise right on dat place."[41] And George Glasker, a former slave on a plantation on the Brazos, recalled that "each cabin had its little yard an' garden an' each family had its chicken house and yard at de back."[42]

The Tait slaves sold their extra eggs and chickens to their mistress. And in a number of cases, the slaves sold not only vegetables to earn spend-ing money, but also cotton and corn. Ashbel Smith allowed each slave who wished it to have his own patch of cotton. His slaves also were allowed to sell wood and to own cattle.[43]

The Perry slaves raised and sold both cotton and corn crops. In 1839 slaves named Bill and Sam each received $38.87 for their cotton crop. In 1840–41 Bill and Peter each were credited with $55.02 for their crop. In 1854 the total crop for seven "boys" was 11,036 pounds. A slave named Purnell was credited in 1855 with 20½ bushels of corn. They also raised hogs. One Perry slave sold 50 pounds of bacon in 1847 and another 61 pounds. Like the Tait slaves, they sold their surplus eggs and chickens to their mistress.[44]

Lu Lee, a slave belonging to Henry Cook, recalled that the blacks on his plantation raised "taters and goobers" as well as cotton on their own patches.[45]

Devereux's slaves did a surprising amount of business for themselves. At least twelve of them had crops, and in 1850 the total value of their crops was $737.05. A merchant at Mt. Pleasant wrote to Devereux in April of 1853:

> Hereby per Mr. Ray I send you $300 in gold with the request to have the same distributed amongst those Negroes of yours who own the cotton which I bought of them. I should be glad to have a chance to sell them any-thing they want of such things as we keep for sale. I would sell goods to them *really very low*.[46]

41. Ibid., Anthony Christopher, p. 718.
42. Ibid., George Glasker, p. 1504.
43. Record book, 1855–1867, and memorandum book, Tait (Charles William) Pa-pers, Barker Texas History Center; Ashbel Smith Papers, Barker Texas History Center.
44. Curlee, "A Study of Texas Slave Plantations," pp. 139–40.
45. Rawick, ed., *Texas Narratives*, Lu Lee, p. 2300.
46. Charles Vinzent to Julien S. Devereux, Apr. 21, 1853, Devereux (Julien Sidney) Papers, Barker Texas History Center.

Just as houses and furnishings on Texas plantations improved as the years passed, so did the variety and quality of food and drink. Up until 1850 almost all home cooking was done in fireplaces. Kitchen fireplaces in the big houses were elaborate. Iron cranes, equipped with S-shaped hooks to hang pots and kettles from, swiveled so the pots could be moved to hotter or cooler positions as the cook desired. The crane could also be swung away from the fire so the pots could be tended. Most of the cooking was done over hot coals, which were raked out onto the hearthstones. The food was set on trivets of various heights above the coals or cooked in pots with little legs.

Large pieces of meat were cooked on roasting spits of different lengths and weights for different sizes of fowl or meat. These spits were held by fire-dogs (andirons) and had handles so they could be turned. The cook used a long-handled basting spoon to keep the meat from drying by moistening it with the juices that were caught in a dripping pan underneath the spit.

Waffle irons, muffin tins, skillets of different sizes, large and small kettles and pots, ladles, tongs, spoons, roasting forks, and skimmers all hung from hooks near the fireplace or sat on the hearth ready for use. A large working table, which sometimes had a dough box underneath, occupied the center of the room. Shelves and cabinets held stoneware crocks, pitchers, basins, and molds; tin or wooden sieves, pastry cutters, pie crimpers, elaborate jelly molds, and eggbeaters; as well as the handmade pewter utensils. Pie safes with pierced tin fronts were used to keep the flies off the food. These sometimes had locks on them, as did the cabinets in which expensive spices were kept.

Remembering the fireplaces of their former homes in the southern states, some planters had ovens (which were called Dutch ovens) built into the chimney to the side of the fireplace. A fire was built right in the oven, and when it had burned to coals, they were removed and the food placed inside.

A deep cast-iron pot, also called a Dutch oven, with a rimmed lid and four little legs was a favorite cooking vessel. Another favorite was the spider, which had a long handle and three legs and resembled a skillet with a cover. Each of these was set directly over hot coals, with more coals piled on its rimmed lid. A good cook could prepare almost anything in a Dutch oven or a spider: breads, biscuits, cakes, potatoes, meats, fowls, soups, and stews.

When wood cooking stoves became available, wealthy plantation homes were among the first houses in Texas to have these newfangled contraptions. There was some resistance, however, by those who thought food did not taste as good if it were not cooked in direct contact with the "real coals" of an open fireplace. Both white mistresses and their black cooks had considerable doubts about using these innovations. An advertisement in the *Southern Rural Almanac* of 1859 encouraged the use of wood stoves by reason-

The plantation kitchen centered on the fireplace, most of them large enough to roast a small steer. Dutch ovens were scattered among the coals, filled with any number of side dishes. Many kitchen fireplaces had brick ovens built alongside, where smaller fires were built, allowed to burn to coals, the coals removed & bread & pies baked to a turn on the hot bricks. Skillets & pots of all sizes abounded. The pots were hung over the fire on a metal arm built to pivot over the flame. The skillets were placed over coals on trivets of various heights. Good-sized work tables were supplied, a dough box under one of them. Pie safes standing in the corners stored finished foods & ingredients like spices & condiments. In stark contrast...

...the simplest sort of cooking was done in the slave quarters. Most of the cooking was done outdoors. The steady diet of pork, corn bread or cornmeal mush & greens of some sort was augmented on occasion by wild game or fish. Most plantation owners allowed the slave population small garden plots for their own use. Families often ate from common dishes because of a lack of tableware. Small children, especially at midday, when their parents were in the field or elsewhere, were fed from a trough, an "aunty" nearby to keep territorial squabbles to a minimum.

ing: "The return to the old system of cooking before a blazing fire, occupy-ing a whole side of a house and consuming half a cord of wood a day, would be as absurd and old-fogyish as to reestablish the old stagecoaches in place of our rail-cars and barges for steamboats on the Mississippi."

In the spring of 1859, one of Lizzie Neblett's friends wrote that she had a nice stove to cook in, but that she had had a "bad time" with it at first. Not knowing how to control the heat, she and her servant had made the fire in it but let all the heat go up the pipe. "One night I cried," she told Lizzie, "because we could not get our supper done 'til midnight." However, they did learn to use the stove and found it "not half the trouble" of cooking in the fireplace.[47]

In the early days of settlement some travelers in Texas complained about the steady diet of corn bread, bacon, and coffee. But those who were the guests at plantation households gave better reports. In 1831 a visitor at one of the McNeel plantations dined on venison, turkey, and "excellent cof-fee."[48] In 1836 Mary Austin Holley spoke of being served "vegetables of every description, wild foul, and other game, beef, pork, venison, butter, eggs, milk . . . with tea, coffee and all the like comforts. . . ."[49] Frederick Roemer mentioned eating roast wild turkey at the New Washington planta-tion of Col. James Morgan and enjoying a breakfast of ham and eggs, corn bread, and coffee at Nassau plantation.[50]

Like the Indians, who were their teachers, early pioneers into Texas used the buffalo, bear, deer, and wild mustang as a general store. From them they obtained skin for clothing and shoes, blankets, and tents; horns for spoons and drinking vessels; shoulder bones to dig and clear land; manes for ropes and girths; wool; tendons for threads and bowstrings; hooves for glue; fat to provide light, to cook with, and to make soap with; and food to eat.

The wild turkey was also plentiful. In the spring when wild onions and wild cayenne peppers were also abundant, there was a saying that the wild turkeys, which would have eaten these plants, were already seasoned. They needed only to be cleaned and roasted.

Deer meat was usually "ripened" or aged by allowing it to hang from four days to two weeks. If the deer was full grown, the meat was marinated in a sauce that might include onion, carrot, celery, parsley, thyme, bay leaf, and whole cloves cooked a few minutes in hot fat and then added to vinegar and simmered. When cool, this mixture was poured over the venison and left for one or two days. The marinating took away some of the gamy taste of the wild animal and tenderized it. Then the venison was larded with salt pork and roasted slowly, with frequent basting with the drippings. A tart red jelly was often served with it.

47. Neblett (Lizzie Scott) Papers, Barker Texas History Center.
48. Fiske, *A Visit to Texas*, pp. 30–31.
49. Mary Austin Holley, *Texas*, p. 140.
50. Roemer, *Texas*, pp. 58, 162.

Small birds such as quail, snipe, partridges, and plover were cleaned and trussed, larded and roasted. They might be served on toast or alone with a gravy to which currant jelly had been added. They were also made into tasty pies. The cook placed the birds in a deep earthen dish; seasoned them with salt, pepper, and butter; and dredged them with flour. After adding cold water to nearly cover them, she topped them with a crust and baked them slowly until they were done. At Evergreen plantation, where Ashbel Smith enjoyed such gifts of the Gulf as oysters and crabs, the cook also made blackbird and wild-duck pies.

After visiting the Perrys and making trips to neighboring plantations, Rutherford B. Hayes wrote in his journal: "These Texans are essentially carnivorous. Pork ribs, pigs' feet, veal beef (grand), chickens, venison and dried meat frequently seen on the table at once."[51] This lavish array of meat dishes was an expression of the bountiful hospitality of the planter and of his wish to give each guest sufficient choices.

In addition to wild game and wild and domestic fowl, beef appeared frequently on the planters' tables. And jerky was often carried by anyone making a trip away from the plantation. It could be made by drying strips of beef or venison in the sun, but it was better if it was smoked after it was dried.

Fish—baked, smoked, roasted, boiled, or fried—was popular. Both blacks and whites on plantations near rivers or lakes enjoyed fishing. The whole population sometimes turned out to fish and have a big fish fry. It included, of course, hush puppies made from cornmeal and fried in the same pan after the fish was done.

Those who lived near the Gulf ate large quantities of oysters. Ashbel Smith and Albert Sidney Johnston enjoyed eating them at an "oyster shanty," as did Rutherford B. Hayes when he and Guy Bryan visited a place called "Sailor Tom's" to feast on the fresh shellfish. In fact, oyster shanties may have been the original fast-food places in Texas.

Pork was by far the most prevalent meat on Texas plantations. At hog butchering time there was an orgy of eating fresh pork and great delight in feasting on chitterlings, commonly called "chitlins." These were sections of the small intestines that had been cleaned, soaked in saltwater, boiled until tender, dipped in cornmeal, and fried crisp. Cracklings were another much-appreciated by-product of hog butchering. They were the solid bits left when the lard of the hog was rendered or melted by heating. Slaves and white children loved to eat them as they were strained from the pot, but white adults usually preferred theirs mixed into corn-bread batter to make crackling bread.

Without refrigeration, milk and its by-products spoiled quickly. In the summer the milk was sometimes put in pails and lowered into a well, or

51. Rutherford B. Hayes, "Texas Diary, 1848–1849," Barker Texas History Center.

the plantation might have a springhouse built over a stream of running water where the milk and butter could be kept cool. A great deal of fresh milk was drunk on plantations by humans and animals. Milking was usually the task of young female slaves, as was churning butter.

Milk for butter was set aside until the cream rose to the top and the milk underneath clabbered (soured and curdled). Then the cream was poured into a churn made out of pottery or wood. An upright churn held about four to five gallons and had a stick through the middle of a tight lid. Inside the churn, on the end of the stick was a paddle or dasher that agitated the cream as the churner pushed the stick up and down, often accompanying herself with a rhythmic chant:

> Come Butter, come; Come Butter, come.
> St. Peter standing at the gate
> Waiting for a butter cake!
> Come Butter, come; Come Butter, come.

Some churns were big oak kegs holding twenty gallons. These were hung sideways between two poles with a crank on one end for the churner to rotate.

When the cream turned to golden lumps of butter and could be gathered (stuck together), it was lifted out of the churn, salted, and worked with a wooden paddle until all the liquid was squeezed out. Then it was rinsed with cold water. Buttermilk, the liquid left in the churn, was a favorite plantation drink. Cheesemaking does not seem to have been common in Texas, although some cooks made cottage cheese by taking the curds of clabbered milk, squeezing the liquid (called whey) from them, and letting them dry. Others preferred to eat their curds and whey together.

It would be hard to exaggerate the importance of corn to the early settlers. More than one settler stated that raising corn was a matter of life or death. On the plantations white and black families watched the corn crop, eagerly anticipating the first tender roasting ears. When the corn got too hard for roasting ears, it was ground into cornmeal. Jared Groce's first crops of corn were ground by pounding them in a hollowed-out tree stump. Eventually there were gristmills on nearly every large plantation, but before that, slaves ground the corn on hand mills.

After the cornmeal was mixed with cold water and a little salt, it could be made into corn bread several different ways. For ashcake it was covered with hot ashes. For johnnycake it was placed in a greased skillet and set over hot coals. Placed on a hoe blade used as a griddle, sometimes in the field, it became hoecake. Cooked in a spider it was corn pone or corn dodgers. Sometimes sugar, eggs, or milk were added, but they were not essential. Hominy was an especially popular dish with both whites and blacks. To make hominy, the grains of the corn were cooked in a weak solution of lye water until the kernels swelled and shed their skins, which floated to the top of the liquid. After repeated washings, the kernels were boiled in two or three changes of water. Then, baked, boiled, or fried, the hominy was often a side dish on the planters' table. For breakfast, dried hominy was ground and served as grits.

Some planters grew wheat and ground it at their own gristmills or took it to a miller so they could enjoy breads made from the flour. Imported flour was expensive, sometimes costing as much as seventy-five dollars a barrel. It was always much scarcer than cornmeal on the plantations, and slaves rarely tasted flour biscuits or bread.

The black-eyed pea or cowpea was the most popular kind in Texas, although many varieties of peas were grown and eaten on plantations. They were nutritious food for humans and animals and could be eaten fresh or dried. Husking peas was a favorite task for the black children because after the peas were put in sacks, the children would stomp barefooted on them until the hulls broke away from the peas. Then, on a windy day, the contents of the sacks were winnowed like wheat until the hulls had blown away.

Whether the peas were eaten green or dried, they were sure to be cooked with a hunk of pork for flavoring, as were all greens, peas, and beans.

Gourds were grown for their usefulness as utensils. One method of cleaning them was to fill them with sugar water. The water was then poured out and the gourd placed over an anthill. In a short time the ants would eat the inside clean. They could be used as dippers, cups, water jugs, bowls, spoons, and storage bins, depending on their sizes.

Salt was important for both human and livestock diets and for curing meat. The plantation residents suffered greatly when salt was hard to come by in the early days of settlement. Later they imported it by wagonloads. When the supply was short, planters on the Gulf Coast obtained salt by digging shallow wells and boiling the saltwater until the water evaporated and left a sediment of salt in the pots.

Sweetening was obtained in several forms. Bee trees could be robbed of their honey, but a surer source was the hives kept on many plantations, where an abundance of clover and wild flowers kept the bees busy. Sorghum and sugarcane provided molasses and sugar. The slaves called syrup "long sweetening" and sugar "short sweetening." Their sweetening was more often long than short. Bought sugar came in loaves and had to be pulverized to use in cooking. Cakes were made in large quantities to satisfy the many sweet tooths of large families. Recipes were handed down from generation to generation and copied by hand in notebooks. Since the slave cooks could not read, the plantation mistresses would teach them to make the family favorites from the treasured cookbooks. One favorite was loaf cake. A recipe that made "four large loaves" called for: "Two cups of butter, five of sugar, two of sour milk, eight of flour, one teaspoonful of saleratus [baking soda], six eggs. Flavor to taste." Usually, directions were not given for baking time or pan size, for each cook had her favorite utensils and knew how long the batter in them needed to bake.

Pyramid cakes were made for weddings and other grand occasions. Round and square layers of cake were baked in graduated tins and elaborately decorated with swags of icing. Candied violets and mint leaves added the final touch. The violets and leaves were prepared by dipping them in beaten egg white after they had been washed and dried. Then the cook held them carefully by the stem and dipped them into the pulverized sugar until they were coated. After they hardened, they could be packed away in boxes, where they would keep for a long time until they were needed for cake decorations or to serve with tea or as candy. In addition to cake, pies of all kinds were popular plantation desserts, as were puddings. The ever-present cornmeal was combined with milk, molasses, eggs, butter, and sugar to make Indian pudding, a nourishing dish for young and old alike.

It took oceans of strong black coffee to run a plantation. Fifteen to twenty cups a day was not considered an unusual amount for an individual to drink. Coffee beans, which were purchased green, had to be roasted or parched on the hearth. Then the roasted beans went into a coffee mill. These small grinders sat on wooden boxes with a drawer below to catch the ground coffee. The cooking method was simple: A handful of grounds were tossed into a pot of cold water that was set over hot coals to boil. After the coffee had boiled sufficiently, a few spoons of cold water settled the grounds, and the potent brew was ready to drink. Often there were not enough of the expensive coffee beans for the slaves. The slaves made coffee substitutes out of whatever was available, including dried okra, potato peelings, wheat grains, and cornmeal.[52]

In addition to water, milk, and coffee, planters' families often had a taste for imported tea, and it is apparent from their grocery bills that fine brandies and liquor were freely served. William Bollaert found that the Texas settlers were making beer by fermenting the native persimmons. In East Texas, cider was made from apples, and some planters like Ashbel Smith made wine from native grapes. Thomas Blackshear was one of those who made their own wine after the Civil War began. In July of 1861 he noted in his journal that the hands had made nine barrels of wine. At Glenblythe, Thomas Affleck reported making one hundred barrels of wine a year from mustang grapes.

In addition to the persimmon beer, individual plantations specialized in various beers made from the first distillation of fermented sorghum juice, from grains such as rice, and of course from corn. Corn could also be made into a very potent whiskey, and honey and water were converted into mead, a smooth amber beverage popular in Europe as far back as written history goes. In the late spring or early summer when the dandelions matured, their blossoms could be picked and made into a light wine. Boiling water was poured over the heads of the flowers and allowed to stand for twenty-four to forty-eight hours. Then it was strained into a large jar, and cut-up lemons and oranges (if available) were added along with sugar and yeast. The mixture was stirred five or six times a day until the fermentation process stopped. After a resting period of five or six weeks, it was ready to bottle or to drink. Another favorite hot-weather drink was lemonade, although lemons were hard to come by in the early days of Texas plantations.

Preserving the harvest of fruits and vegetables was of the utmost importance if the planter and his family and slaves were to eat well during the winter. Much of the produce was stored in food mounds, barns, or cribs, but much was preserved by the women of the plantation. Many fruits and vegetables could be dried—either in the sun or by the fireplace. As the dried food was put away, chinaberry leaves were placed between layers to discourage insects and worms. Beans, peas, pumpkins, sweet potatoes, corn, okra, peaches, figs, and pears could all be enjoyed dried. Peach leather was a delicious way of saving fresh peaches to use in peach dumplings, cobblers, and

52. Rawick, ed., *Texas Narratives*, Calvin Moye (wheat), p. 2849, Mary Kindred (peanuts, okra seed), p. 2203, for example.

other dishes. Ripe peaches were mashed and the pulp spread about a half inch thick and dried for a few days. When it was leathery, it was rolled or folded and put away for future use. Pickling was another way of keeping food. Watermelon rinds, tomatoes, cabbages, cucumbers, and the feet of hogs were among the many items pickled in solutions of salt, vinegar, and spices to enjoy during the winter season.

Strings of dried red peppers decorated the kitchens, as did bunches of herbs. Every sizable plantation had next to its kitchen an herb garden where mint, sage, parsley, thyme, and savory grew, and most plantation mistresses observed the old rhyme about these seasonings: "Cut herbs just as the dew does dry. Tie them loosely and hang them high."

Glazed ceramic jars or crocks were used for preserving fruits, and tasty jams and jellies were made from both wild and domestic fruits. As glass jars became more easily obtainable, they were used for canning and preserving as well as pickling.

Many planters preferred to have a common kitchen for feeding their slaves, but on other plantations a weekly ration was meted out to the bondsmen for them to cook on their own mud-and-stick fireplaces. The efficient Charles William Tait gave his overseers detailed instructions for the weekly distribution on his plantation:

> Serve out to every working hand once a week from two and a half to three and a half pounds of bacon according to circumstances. If milk & butter is plenty then less meat; if molasses is served out then one quart in place of one pound of meat. Of dried beef five or six pounds is the weekly allowance, also one peck of meal. When potatoes are served then less meal. Lying-in women to be allowed one quart of coffee and two quarts of sugar and fed from the overseer's kitchen for two weeks.

> The negroes are to be allowed to commence using the potatoes and sugar-cane on the first of October.[53]

Memories of food we've enjoyed as children are among our most lasting impressions. What did former slaves remember about the food they ate on Texas plantations? Some recalled scanty and monotonous diets, but many remembered eating well. Some recalled supplementing their usual rations with the abundant wild fruit and game in nearby woods. Pragmatic masters fed their slaves well not only to keep them strong and prevent illness, but also to keep them contented. In their extreme old age, many former slaves still remembered with pleasure eating roasting ears of corn, sweet potatoes, and corn pone cooked in the hot embers of a fireplace;[54] savoring molasses poured over hot corn bread; eating hog jowls and greens, chitlins,

53. "Particular Rules," C. W. Tait's record book, Tait (Charles William) Papers, Barker Texas History Center.
54. "Corn Pone: Mix 1 cup cornmeal, ½ teaspoon salt and 1 teaspoon sugar together. Stir in boiling water until thick enough to form patties. Make patties little larger than 4-bit pieces [fifty-cent piece]. Brown in hog lard."—old recipe

cracklings, and souse (hogs headcheese). A dish fondly recalled by many was baked opossum in a ring of sweet potatoes swimming in molasses.

Richard Carruthers, who had lived on a plantation in Bastrop County, told his interviewer:

> If they didn't provishun you right on Saturday night, you jus' had to slip around and git you a chicken. That was easy enough, but grabbin' a pig was a sure 'nuff problem. You have to cotch him by his snoot so he won't squeal and clomp down tight while you take a knife and stick him till he die. Then you take the hide and insides and put them in a sack and throw them in the crick. Some folks mought call that stealin' but it ain't stealin', is it? When you don't git 'lowanced right, you has to keep right on workin' in the field and no nigger like to work with his belly groanin'.[55]

Sarah Ashley, from a plantation near Coldspring, also remembered short rations, pilfering, and spying.

55. Rawick, ed., *Texas Narratives*, Uncle Richard Carruthers, p. 630.

D' niggers 'roun' dere neber git 'nuf t' eat so dey kep' stealin' stuff all d' time. Dey gib 'em a peck 'r' meal t' las' a week 'n' two 'r' t'ree poun' 'r' bacon in chunk. Us neber seed no flour 'n' sugar, jus' co'n meal, meat 'n' 'taters. Iffen you raise' hawg d' uder niggers steal 'em. Dey had a big box under d' fireplace w'ere dey kep' all de pig 'n' chickens w'at dey steal down in salt. Us hafter be keerful wid dat how us eat it cause iffen some 'r' d' nigger fin' out 'bout it dey run 'n' tell d' boss so he not mek 'em wuk so hard.[56]

And another former slave recalled, "Lots of times, I went down to de potato patch a long time after all de others were in bed, and stole some potatoes, so we wouldn't be haungry de next day."[57]

In contrast, for many former slaves their most pleasant memory of life on the plantation was of fresh, abundant food. Anna Humphrey had the job of "allowancing" the food for her master's two hundred slaves. "Seem like the earth was just full of people. Seem like the earth was just full of vittles," she said. "Lord I get the mouf watering when I think of the quinces and blue plums and damsons and pears and the hogs walking round for the killing."[58]

Mollie Dawson reported eating corn pones three times a day except for Sundays and Christmas, when they had flour for biscuits.[59] Jeff Calhoun described cooking the pones: "Our bread wuz roasted like you roast potatoes if you eveh roasted any. We put one leaf down and put corn bread battah on it and put enouther big leaf oveh it and cover wid hot ashes and by noon it would be done."[60]

Thomas Cole remembered:

We allus had plenty of meat ter eat. And marster Cole tried to fix it so each person on de plantation got his share of de meat and lard. Once a week all de slaves had biscuits. Der was a orchard of bout five or six acres of peaches and apples on de plantation and we had all de fruit we wanted and in de fall we had all de pumpkin pies we wanted, we planted pumpkins and he would let us have bout one or two acres fer water melons if we work dem on Satidy evenins. . . . We allus had plenty vegetables ter eat too, and iffen any of dem didnt hit was der own fault.[61]

Many of the slaves were well aware of the motivation on the part of their owners for feeding them well. "Massa always fed us good, cause he said we couldn't work like we oughtta iffen we got too poor, and den we git sick too," one former slave noted.[62] Jacob Branch said: "Us li'l chillen would go to de smokehouse mos' any time us want to and git all de cracklin's or sweet 'taters us want. Dey like for us to eat all de time us want 'cause dat mek us fat and healthy."[63]

On some plantations the younger slave children were fed from long troughs or trays dug out of soft wood. In summer the trough was set in the

56. Ibid., Sarah Ashley, p. 89.
57. Ibid., Emma Taylor, p. 3764.
58. Ibid., Anna Humphrey, p. 1825.
59. Ibid., Mollie Dawson, p. 1126.
60. Ibid., Jeff Calhoun, p. 603.
61. Ibid., Thomas Cole, pp. 788–89.
62. Ibid., Willis Woodsen, p. 4277.
63. Ibid., Jacob Branch, p. 407.

shade of a large tree. Often the meal was pot liquor over crumbled corn bread. The barefooted children, dressed only in their long ducking shirttails, gathered around the trough. An old aunty usually stood by with a switch in her hand to settle any arguments. Abram Sells, raised on a plantation near Newton, described the meal:

> De mos' 'r' de food us et outn' de trough was potlicker, jes' common ol' potlicker. Turnip green 'n' juice, Irish 'taters 'n' juice, cabbages 'n' peas 'n' beans, jes' anyt'ing dat mek potlicker. All t'ings like dat wid lots 'r' juice dey jes' po it in de trough 'n' all 'r' us git 'roun' it like so many li'l pig', sometime seben 'r' eight 'r' mo'. Den us dish in wid our wood spoon 'til it gone.[64]

CLOTHING

In Victorian times clothes were indicators of status, and the elite group of planters brought along at least some of their finery. As a result, visitors like Mary Austin Holley were astonished to see elegantly dressed men and women amid the primitive environment in the early days of Anglo-American settlement. In the first years of getting started, homespun and buckskin were frequently used for everyday wear and the fine clothes saved for "best." During the plantations' heyday it was fine imported material and clothing for the white family and homespun or cheaply manufactured material for the slaves. After the Civil War interfered with shipping and made luxuries impossible to come by, it was homespun again for both. When Texas stores received a new shipment of goods, they advertised the arrival in the newspaper. In November of 1836, the *Telegraph and Texas Register* (Houston) carried the information that Handy & Lusk, merchants in Galveston, had received from the schooner "*Col. Fanin,*" in addition to "brown Havanna seegars, double refined loaf sugar, coffee & Imperial tea, French & Peach brandy, Holland gin," a "very extensive assortment of ready made winter clothing . . . red and white flannels, black & white silk, and fur hats, boots and shoes . . . and the finest lot of belt and holster pistols ever offered for sale in Texas."

Godey's Lady's Book was the fashion bible for planters' wives. They bought fine materials and hired skilled seamstresses to copy the beautiful hand-tinted fashion plates found in its pages. They also studied the *Illustrated London News* for the latest styles and fabrics. In addition, they wrote to friends and relatives back in the States begging for information on the latest styles in gowns and bonnets. And they ordered silks and satins, brocades, laces and velvets, feather plumes, and soft leather high-button shoes through their merchants. Mary Austin Holley described three planters' wives' dresses at the San Jacinto Ball in 1837 as "white satin with a black lace overdress; a

64. Ibid., Abram Sells, pp. 3486–87.

bouffant white velvet; and a full-skirted off shoulders gown with lace bertha and parure [set of matched jewelry] of amethyest and pearls."[65]

The invention of corsets with grommets in 1828 enabled women to lace tightly, to the enhancement of their figures and the endangerment of their health. The more nearly her figure resembled that of an ant, the happier the woman. Next to her skin the well-dressed woman wore a chemise, a loose-fitting garment. Over that went the tightly laced stiff corset, topped by a camisole. Her drawers were of fine material sewn with tiny stitches. Victorian ethics dictated that only the edges of her underclothing be trimmed in lace or embroidery. It was "not nice" to have lace on the portions of a lady's "unmentionables" that were never expected to be glimpsed. As skirts grew wider, a woman might wear from four to six petticoats, measuring from six to eight feet around their hems and stiffened with hoops of crinoline (a combination of horsehair and linen). Crinoline or whalebone cages padded and tied at the waist lessened the need for so many petticoats but made navigation hazardous both for the wearer and for those near her. Linen, muslin, or flannel undergarments were worn according to the season. As the Civil War approached, women's fashions began to change. The fullness moved to the back, and eventually the bustle replaced the hoop.

Although they dressed more casually at home, in public planters wore black frock coats, high collars, ruffled shirtfronts, and black string cravats, and they often carried canes. The only colorful part of their clothing was their vests, which were often made of rich materials and in vivid hues. In 1838, Mary Austin Holley, who hobnobbed mostly with plantation families, wrote to her daughter: "The gentlemen dress remarkably well—the clothes being all brought from N. York ready made of the newest fashions."[66] A planter's usual footwear was boots made of fine leather, but he had white dancing slippers for balls and other grand occasions.

No lady or gentleman went bareheaded in public. Planters favored low-crowned, wide-brimmed hats of felt or straw. Their ladies wore bonnets trimmed with ruffles, veils, ribbons, bows, and feathers.[67]

An important accessory to the planter's dress was his pistol, usually a revolver such as the Colt. After the mid-1850s, small pistols called derringers gained popularity among those who wanted an inconspicuous, easily concealed weapon. They also carried knives such as the Bowie knife, in leather sheaths.

The clothing for white children on plantations was very much like that of their parents. Little boys wore jeans and shirts for everyday and trousers, short jackets, and vests for dress. White pantalettes with lace ruffles,

65. Holley (Mary Austin) Papers, Barker Texas History Center.
66. Mary Austin Holley to Harriette Holley Brand, Feb. 21, 1838, Holley (Mary Austin) Papers, Barker Texas History Center.
67. C. Willett and Phillis Cunnington, *The History of Underclothes*, pp. 76–105; Pamela Ashworth Puryear, private files, Navasota, Tex.

although often pictured on southern belles, were actually a short-lived fashion for adult women and were usually worn only by little girls. Instead of hoopskirts, a young girl wore two or three tucked petticoats over her pantalettes. Children, too, wore hats; the girls especially were never allowed to venture into the sunlight without sunbonnets to protect their complexions.

Black boys and girls wore the long cotton shirts called "duckings" until they reached their teens and sometimes beyond. Adult slaves were usually issued two sets of clothes each year. For the men it was two pair of pants and two shirts; for the women, two dresses and two sets of underwear. Many planters gave their slaves a set of better clothes to wear to worship services—often a white dress for the women and a white shirt and better pair of jeans for the men. Slaves who were allowed to earn a little money of their own were likely to spend it on store-bought clothes to fill out their meager wardrobes.

Cobblers were held in high regard on plantations, although the shoes they produced were not. After cattle were slaughtered, the hides were given to the cobbler, who tanned the hides by soaking them in a vat containing oak bark. Shoes produced from the resulting leather were almost impossible to wear out. Called "red russets" or "everlasting brogans" by the slaves, these shoes hardened and stiffened when dry, making it necessary to grease them regularly with tallow. To cover the red color, many of the young males painted their homemade shoes with a mixture of grease and soot, especially when they were going to a dance. Store-bought shoes with brass toes were highly prized for their appearance, not because they were much more comfortable than the homemade red russets.

The reason planters could get by with issuing only two sets of work clothes a year to slaves was that the cloth turned out by the plantation spinners and weavers was as everlasting as the shoes made by the cobblers. As one slave put it, "Them wuz shirts that *wuz* shirts. If someone gets cot by his shirt on a limb of a tree he had to die there if he wern't cut down. Them shirts wouldn't rip no more than buckskin."[68]

The spinning wheel was as common then as the sewing machine is today, and on large plantations there were a number of wheels and looms. Cotton or wool was spun separately, or the threads could be spun together to be woven into linsey cloth for cool weather. It took skill to coordinate hand, eye, and foot movements to spin the raw cotton or wool into thread and even more skill to weave the threads into cloth. A good weaver could turn out five or six yards of cloth about three feet in width a day. An expert might finish ten. Many planters, however, found it cheaper to use their slaves in the fields and to buy the Osnaburg, jean, kersey, lowell, and linsey woolsey material needed for making the slaves' clothing.

Seamstresses turned cloth into shirts, pants, dresses, duckings, or whatever was required. Needles were scarce, and mistresses guarded them

68. Rawick, ed., *Texas Narratives*, Felix Haywood, p. 1691.

A.

B.

C.

Cotton was set aside and crafted into cloth & clothing by the women. Brought in from the field Ⓐ, the cotton was ginned to get the seeds & husks out, then turned over to the women for carding. Cards Ⓑ were flat paddles with tines, used to break down fibers Ⓒ until they could be formed into rolls Ⓓ and passed on to the spinners Ⓔ. At the wheel, spinners turned the rolls into thread on corn husk bobbins Ⓕ, cheap and plentiful. When they had enough bobbins for a warp & weft, the thread was passed on to the reeler Ⓖ. Then...

E.

Take the inside leaf from an
Ear of corn. Trim it flat on
the bottom.   Roll it up   tight
in a cone   shape and   then
sew it   to hold.   the
shape.   Slip it   on the
spindle   then re-   more
when   it's   full.

F.

G.

D.

...the skeins were taken from the reelers to boiling pots of dye Ⓗ. Store-bought dyes were scarce & expensive, so many colors were made from handy organic sources: oak bark for yellow; Spanish moss for blue; pokeberries, blackberries, or clay made red; oak leaves for green. Once the color was set, the thread was put on spools & passed to the weavers at the loom Ⓘ. The cloth from the loom was used for everything from curtains & sacks to the plantation owners' everyday wear & the smallest black child's skivvy shirt.

I.

carefully. In the 1850s home sewing machines entered the market, and by the time of the Civil War several brands were advertised in planters' magazines. The Singer company advertised its "family and plantation sewing machines" as being "so substantial that they cannot be put out of order except by violent misusage or abuse" and stressed the fact that servants could easily learn to use them in "one or two hours." The prices started at thirty-five dollars.[69]

Apparently, making the clothing more colorful was not considered important, but some masters allowed individuals to dye their own. Indigo, obtainable from several different plants, was boiled and the clothing dipped into it to achieve a blue color. For other colors, pokeberries, wild-peach bark, sweet-gum bark, and sumac were boiled down to a thick ooze. A little indigo was always mixed in to make the colors hold. Clay could be used as a dye by wrapping the cloth in a layer of it. Almost all the women living in the manor house could do fine handwork, and both servants and mistresses knitted socks, scarfs, sweaters, and stockings.

In addition to keeping the white families' wardrobes clean, the slaves were required to clean their own clothes, usually on Saturday afternoons. In the plantation washhouses or outdoors if the weather permitted, the laundresses scrubbed the clothes with homemade lye soap, boiled them in huge black washpots over wood fires, scrubbed them again, rinsed them in several tubs of water, lifted them out on broomsticks, wrung them out by hand, and hung them to dry. Quilts, heavy rag rugs, and other large items were beaten with wooden "battling sticks" to remove the dirt. The fire had to be fed constantly to keep the water boiling, and the heavy washpots were dumped and refilled when the water became dirty. When the laundry was dry, most of it was ironed with "sad irons"—cast-iron wedges that were set over coals to heat. As one iron cooled, it was put back to reheat and another iron taken up to be used until it lost its heat. Many of the clothes were heavily starched and had pleats and ruffles. These were pressed with special devices called fluting irons that had ridged cylinders and hollow centers where heated metal spokes could be inserted.

As their cotton and cane empires gave them wealth and their domains spread, the planters' standards of living increased. From buckskin and homespun they changed to cassimere and silk. They moved from log cabin to mansion. And their diets expanded from corn bread and bacon to lobster and champagne. The slaves profited little from the master's luxuries, and in fact often had their labor increased because of them. The more lavish the entertainments, the more work required to prepare for them. Log cabins, homespun, corn bread, and bacon were still very much a way of life for the slaves.

69. *Texas Almanac*, 1959, advertisement.

CHAPTER FOUR

The Seasons

"As a planting country, Texas is unrivalled."
—Ashbel Smith

The pioneer planter's livelihood was closely tied to the land and the weather, and to his livestock as well, for he depended on them to run his plantation. Every plantation had a good supply of domestic animals. Horses, oxen, and mules were necessary for transportation, for hauling goods, and for helping with the farm labor. Cattle provided beef, milk, butter, and hides. Chickens, ducks, and geese supplied feathers for bedding and pillows as well as eggs and many delicious dishes for the table. Hogs yielded bacon, sausage, hams, and the all-important lard, while sheep and goats gave wool and meat. Dogs were kept for hunting, herding other animals, and for protection. And cats helped keep the rodent population under control.

Lush prairies, rich river–bottom land with wooded areas, and a mild climate made it easy to raise livestock. But wild grasses and mast (nuts and acorns) alone were not enough to feed all the animals. Crops had to be raised for animal as well as human consumption.

Although each planter had his own methods of planting crops, on every plantation slaves, mules, horses, and oxen provided the power needed to operate the establishment. Most of the slaves' labor was done by hand or with simple tools such as plows and hoes. Until the Civil War ended the slave system, planters generally were not interested in buying complicated machinery. It could easily be broken, and many of the early farm machines were difficult to repair.

Blacksmiths held important positions on plantations. They shod the horses and oxen and made the iron fasteners and hardware needed for houses and wagons and carriages. They made iron parts for plows, harrows, hoes, and hand tools. Often they were quite creative in designing these tools to suit a particular planter's needs and desires. In addition, the blacksmiths might be called on to make kitchen utensils or parts for guns, or to repair these items. Keeping tools sharp and in good repair was an essential part of the blacksmith's art.

Like all farmers, the Texas planters were acutely aware of the seasons and tried to unite their efforts with the natural order of things. Changes in the seasons on southern farmlands were not as dramatic as they were on more northern farms, but they were still the planters' guideposts. On Texas plantations, late winter and early spring were planting and cultivating time.

SPRING

If cotton was king of the Republic of Texas, corn was its queen. Cotton provided the chief source of revenue for the planter, but corn was his basic means of subsistence. During the first favorable weather after the middle of February, Texas farmers began planting their corn or maize—the staff of life for man and beast on the plantation. Humans enjoyed it first as roasting ears. After that it appeared on their tables in many guises: bread, mush, grits, hominy, succotash, chowder, pudding, porridge, corn-fed pork and chicken, and corn whiskey. The variety called popcorn was enjoyed by all ages and used to decorate Christmas trees. The livestock ate the corn as fodder, as shelled kernels, and as dry shucks. The shucks were also used to fill mattresses, to weave chair bottoms, to make braided horse harnesses, and as toilet tissue (as were the cobs). The cobs furnished fuel, fertilizer, bottle stoppers, corncob pipes, and checkerboard men, and were sliced to make knife handles. Corn could also be used to make starch.

According to Thomas Affleck, a careful farmer tarred his seed corn before planting it. Water was added to a barrel two-thirds full of seed and allowed to stand for about twenty hours. Then the water was drained off and hot water added. When the seed was warm, a gallon of hot water mixed with a pint of tar was stirred into the corn until every grain was coated with the tar. Finally, the corn was drained and rolled in ashes to dry. This tarring provided protection against thievery by birds, squirrels, raccoons, cutworms, and other varmints. Julien Devereux used a similar tarring method and noted that it worked well for him.[1]

Slaves dropped the corn by hand in furrows or "drills," about two and a half to three feet apart, and covered it shallowly or deeply depending on how quickly the farmer wanted it to mature. Usually at intervals of about two weeks more corn was sown. As soon as the first shoots were well up, hoe gangs carefully harrowed (broke up the ground) around them. When the stalks were large enough, both hoe and plow gangs worked them.

As the corn grew, the planter measured it as being "ankle high," "knee high," "thigh high," "waist high," and "head high." Young slave boys who were not yet strong enough to do hard work were set to pulling the

---

1. Thomas Affleck, *Southern Rural Almanac*, p. 32; Dorman H. Winfrey, *Julien Sidney Devereux and His Monte Verdi Plantation*, p. 81.

"suckers" or excessive shoots from the corn rows. As soon as the tassels ripened, the corn was topped, or cut, right down to the first ear. The tops were laid out to dry in the sun and then bundled into shocks to use as winter fodder for the livestock. By May, the plantation residents could expect to enjoy the first tender ears of corn.

The Texas planter who wanted early vegetables and cereal risked planting his beans, peas, and cabbage in late January or early February. He had to be prepared to cover the tender plants in case of severe weather, and he knew that he needed luck for them to survive. Thomas Blackshear, owner of two plantations in Grimes County, noted in his diary one spring near the end of March: "Wet and cold weather destroyed my stand of millet. Concluded to plant it over again." Late in April of the same year, a killing frost damaged part of his corn crop. The next day he had his slaves replanting the corn with hoes.[2] Such stoic persistence was necessary for the successful planter. He soon learned that Texas weather was not predictable, no matter how carefully he kept his records of it.

Monoculture was a way of life for most Texas planters. Although Ashbel Smith, the first president of the Texas State Agricultural Society, urged them to diversify and deplored the "too great sameness of cotton and cane culture,"[3] the majority of the planters persisted in cultivating one or the other of these products as their cash crop.

Cotton production was a yearlong endeavor. From January to December there was always some work to be done in connection with it. The ground had to be prepared; the seeds planted; the plants tended; the bolls picked; the fiber ginned; and the bales packed, sold or traded, and shipped to market. Then, and sometimes even before the marketing was done, it was time to prepare the ground again.

Plantation owners on the lower Brazos and Colorado river bottoms began planting or "pitching" their cotton in late February, while those on the Red River did not begin until about a month later. The wise farmer planted only one-third to one-half of his cotton crop early, and the rest later in order to avoid disaster, if the weather should prove treacherous. The cottonseed was usually planted thickly in shallow furrows on top of ridges, and then covered over with dirt. A gang of plow boys, perhaps eight or ten, opened the furrows. All plows were walking plows made of hardwood with iron points. The plow lines, usually attached to mules, might be made of cotton or bear grass. Another gang followed the plow boys, planting the seed, and another group closed the drills by pulling dirt over them.

When the cotton plants had pushed up out of the ground a couple of inches, hoe gangs cultivated them by scraping away or "chopping" the weeds and grass. If the weeds were not controlled while the cotton plants were

2. Blackshear (Thomas Edward) Papers, Barker Texas History Center.
3. Elizabeth Silverthorne, *Ashbel Smith of Texas*, p. 131.

small, they could choke the tiny seedlings and ruin the crop. Sometimes this happened when a great deal of rain made it impossible to work in the fields for weeks. Some planters put their geese to work by letting them eat the grass out of the cotton.

      The backbreaking chopping continued until the bolls began to form. When the plants had grown a few inches, field hands chopped out the excess seedlings, leaving stands of two or three cotton plants in clusters about six inches apart, to protect against such enemies as cold and cutworms. Later, the chopping gangs thinned the large cotton plants for the last time, leaving stalks about every two feet. Early cotton put on buds, or squares, sometime in May. On one May 16, Thomas Blackshear noticed two to four squares on some of his young cotton. A week later he noted it was "branching and squaring finely." Two weeks later he saw cotton blooms.[4] Creamy cotton

    4. Blackshear (Thomas Edward) Papers, Barker Texas History Center.

blooms opened in the midmorning sun and began to wither the next day. After they dried, they turned pink, blue, and purple before dropping from the plant. As the flowers withered, a tiny boll began to form. Now the planter watched his crop intently because he knew that if nothing happened to the boll, which contained the cotton, it would mature in a month and a half to two months. At this point the cotton crop was said to be "laid by," and the chopping could cease. This was the "breathing time" on cotton plantations before the labor of picking began.

Almost from the beginning of the plantation system in Texas, some planters raised a small amount of sugarcane. In the early 1840s, cotton worms, extremely wet weather, and a fall in cotton prices brought on by the panic and depression of 1837 caused many more of them to turn to sugarcane as their cash crop. In Brazoria County and on plantations in and around Egypt in Wharton County, there were so many sugar growers that newspapers referred to the area as the "sugar bowl."

The cane was planted during the winter. After plow boys opened deep furrows, "droppers" placed two or three rows of stalks parallel with one stalk overlapping. "Cutters" followed the "droppers" cutting each stalk in three parts with cane knives. Then plows covered the joints with up to six inches of earth to protect them against freezing.

In the spring, hoe gangs scraped some of the dirt off, leaving about two or three inches as cover. As the sun warmed the earth, shoots sprouted from the eyes of the buried cane joints and pushed their way to the surface. Cultivation with hoe and plow continued throughout the spring until about mid-June, when the cane was high enough to smother the weeds and grass on its own.

A large bell mounted between posts controlled the activity on most plantations. Sometimes a shell or a horn was used to summon the little kingdom to life. By four o'clock or half past four the bell, shell, or horn sounded through the quarters, and the slaves came stumbling out of their cabins, pulling on their clothes. They had to do their chores, eat a quick breakfast, and in the case of the field hands, have the mules hitched to the plows and in the fields ready to start work by the first light.

March was the time to plant sweet-potato sprouts grown from roots that had been bedded earlier in the year. This popular vegetable had various names, including "leather coat" and "red," and was often incorrectly referred to as a yam. By whatever name, it was a rich source of vitamins and energy for the plantation workers, although they probably had no idea of its worth beyond its delicious taste after being baked in the red-hot ashes of an open fireplace.

As the weather warmed, it was time to pick the burs off the sheep and shear them for their wool. Although a number of early plantation owners kept sheep for their own convenience, the "mania" for raising sheep in the state did not catch on until the mid-1850s.

When the sap was up, trees were cut and rails split and laid aside to be used for making fences in the fall. The cutting was done in the spring by many planters who thought that the green trees were easier to split than the dry ones would be later on.

SUMMER

As spring turned into summer, the planter enjoyed the roasting ears of his early corn and was reminded to plant his second crop to ensure that he would enjoy the same treat in the fall. It was also time to plant second crops of such vegetables as black-eyed peas, to set the women to weeding the potatoes, and to clean debris from the wells. It was also time to cut the grains: barley, oats, and wheat.

Wheat was the source of flour for the bread and biscuits that provided a welcome change from the ever-present corn bread. Before the use of the reaper, wheat was cut by hand with a cradle. The cradle had a long, bent wooden handle called a snath, with a short bar for each hand and wooden fingers above the blade to catch the grain and keep it from falling on the ground and scattering. The cradle weighed about ten pounds. The worker started the cradle from the right and swung it to the left through the grain, close to the ground. The grain caught on the fingers and slid off in piles as the cutter tipped the cradle. It took strong arms to swing a cradle all day. Bundlers followed the cutters, tying the grain into bundles and putting them into shocks to dry. When the wheat was thoroughly dry, it was hung on rails with canvas spread underneath. Using tough tree limbs with lots of switches on them, slaves beat and thrashed the heads of wheat until the kernels fell out onto the canvas. The straw was picked up and stored in piles to be used as fodder.

To clean the wheat, it was necessary to have a day when the wind was blowing just right. When that day came, the workers picked the wheat up in pails, raised it three or four feet, and poured it slowly into other pails. The wind blew away the chaff and dirt as the grains fell from one pail to the other, and the procedure was repeated several times until the wheat was clean. Often the dried wheat was stored in sheds to be worked on on days when the weather was too inclement for field work. The grain was usually "winded" again just before it was made into flour or roasted as a substitute for coffee.

During early summer, preparations for the great business of the plantation—harvesting the cotton—went ahead full speed. If the planter needed more hands for picking, he made arrangements for hiring them. Wagons and teams must be readied, gin houses and machinery put in order, beams and scales arranged for weighing, and sacks and baskets counted and additional ones made if needed. The cotton baskets were woven from the split wood of trees such as white oak and wild chinaberry, from reeds, or from other flexible

woody materials. The sacks were long, tough cotton sacks, usually made by the plantation's female slaves.

The Fourth of July provided a welcome break in the work on most Texas plantations. In election years the celebration had a strong political flavor, with candidates invited to do the orating. Plantation dwellers came from miles in wagons, carriages, carts, and on horseback. Long tables set up under the shade of a brush arbor groaned with the feast. The day before, slaves would have prepared for the holiday by digging a big pit to barbecue deer, beef, hogs, and wild turkey. Plantation mistresses proudly produced the pound cakes and the dewberry, grape, and wild-plum pies they and their cooks made from treasured recipes. Roasting ears; watermelons; cantaloupe; potatoes, white or sweet; and various other vegetables and fruits in season filled every available space.

Long-winded, strong-lunged speakers entertained the crowd before and after the eating, which usually took place about midafternoon. On one Fourth in Andersonville, there were "how-to" speeches on such agricultural subjects as hillside ditching, manuring, and fruit growing. Then Sam Houston made a speech, which one of the young plantation belles reported to a friend was "all about himself."[5]

For sound effects a small cannon was fired if one was available; if not, lighter firearms had to do. Another entertainment was one called "shooting the anvil." Black powder was packed into the hollow in the bottom of an anvil, which was set upright on a stump. When the powder was set off with a fuse, the anvil went into the air with a sound like a cannon.

There was also usually a band to play patriotic tunes such as "Yankee Doodle" and "Hail Columbia." At night there were dances: an elaborate ball for the whites and a simple dance for the blacks. On Stephen Blount's plantation the slaves were annually the hosts to the other blacks in the neighborhood on the Fourth of July. The pits for barbecuing sheep, shoats, and beef were prepared on the third, and much time was spent preparing pies and cakes. The celebration lasted until late into the night of the Fourth, and the next day was also a holiday from work to allow the celebrants to recuperate.[6]

In July or August, according to when it was planted and how wet or dry the weather had been, the green, golf-ball-size cotton bolls began to crack. The cracks ran in four or five straight lines from the tip. As the bolls split open, they showed groups of eight to ten seeds covered with fibers. In the hot sun the dried boll, or bur, opened at last and offered up its handful of white treasure.

As soon as enough bolls had opened so the light hands could pick forty to fifty pounds a day, the slaves were set to work. By late July or August, when the acres of white stretched as far as the eye could see, every avail-

5. Neblett (Lizzie Scott) Papers, Barker Texas History Center.
6. Abigail Curlee Holbrook, "A Glimpse of Life on Antebellum Slave Plantations in Texas," *Southwestern Historical Quarterly* 76 (Apr., 1973): 378.

Cotton seed Ⓐ, recovered from the previous year's crop, is planted, grows to a height of two to six feet & produces blossoms Ⓑ. Creamy white at first, the blossoms soon turn pink & fall off, leaving small green seed pods Ⓒ, or cotton bolls, containing new seeds. When the plant matures, the boll bursts open, revealing soft masses of cotton fiber Ⓓ. When the cotton is ginned, the seed is separated from the fiber for planting next season. Cotton is classified into three broad groups based on the length of the individual fibers, the highest quality being the longest fiber, the lowest quality the shorter, coarser fiber strains.

able hand was assigned to picking. The plantation bell roused the workers in the predawn coolness, and they hurried to their places in the fields, pushing and jostling and singing snatches of song to wake themselves up lest the overseer prompt them with his whip. Thomas Cole remembered that "When de slaves leaves de quarters every morning goin ter work, it was jest lak a bunch of youngsters now a days goin ter a ball game. Dey was all hollerin and . . . runnin but dey didnt come in dat way, when we comes in it was jest lak drivin an ole give out mule."[7]

On some plantations, a breakfast of corn bread and molasses and bacon was brought to the workers by young slaves. These children also went up and down the rows bringing gourds filled with water to the individual pickers so that there would be as little interruption in the picking as possible. The need for water increased as the summer sun rose relentlessly in the blue, cloudless sky. As the pickers moved along the rows, their hands moved swiftly among the stalks, fingers thrusting into the open bolls, snatching the lint and quickly stuffing it into the long sacks. The dried bolls were sharp, and even skilled pickers got painful jabs from time to time.

Often the cotton pickers sang to accompany the rhythm of their work and to make it more pleasant. They sang spirituals or slow, sad songs that expressed a longing for other places and other times, such as "My Old Kentucky Home" and "Old Folks at Home." Some of their songs were the ones Stephen Foster heard on the Ohio River and at church meetings that he attended with the family's slaves. He turned this music into minstrel tunes that immediately became popular with whites and blacks and in turn were sung in the cotton fields. A favorite in Texas was "Old Black Joe":

> Gone are the days when my heart was young and gay,
> Gone are my friends from the cotton fields away,
> Gone from the earth to a better land I know,
> I hear their gentle voices calling,
> Old Black Joe.

About two hundred to three hundred pounds of cotton a day was considered good for a picker. Having one who could snatch five hundred pounds or more was a feat for the whole plantation to brag about and was considered worthy of notice in the newspapers. According to their natures, plantation owners encouraged their pickers by threats of punishment or by promises of prizes. The punishment for dawdling might be immediate; an overseer would often ride between the rows brandishing his bullwhip. Or it might be a whipping administered when a picker's daily quota of so many pounds was not met. Prizes varied from extra clothing to gold coins to tobacco.

7. George P. Rawick, ed., *The American Slave: A Composite Autobiography*, series 2, *Texas Narratives*, Thomas Cole, p. 798.

The planters themselves were urged to early production and marketing by merchants, who offered silver or gold cups for the first bales of cotton ginned each year. In 1842 Houston merchants offered a silver cup for the first five bales of cotton and a gold cup for the first twenty bales thereafter. Leonard Groce, who was then on Bernardo, won both prizes. In congratulating him, the president of the merchants' group said the prizes were given as evidence that the merchants of Houston "support the most noble exertions of the Planter."[8]

By 1842 cotton production in Texas had come a long way, as far as quantity was concerned, from the early crops planted by Leonard Groce's father. But the method of picking had not changed. On some plantations baskets were used instead of sacks, but in either case, when the container was full, the picker carried it to the wagon and hoisted it up to be weighed. It took about fifteen hundred pounds of cotton to fill a wagon, and about this much to make a bale. In Texas a rule of thumb for normal cotton production was eight to ten bales for each field worker or a bale to an acre. However, on his plantation on the Guadalupe River, Preston Robinson Rose reported a yield of twenty-five bales of cotton to the hand.[9]

In the pioneer planting days in Texas, seed was picked from cotton by hand. Although a few planters like Ashbel Smith experimented with a long-fibered Sea Island cotton, most Texans grew the shorter-stapled variety, which gave a better yield per acre. Its small, furry green seed was firmly attached to the fiber, and removing it was tedious, even though it was a task easy enough to be done by children. The first cotton gin in Texas was built by John Cartwright in Shelby County in East Texas, probably in 1822. The second was erected by Leonard Groce in Brazoria County about 1825.[10]

The early gins were large wooden structures, usually of three stories. The top area was divided into stalls for storing seed cotton for use the next season. The middle area contained the gin, and the first floor housed the large wooden wheel that was operated by the turning of a series of cog-wheels. Horses or mules walking in a circle powered the machinery. The raw cotton was unloaded from the wagons and carried upstairs in baskets to the gin room. One slave stood at the gin feeding the cotton into it, spreading it evenly to the metal saws, whose teeth pulled the cotton from the seeds. The slave constantly risked the loss of a finger in them. As the fiber, or lint, separated from the seeds, it fell into a room below at the rear of the gin house.[11] In

8. *Telegraph and Texas Register* (Houston), Aug. 14, 1842.
9. *Handbook of Texas* II, 503.
10. Some of Groce's descendants maintained that he established the first gin. See Adela B. Looscan, "Harris County, 1822–1845," *Southwestern Historical Quarterly* 19 (July, 1915): 37–64; Rosa Groce Bertleth, "Jared Elison Groce, *Southwestern Historical Quarterly* 20 (Apr., 1917): 358–68; *Handbook of Texas* I, 739.
11. Generally Texas planters considered left-over cottonseed a nuisance. Although a few used it as fertilizer or as cattle feed, they were unaware of the many uses that would be

As plantations grew & crops increased, the hand-turned gin was replaced by a larger model powered by horses or mules.

Generally built to 2½ or 3 stories, the top floor was divided into bins for storing seed for next year's crop. The gin was installed on the second floor. The ground floor was given over to the "power plant", a large wooden wheel operated by the turning of a series of cog wheels, all powered by horses or mules walking around in a circle.

Wagons brought the raw cotton in from the field; then it was unloaded into the second floor. There, one slave fed the cotton into the gin, where the turning blades separated the seed & chaff from the lint.

The lint fell out the back of the gin to the floor below, where other slaves raked it into baskets. From there, the cotton was packed into the press, where pressure was applied from the massive screw, again turned by horses or mules, compressing the cotton into bales to be wrapped & bound for shipment.

Finished cotton bales weighed from 400 to 600 pounds each.

the lower room, other slaves raked the lint into baskets, covering themselves from head to toe with wisps of white. Then they carried it to the homemade cotton press. The most important part of this type of old-time press was a huge wooden screw made from a tree trunk. Finding just the right size tree trunk, cutting it to the right height, and carving it into a screw took skill. Under the screw was a rectangular box the size of a cotton bale. Strong wooden beams were attached to the screw like giant legs. A mule hitched to each beam walked around in a circle, pulling the screw slowly downward into the press. It was the delight of the small boys on the plantation, white and black, to ride these mules. When the cotton fiber was pressed into bales of between four hundred and six hundred pounds, bagging was drawn around them and the whole thing tied with rope.

Over the years, manufactured gins improved greatly. In Texas the ones manufactured by Daniel Pratt of Prattville, Alabama, were the most popular. Only a few bales a day could be made on the older gins, but by 1859 the sixty-saw Pratt gin was capable of making ten bales a day.

From the days when Groce marketed his first cotton by pack mules until the expansion of the railroads after the Civil War, the planters had a hard time getting their produce to market. Inland planters had no choice but to haul their cotton to coastal markets or river towns by ox-drawn wagons. The roads were mud bogs in wet weather and trails of dust in dry weather.

When the Spanish occupied Texas, they built three main roads from Mexico to Louisiana. In 1836, the main overland routes were still these three: the Old San Antonio Road, the La Bahía Road, and the Atascosito Road. One of the first concerns of the new republic was to construct and maintain more roads. Each plantation owner was expected to use his slaves to help build and maintain the roads in his area or suffer a fine. But beyond the plantations, the roads were little better than trailways.

The large, heavy wagons used for freighting could carry ten or twelve bales of cotton, weighing a total of four thousand to five thousand pounds. Even with oxen pulling them, the wagons often got stuck in the mud and had to be pried out—an exasperating job usually accompanied by much cursing of the oxen and swearing of oaths. Although they were slower than horses or mules and more stubborn, oxen were preferred for pulling the wagons because they could subsist by grazing on the grass along the way and because they had broad hooves that resisted sinking into the mud. It took a special kind of tact to manage an ox, and many slaves hated them. As one of them recalled: "They call the work 'driving the ox.' Well, 'taint so. The ox drives you, and him drives you mad."[12]

It was common for the wagons to travel in long caravans for protection. Ten to fifteen miles per day was considered average. At night the oxen

found for it in the next century.
    12. Rawick, ed., *Texas Narratives*, Bill Homer, p. 1787.

were turned loose to graze with bells on their necks to make them easy to find the next morning. The drivers cooked supper and sat around campfires, telling tall tales of encounters with panthers, alligators, snakes, and other Texas wildlife.

A trip to market or a port might take several weeks, and the return trip was equally long since the wagons came back loaded with supplies and equipment of all kinds for the plantation. The crack of the driver's whip, like the whistle of the steamboats, carried for long distances and was as eagerly anticipated. The occupants of the plantations knew that in addition to the usual provisions, there would almost certainly be special treats such as candy, spices, snuff, store-bought clothes, magazines, and newspapers. Some planters hired wagons and drivers from organized firms to haul their cotton and deliver their goods. The teamsters who drove these wagons were known for their colorful cursing and prodigious capacity for hard liquor, as well as for their ability to handle oxen.[13]

Marketing produce via waterways was not much easier nor was it more satisfactory, even though Texas had plenty of rivers. Often they were dangerously low, and sometimes they were dangerously high. And they had unpleasant surprises such as low overhanging branches, snags, rafts (barriers of tangled logs and driftwood), and treacherous sandbars. Nevertheless, planters located near the rivers made use of them to get their produce to factors in Houston, Galveston, and New Orleans, especially in the rainy season.

Flatboats, keelboats, and steamboats were used on Texas rivers. William Bollaert noticed flatboats being built on the San Jacinto River and a large keelboat under construction at La Grange. He saw a flatboat carrying two hundred bales of cotton from La Grange to the raft near the mouth of the Colorado River. From that point the cotton would be loaded onto wagons to be hauled to Matagorda.[14]

The earlier flatboats were crude crafts capable of traveling in only one direction, as they had to follow the river current. They were built of squared logs bound together. Looking like long, shallow boxes with straight sides, they were covered with a roof of timbers to protect the cotton bales. The navigators, usually slaves, poled the boats along with strong saplings. When the flatboats reached their destinations, the cargo was transferred to a larger boat or to wagons and the boats were sold for their lumber.

A keelboat could be used for round-trips. Shaped like a long, narrow oval, pointed at each end, it had a roomy hold and a small cabin at deck level. The cabin had windows and was furnished with a table, bunks, and a fireplace. The enormous rudder, supported by a long, bent pole, could be used at either end of the boat. To propel the boat upriver, slaves either poled it along or pulled it from the bank, using oxen and steering it with the sturdy

---

13. "Freighting," *Commerce* (pamphlet), pp. 17–20.
14. William Bollaert, *William Bollaert's Texas*, ed. William Eugene Hollon and Ruth Lapham Butler, pp. 185, 261, 267.

When fall rains turned Texas' roads into quagmires, planters put their produce on the rivers in a variety of craft.

The most basic was a simple raft; logs tied together, loaded up & poled down river.

Flatboats were slightly more elaborate, with shelter for the cargo, but neither had a steering mechanism beyond poles wielded by slaves. Both, however, were totally marketable, the cargo & the timber they were made of being sold at the final destination. The people went home over land.

Keelboats depended on the current & men with poles for power but could maneuver past obstacles by using the long-armed rudder, adaptable to either end of the craft. The cabin made for some creature comforts not found on flatboats or rafts.

Top of the line transportation was the steamboat, carrying cargo aplenty & passengers in comfort. While paddle wheelers & side wheelers both worked the rivers, the side wheeler, with its shallow draft & greater agility, fared better on Texas' narrow streams, with their changeable depths.

rudder. On their return trips upriver the keelboats carried supplies for merchants and plantations.

Steamboats were the most desirable vessels for shipping cotton to market. Both sidewheelers and sternwheelers were used on Texas rivers, although the sternwheelers had the advantage of drawing less water and of having the paddlewheel better protected from snags and driftwood.[15] At best, the planter who entrusted his cargo to a steamboat had much to worry him until he learned that it had arrived safely. The boilers of paddlewheelers blew up; the boats foundered in high water, ran aground in shallow water, and had other accidents with alarming frequency when they encountered obstacles.

The Brazos River, which ran through the richest cotton-producing region of Texas, was a desirable route, although it had a nasty sandbar at its mouth. In the fall of 1833 a number of planters signed a subscription list, promising to donate land and money if the owners of the sidewheeler *Cayuga* would bring it to Texas to carry produce and merchandise for them. When the *Cayuga* got as far as San Felipe in January, 1834, a grand ball was held to celebrate its arrival.[16]

The sidewheeler *Yellow Stone* was half loaded with cotton and tied up at Groce's Landing in March, 1836, when Sam Houston arrived and impressed the ship to carry the Texas Army across the Brazos. After completing this mission, the *Yellow Stone* raced down the river under a full head of steam past a company of Mexican soldiers, who fired their muskets at her and attempted to lasso her smokestack. Although she spun completely around in midcurrent and struck the bank, the *Yellow Stone* eventually reached Quintana on the Gulf with her cargo of cotton still intact.[17]

Capt. Basil Muse Hatfield, owner of a plantation near Washington, also commanded the steamboats *Washington* and *Brazos*. He pushed steamboat navigation in Texas to the limit by taking the *Washington* up the Little River as far as Cameron, where he threw a ball that lasted three days and where a marker still acclaims his feat.[18]

For East Texas planters, the Red River was the important shipping route. But navigation of its upper waters was hampered by a huge log raft. This raft, which obstructed the river for thirty miles above Shreveport, created Caddo Lake and made Jefferson an important shipping point for cotton growers. The first steamboat reached Jefferson in the early 1840s.[19]

Steamboats needed large quantities of wood and water to operate their boilers. River water was easy to come by, but the wood had to be cut

---

15. Pamela Ashworth Puryear and Nath Winfield, Jr., *Sandbars and Sternwheelers: Steam Navigation on the Brazos*, pp. 38–39.

16. William Ransom Hogan, *The Texas Republic: A Social and Economic History*, p. 70.

17. Puryear and Winfield, *Sandbars and Sternwheelers*, p. 47.

18. Ibid., p. 68.

19. Traylor Russell, *Carpetbaggers, Scalawags, and Others*, pp. 4–5; *Handbook of Texas* II, 451.

and stacked for pickup along the boat's route. For example, the *Yellow Stone* on its trip downriver required one hundred cords of wood between Washington and Groce's Landing, fifty cords at the Landing, another fifty at San Felipe, and so on until it reached its destination at Quintana on the Gulf. The ships' owners paid three dollars per cord, and the large plantation owners saw that the wood was ready and waiting along with their bales of cotton.[20]

The dream and constant hope of the cotton planter was for rail transportation to get his produce to market. Many of the planters who were also legislators used their positions to promote the building of railroads in Texas. William T. Scott, who served eight terms in Texas legislatures, was especially influential in this effort.[21] By the time of the Civil War there were eleven short railroads in Texas, one of which ran between Houston and Columbia. The Civil War interrupted plans for extensive railroad building in Texas, and they arrived essentially too late to solve the marketing problems of the majority of plantation owners.

As marketing methods became more sophisticated, some mercantile houses in small towns offered their services as agents for Galveston cotton factors and acted as middlemen for the planters. The price paid for cotton fluctuated according to the demand for it, from a few cents per pound to a dollar. In 1840 the *Brazos Courier* carried an editorial advising planters to get their crops ready to send on a British ship that was expected to dock at San Luis. The editor reported that Texas planters who shipped to Liverpool the previous season had realized from one to two cents per pound more than those who shipped to New Orleans.[22]

Usually the cotton fields were picked over until all the scrap cotton was gathered. Ginning and baling and shipping sometimes continued into the winter, depending on the weather, the conditions on the rivers and roads, and the number of hands available. After the cotton had been picked over once, winter oats and rye could be sown among the cotton plants. These crops made good winter pasturage and hay. August was an important month for planting the kitchen garden, especially cabbage and cauliflower, turnips, mustard, and beets. By the 1850s some planters had such an abundance of food in good years that one observer was moved to exclaim:

> Above and below the thriving town of Washington on the Brazos, for many miles the cotton, corn and every other vegetable substance seems to overload the earth, and when I viewed the fields and saw the corn and pumpkins rotting and the hogs so fat that they could scarcely wallow, and passing the plump ears of corn and large orange-colored pumpkins without regarding them, I almost thought it a wanton waste of nature.[23]

20. *Commerce* (pamphlet), p. 29.
21. *Handbook of Texas* II, 583.
22. *Brazos Courier* (Brazoria, Texas), Aug. 4, 1840.
23. "Agricultural Capacities of Western Texas," *DeBow's Review* 18 (Jan., 1855): 54–55.

A few Texas planters raised enough tobacco to sell. Captain Hatfield had at least two large tobacco barns on his plantation near Washington. Many others grew it as a luxury crop for the use of the plantation residents. After the leaves matured, they were dried by being spread out in the air, usually on the roofs of some of the outbuildings. The leaves were soaked in sugar or honey to make chewing tobacco or powdered to make snuff. White women as well as black used snuff, and sometimes mistresses gave a bit of snuff to young house slaves as a treat. Fancy snuffboxes of papier-mâché or japanning (lacquering) sat on parlor tables in plantation manor houses. Snuff was used in various ways. It was sniffed through the nostrils, tucked between the gums and teeth, or applied to the gums with a "dip" stick (made from a well-chewed twig). Both sexes enjoyed smoking tobacco in clay or corncob pipes.

FALL

When the pressure of gathering the main part of the cotton crop eased, the hands could be used to gather in the corn and other crops. Proper storage of the produce was essential. Pumpkins might be stored in rail pens, covered with crabgrass hay, and then covered with clapboards. Barns were used for storage, but many planters used dirt banks to keep their produce fresh. Sweet potatoes, white potatoes, and other vegetables were bedded in deep holes on mounds of dry sand, dry cornstalks, straw, and grass. Each kind of vegetable, such as turnips or beets, was put by itself in the mounds. Cornstalks made a sort of Indian tepee over the food, with a small hole on the south side big enough for a child to crawl through. A board fitted tightly over the crawl hole. Straw and grass covered the cornstalks, and dirt was piled thickly all around so the rains would not wash it off or seep through to the vegetables. The storage area of a prosperous plantation might be dotted with a number of these food banks. Of course, after a hard rain, they had to be repaired and built up, but if they were properly maintained, they kept the food in good condition until new crops provided fresh vegetables.

When the weather was too harsh for field work, or sometimes at night, planters held "corn shuckings." Holding the huskings on different plantations added to the party spirit. The host planter provided the corn, whiskey, and the food. The slaves shucked the corn, laughing, joking, singing, and hoping to find a red ear, which entitled them to kiss the one of their choice. Sometimes the shuckings lasted all night. After the work, a big fire was built and a dance held, with the music provided by slaves scratching on skillet lids, beating bones together, or plucking homemade banjos and fiddles.

On many plantations another communal work and party time was connected with log rolling. Plantation owners were constantly acquiring and clearing more land, and it was the custom to have neighboring owners and their slaves come to help. The cleared logs and brush were piled high and

Just before the first frost was expected,
sugar cane was cut, brought in from the field &
stripped of its leaves. Cut into manageable lengths,
the cane was fed into a hopper where mule power
drove the press, turning rollers that extracted the
juice. The dry, pulverized cane was used for animal
fodder; the juice was collected in buckets to
be poured into kettles where the process of
making syrup & brown sugar became
a serious business.

24"–30" Long

Everyone on the plantation was involved in a week or more of 18-hour days with the most experienced hands stationed at the kettles. The large sugar crystals that formed on top of the liquid had to be skimmed off at just the right moment to avoid scorching. The fires had to be carefully managed to provide enough heat to cook the juice down to a molasse s-like thickness without burning it.

By the early 1850's sugar production had peaked in Texas, & when the cane crop was heavily damaged by severe cold in 1856, many planters lost interest & returned to cotton as their cash crop.

burned in a great, roaring fire. Again the host provided food and drink, and there was singing and dancing.

Halloween was a time for telling ghost stories and for the larger children to play tricks to scare the smaller ones. For the planter it was a reminder that cold weather was coming, and it was time to get up the hogs he intended to butcher. These hogs, having eaten the mast in the woods and foraged in the clover lots as well as oat and pea lots in succession, were now turned in to the harvested cornfields to fatten up or were penned and fed corn.

Fall was also the time to attend to soap making, if it had not been done earlier in the year. Lye, grease, and water were the necessary ingredients for making soap. To make the lye, ashes from the fireplaces were kept in an ash hopper. Sometimes these hoppers were simply big hogshead barrels with holes punched in the bottom. More often the hoppers were built of boards that slanted up in a V from a wooden trough that was shaped at one end to make a spout. When the hopper was filled with ashes, boiling water was poured over them. A thick layer of corn shucks or straw in the bottom of the hopper kept the ashes from running out the spout with the lye water, which was caught in a container.

It took about two pounds of grease to a gallon of dripped lye to make soap. Any kind of fat or grease could be used: leftover cooking grease, fatty meat scraps, yellow lard cut from meat hanging in the smokehouse, hog or mutton tallow from butchering, or bear fat. Women slaves stirred the mixture in huge iron kettles and kept a hot fire underneath the pot to keep it bubbling. Greasy bones were sometimes thrown into the pot. The strong lye dissolved them, and they became part of the soap. When the mixture had boiled down to a jelly-like stage, it could be stored for use as soft soap. For cakes of soap, the mixture had to be boiled some more and then placed in shallow pans to harden. It was then cut into bars for use in all kinds of washing, from scrubbing floors to scrubbing humans.

Just before the first frost was expected, the sugarcane was cut with cane knives and the leaves stripped. The work day stretched to eighteen hours as the cane-grinding season began. After harvesting, the stalks were poured into a hopper about five feet from the ground. Oxen, mules, or horses harnessed to spokes walked in endless circles, moving the rollers that pressed the juice from the stalks. The stalks could be used as livestock feed, and the juice was boiled down to evaporate the water, producing syrup and brown sugar.

Sweet sorghum, which was cultivated in much the same way as corn, was also used to make syrup. The initial investment in equipment for sugar making was expensive, and the process required a large labor force. After the juice was pressed from the cane or sorghum, it was boiled over wood fires in big cast-iron kettles until it became thick and syrupy and formed sugar crystals. It had to be skimmed at just the right stage, and care had to be taken not to burn the sugar and syrup and to keep applying heat until large sugar crystals formed and the syrup thickened to molasses. All the children on the

plantation enjoyed eating the raw sugarcane joints and drinking the juice before it became syrup.

First attempts to make sugar in Texas from sugarcane were disappoint-
ing. It turned out a brown, sticky substance that leaked if carried wrapped in
paper. But during the 1840s sugar production increased as the planters learned
better methods of refining it. And sugarhouses sprang up alongside cotton
gins. By 1845 Peach Point was shipping hogsheads of sugar and molasses to
New York to sell. Col. James Morgan grew sugarcane successfully along the
shores of Galveston Bay, as did Ashbel Smith. Always an innovator, Smith
experimented in sugar and molasses production and wrote articles for his fellow planters on the art of cultivating cane and making sugar, which he claimed
was as easy as making soap. By the early 1850s sugar production had peaked
in Texas, and when the cane crop was heavily damaged by severe cold weather
in 1856, many Texas planters returned to cotton as their cash crop.

After the crops were gathered in the fall, it was time to issue winter
clothing to the slaves, chink up the cabins in the quarters, and haul wood to
the big woodpiles that would supply fuel for heating and cooking all through
the winter. In the fall the planter built new fences and had the old ones mended.
Since cattle grazed on an open range, it was necessary to keep the fences
around fields and yards in good repair. Cornfields especially needed to be
well fenced to keep cattle and other animals out. A cedar picket fence, which
might last as long as a stone fence, was built of pointed stakes driven upright
into the ground one against the next. It took a great deal of wood and work
but was a long-lasting investment. The most common fence was the split-rail
worm fence, which was considerably easier to build. Each section of rails was
at an angle to the next section so the fence zigzagged back and forth.

Hedgerows of Cherokee rose, pyracantha, or Osage orange (also
called bois d'arc) also made effective fences. The Cherokee rose, a vigorous
evergreen with many sharp thorns, could be grown readily from cuttings and
if well tended formed an impervious fence in four years. The long shoots
interlaced so that no animal could force its way through when the hedge was
four feet high or more. The pyracantha required more care than the rose. It
had to be planted from rooted plants and protected in its early stages, and it
needed clipping at least once a year. But it grew into a beautiful solid wall of
green, which in spring was covered with snowy blossoms and in fall and
winter with masses of bright scarlet berries. The spiny bois d'arc made a for-
midable tree hedge. In one year the town of Jefferson exported more than
nine thousand bushels of bois d'arc seed to the prairie areas of Texas, where
they were planted in hedges to serve as fences.[24]

Cool weather was time for making candles from melted tallow or
beeswax. Wicks of spun cotton were dipped repeatedly into the melted tallow
until they were the right thickness. Or the candlemakers might use molds

24. Affleck, *Southern Rural Almanac*, pp. 104–105, 114–15.

into which they poured the melted wax. Various plants and bark could be used to make colored candles. After the candles cooled, they were put away in tin candle boxes to protect them from mice, which were attracted to the tallow.

When the pecans matured and fell off the trees, it was usually the women and young black children who went to pick them up. The men on the plantation, masters and servants, enjoyed hunting at all times of the year, but particularly in the fall when the weather was cool enough for the meat to be preserved. To save ammunition they hunted deer with pine-knot torches or pan fires. The hunter, on foot or horseback, proceeded cautiously through the woods. The startled deer looked toward the pan of fire and the hunter saw a reflection of light in the eyes of the deer, which remained frozen in terror, allowing the hunters to walk right up to them. Bollaert said that this procedure, called "shining the eyes," was effective at a hundred yards or more.[25]

WINTER

As northers began to arrive with regularity and periods of prolonged chill prompted the planter to don his flannel underwear, he concentrated his attention on the care of his livestock. Even in the mildest parts of Texas the planter usually provided some kind of shelter, stable, or barn to protect his domestic animals. And he planned his crops to provide enough food for them when grazing was not sufficient.

During most of the year the hogs might be left in the woods with the advice to "root, hog, or die," but as butchering time approached, they were rounded up and fattened by generous feeding. On a large plantation there were several hog-killing times—from the first cold day in November or December through January. A hundred hogs might be killed at one time, and the whole plantation became a meat factory.

One group of slaves did the sticking and killing. Another group scalded the hogs in huge iron tubs to loosen the hair, which another group scraped off down to the bare skin. Then the carcass was hung over a tub, and workers quickly gutted it, throwing the insides into the tub. The anxiously waiting dogs got their share of the entrails after the women had saved the lard, the liver, and other desirable bits. The fat around the kidneys, known as "leaf lard" or "leaf fat," was especially valued for its fine quality. The bladders were carefully cleaned and saved, as were the small intestines. Skilled slaves cut the meat up into hams, shoulders, ribs, backbone, and slabs of bacon.

Some of the best lean pieces were made into sausage to be eaten fresh or sent to the smokehouse. These might include trimmings from hams, shoulders, the tenderloin, meat from the head, and even the jowls. Each cook

25. Bollaert, *William Bollaert's Texas*, p. 277.

had her favorite recipe for sausage, which included differing amounts of salt, pepper, sage, red pepper, and brown sugar. To test for taste, a small amount was run through the grinder and fried. When the taster was satisfied, the sausage making proceeded, with even the children helping with the grinding. The sausage might be packed in muslin bags or in the sections of cleaned small intestine, tied, and hung from the joists of the smokehouse for curing.

Nothing was wasted. The tongue, ears, and tail were enjoyed by the slaves, and the feet and ankles ("knuckles") were pickled. The jowls were cooked with vegetables. The fat was rendered, or melted, by cooking, to be used in preparing food and in making soap. Cracklings, left after the lard was rendered, were a special treat. Chitlings, made from the fried small intestines, were another great favorite. What was left of the head was made into headcheese, or souse. The hams, bacon sides, shoulders, and other large pieces were "cured"; after they were generously salted, they were packed down in a meat box for several weeks. Then they were washed and hung in the smokehouse. Hickory wood was preferred for the long, slow smoking that preserved the meat and gave it a delicious flavor, but if hickory was not available, the ever-present corncobs also gave the meat a good flavor.

In the mid-nineteenth century, Texas, along with the other states, joyfully adopted the kind of Christmas popularized in the works of Charles Dickens. With few exceptions Christmas was the biggest holiday on Texas plantations. Many planters gave their slaves the whole week between Christmas and New Year's as a holiday except for necessary chores such as feeding livestock, milking, and gathering eggs. The household chores were shared among the house servants so each got some days off.

Under the mistress's supervision the house was decorated from top to bottom with holly, wreaths, evergreen branches, and candles. The slaves were sent to cut and haul to the big house an enormous tree, which was decorated with popcorn strings and handmade ornaments, including cotton balls. The slaves took particular care in choosing the large yule log to place at the back of the parlor fireplace, for the traditional belief on many plantations was that the holidays would last as long as the yule log burned. The slaves were also adept at keeping the log burning by judiciously dampening it from time to time.

Exquisitely dressed china dolls and brightly painted wooden rocking horses were typical gifts for the white children. Gifts for the slaves might be pennies for the children, a sack of candy and a popcorn ball, or a pair of shoes for the adults. One planter gave each slave family a present of twenty-five dollars, a generous sum in the mid-nineteenth century.[26]

Between Christmas Eve and New Year's Day there was a constant round of visiting on plantations. The families took turns hosting dinners, suppers, parties, and dances. Young black servants holding the gates open for

26. Rawick, ed., *Texas Narratives*, p. 2842.

Left out in the woods most of the year, fattening themselves on acorns, nuts & whatever they could find, the plantation's hogs were gathered at the end of fall & penned close by the plantation's buildings. With the onset of the first cold weather—& after spending a month or more eating corn—as many as one hundred hogs might find their way to the butcher's table. After a hog was killed, usually by a sharp blow to the head, the jugular was punctured & the carcass allowed to bleed as dry as possible.

Passed along from one group of slaves to another, the body of the hog was scalded Ⓐ & the hair scraped off with knives Ⓑ leaving only bare skin. Hung up by the tendons in its hind legs, the hog was dressed Ⓒ with the liver, heart, lungs, kidneys, small intestine, stomach & head being saved, the remainder going, literally, to the dogs.

A

B

C

Turned over to practiced butchers, the carcass was decapitated & split down either side of the backbone ⒟ with the hams, shoulders & bacon (from the sides) cut out & trimmed of fat. These prime cuts were tucked away under piles of salt — sometimes mixed with shelled corn or peppers — in the smokehouse or the cellar of the big house — awaiting smoke curing in the spring.

Sausage was prepared ⒠ from cuts of lean meat mixed with lard, peppers & "secret" spices, stuffed into the cleaned small intestine, parboiled & smoked.

The fat trimmed from the hogs was rendered to lard ⒡ for cooking & a variety of other uses.

The backbone was sectioned between the vertebrae & with the feet, pickled.

The tenderloin, internal organs & head were used immediately, being too fragile, or tasty, to salt or smoke.

Each plantation had its own recipes & proportions of measure, but a lot of salt figured in all of them. More than one tale comes from the Civil War years of the mistress of the plantation leading a crew of slaves to the smokehouse, where they shoveled & sifted through the dirt floor to recycle salt they couldn't buy.

D

E

F

the white guests eagerly received the small gifts or pieces of money tossed to them by visitors. At the front door the slave girls who took the wraps of the guests expected and received the same small favors.

Eggnog and syllabub were the favored drinks of the season. As early as 1843 William Bollaert, who was traveling in Texas, mentioned Christmas Day as a time for "visitings amongst the neighbors; dinner and merry makings." And he described "egg nogs, the favourite beverage this morning (made of the white and yellow of eggs, beaten up separately, the yellow with sugar, then both mixed with whiskey, brandy and new milk to thin it—somewhat pleasant, but of a bilious nature)."[27] Syllabub, a lighter mixture of eggs, milk, wine, and spices, was sometimes eaten as a custard with a spoon, but more often drunk from fine glass goblets. Since it contained wine instead of whiskey, syllabub was considered a better drink for ladies.

Christmas dinner was a feast. At Eagle Island it began with raw oysters and included stuffed turkey, wild ducks, turnips, greens, sweet potatoes, and rice and ended with plum pudding. On other plantations beef and pork roasts, creamed potatoes, varieties of preserved vegetables and fruits, biscuits, and many kinds of pies and cakes and sweetmeats were served.

When everyone was sated, it was time for the fireworks. Hog bladders, saved from hog-killing time, were filled with air, tied tightly, and hung up to dry. On Christmas night, a big fire was built, and the children, with the hog bladders on sticks, darted to the fire to hold them in the heat until they exploded with a satisfying BANG! The fireworks went on for a long, noisy time as there were often more than a hundred bladders to pop. The evening usually ended with a big dance. During the holiday week there would also be religious services, taffy pulls, and singing by the slaves to entertain their owners. Some planters included New Year's Day in the holiday time, but others, believing in an old superstition that says that whatever one does on that day presages what will happen during the rest of the year, insisted that it be a full day of work.

As the old year ended, the planter looked over his estate, thinking about the improvements he had made during the past year and determining those he wanted to carry out the next. Thomas Affleck, planter and nurseryman and publisher of planters' record books, warned plantation owners "not to enter upon the new year without duly weighing both the past and the future." He advised them to "keep the plow in motion" during the winter, whenever the weather permitted. He thought it a "misfortune" if the cotton crop had not all been picked, baled, and sent to market by the close of the year so that the efforts of master and slaves could be turned to preparation for a new crop.[28]

There was plenty to do even in bad weather. Tools and instruments

---

27. Bollaert, *William Bollaert's Texas*, p. 293.
28. Affleck, *Southern Rural Almanac*, pp. 20, 134.

needed repairing; harnesses and shoes needed mending. Spinning, weaving, basket making, and corn shelling could be done in any weather. Many Texans, like Sam Houston, were skillful whittlers, and so were many of the slaves, who whittled dishes, bowls, troughs, spoons, trays, churn paddles, and other useful items during the long winter evenings. Both white and black women enjoyed the creative art of quilting. Although some planters referred to such tasks as "piddling," they were important to the smooth operation of a plantation.

In addition to hog butchering, outside winter tasks included spreading manure in the garden; repairing fences and buildings; planting fruit trees and shrubs; and, weather permitting, "keeping the plows moving."

By mid-February, thoughts turned to spring. It was time to plan vegetable and flower gardens. In a month or less the wild buffalo clover (bluebonnets), primroses, and other colorful flowers would appear to mark the reawakening of nature after the dormant season. By then the planter's first crops would be in the ground, and he would be praying that nature would be kind to this year's crops, sparing them from too much pestilence, too much heat or cold, drought or flood.

In a letter to his father, Charles William Tait summed up the obstacles to a successful cotton crop: "I am afraid that with the rains in the spring, the drought in the summer and the catterpillars in the fall, together with the sickness among the negroes, my chance for cotton will be slim." However, the next day he showed the persistence that characterized the successful planter, for he told his father that they were "picking cotton as fast as we can."[29]

29. Tait (Charles William) Papers, Barker Texas History Center.

CHAPTER FIVE

Body & Soul

"We hummed our religious songs in the field while we was working. It was our way of praying for freedom, but the white folks didn't know it."
—Millie Ann Smith, Texas Slave Narratives

MEDICINE

When Jared Groce built his inland plantation to get away from the malaria-plagued river bottom, he made the right move, although he didn't know why. Nobody associated the tiresome mosquitoes of the low country with the chills and fevers that racked many newcomers, but it was generally believed that those living in higher and drier locations suffered less. Sickly slaves cut into their owners' income, and advertisements often mentioned that a group of slaves offered for sale were "acclimated," meaning they were less likely to get malaria. An often-quoted poem had these lines:

> Did you ever? No I never!
> Have the racking chills and fever?
> Then you surely cannot know
> All the pangs of human woe![1]

Malaria went by different names: intermittent fever, remittent fever, ague, and bilious fever. In whatever form and by whatever name, it caused excruciating pain in muscles, bones, and joints; severe headaches; uncontrollable shivering; burning fever; drenching sweats; and in severe cases, emaciation, anemia, great weakness, depression, and disorientation. Quinine was the most widely used medicine for malaria. But when it was not available, boneset, a common herb, was nearly as good at breaking the chills and fever of mild cases. Patients regarded either remedy, quinine or boneset, as equally evil tasting.

Not surprisingly, in those days of bad sanitation and poor hygiene, dysentery (also called summer complaint or blood flux) was another com-

1. William Ransom Hogan, *The Texas Republic: A Social and Economic History*, p. 224.

mon ailment. Home remedies included rice water (water in which rice had been boiled); blackjack oak-bark tea; broth made from pulverized dried linings of chicken gizzards; and oak leaves, which were chewed. Or, for fifty cents the sufferer could purchase Dr. Browning's Celebrated Cholera and Diarrhea Remedy, which was advertised as a "Sovereign and never-failing remedy for all Bowel Affections." The advertiser modestly admitted that Dr. Browning's would not cure "all the diseases to which the human race is subject" but promised a "speedy cure" for the "worst forms" of diarrhea, dysentery, and cholera morbus.[2]

Epidemics of the dreaded cholera caused panic in Texas cities and among plantation residents in the lower Brazos area in 1833–34 and again in 1850 and 1852. Hundreds died in Austin's colony in the first epidemic, including the eleven-year-old daughter of Emily Perry by her first marriage. Texans referred to 1833 as the year of the "Big Cholera." The towns of Brazoria and Velasco were devastated by the disease, and the plantation families suffered proportionately.

The plantation of Thomas Westall, a successful cotton planter on Gulf Prairie, was particularly hard hit. Westall and two of his children as well as many of his slaves died of the disease. James Perry wrote to Stephen F. Austin that at one time there were six or seven corpses at the James Westall plantation because "the neighbours were afraid to approach them." Two of Josiah Bell's sons were killed by cholera. The effects of the epidemic were felt economically and politically. So many slaves were stricken that the crops suffered, and everyone was so caught up in nursing the sick and trying to keep their families alive during the crisis that even the "War Dogs" suspended their agitation for Texas independence. The disease spread to Mexico, where Stephen F. Austin, there to straighten out his colony's affairs, was infected. He recovered, but was handicapped in carrying out his business because so many officials were involved in trying to overcome the effects of the disease in that country.

In 1849 and 1850 cholera appeared on the Red River and killed a number of plantation slaves there. As Williamson Freeman and his family and slaves were making their way from Georgia to their new life in Texas, the cholera caught up with them in New Orleans and killed several of the slaves. It rolled on relentlessly, and on a plantation near Huntsville it killed more than a dozen slaves and the owner's son. When sixteen slaves died of cholera on one Brazoria County plantation and thirty-three on another, some of the planters suspended all work and had their slaves scatter in the woods to avoid exposure to victims of the disease.

The cause of the disease was not understood, but intelligent doctors connected its onset with a lack of cleanliness and inadequate sanitation relating to food and water. All kinds of quack remedies were tried. Some were as

2. *Texas Almanac*, 1861, advertisement.

harmless as eating garlic and going to bed early. Other "cures" that were published included pills made from black pepper and opium, tobacco enemas, pills of sulfur mixed with powdered charcoal, and throwing cold water on the patient. Large doses of the much-overused calomel as well as copious bloodletting were prescribed. Thus the poor cholera victim had to survive not only his disease but also its treatment.[3]

Yellow fever, commonly called yellow jack, was another terrifying disease for which neither cause nor remedy was known. The frightful epidemics that hit Texas in 1839, 1844, and again in 1854 were confined mostly to the seaport towns of Houston and Galveston, and the plantations escaped with only a few scattered cases. However, James Perry and his son Henry, who were in New Orleans in August of 1853, fell victim to the epidemic that swept the south that summer, and both died there of yellow fever.

Just as dysentery and malaria were recurrent summer diseases for plantation dwellers, pneumonia, pleurisy, diphtheria, and whooping cough were the dreaded diseases of cold weather. Older people were more apt to die from pneumonia, while children died frequently from diphtheria or whooping cough.

The infant and child mortality rate was terribly high in the large families that were common to plantations. In East Texas, plantation owner John B. Webster lost four of his nine children during their infancy or childhood. Of Josiah Bell's eight children, only three reached maturity. In 1864 Rebecca Adams wrote her physician husband from their Fairfield plantation that all six of their children were suffering with whooping cough and that she had them all in her bedroom. "You can easily imagine what kind of noise we have at night," she told him.[4] In the same letter Rebecca mentioned that smallpox was spreading in Texas, so she had had all the children vaccinated against it. Most of the planters belonged to the group of enlightened Texans who were eagerly accepting use of the controversial smallpox vaccine, discovered in 1796. One of the Perrys' doctor bills included this charge:

April 21	
To visit and vaccinating your children	5.50
Also vaccinating about 16 or 18 little negros	5.00[5]

3. P. A. Davenport to John Adriance, Aug. 6, 1850, Adriance (John) Papers, Barker Texas History Center; James Perry to Stephen F. Austin, Oct. 26, 1933; Eugene C. Barker, ed., *The Austin Papers* II, 1009; *Standard* (Clarksville, Tex.), July 7, 1849; *Texas State Gazette* (Austin), Feb. 2, 1850; Freeman Family Papers, privately held, Jesse M. DeWare IV, Jefferson, Tex.; Marie Beth Jones, *Peach Point Plantation: The First 150 Years*, pp. 35–39; *Washington-on-the-Brazos*, summer, 1983.

4. Rebecca Adams to Dr. Robert Adams, Jan. 28, 1864, Gary D. Woods, comp., *The Hicks-Adams-Bass-Floyd-Pattillo and Collateral Lines, Together with Family Papers, 1840–1868*, p. 356.

5. Bill from Dr. W. C. Goodlett to James F. Perry, 1857, Perry (James F. and Stephen S.) Papers, Barker Texas History Center.

Some plantations like Thomas Affleck's Glenblythe had a separate hospital building for slaves. On others the slaves might be taken to the big house to recover, while on others they were confined to their own quarters. When the Adamses' servant Jim became seriously ill during Dr. Adams's absence, Rebecca had him brought into the dining room where she could see after him during the night and give him every dose of the medicine prescribed by the doctor, who visited twice a day. Rebecca was distressed when the faithful Jim died from "bilious fever," despite large doses of quinine, calomel, ipecac, and blister plasters placed over his abdomen.[6]

On small plantations masters and mistresses kept close watch over the health of their slaves. From necessity the white women learned nursing skills. Rutherford B. Hayes, on his visit to Peach Point, wrote:

> Mrs. Perry . . . instead of having the care of one family, is the nurse, physician, and spiritual advisor of a whole settlement of careless slaves. She feels it her duty to see to their comfort when sick or hurt, and among so many there is always some little brat with a scalded foot or a hand half cut off, and 'Missus' must always see to it. . . .[7]

Leonard Groce remembered: "One of my earliest recollections of my mother was her visiting the sick at the 'Quarters' accompanied by a maid with a basket filled with dainties, and seeing that they were comfortable and well cared for."[8] Many of the black women, especially the mammies, were skillful nurses, midwives, and concocters of medicines.

On large plantations, in the case of the illness of a slave, the patient or another servant reported to the overseer, who decided whether it was a real or pretended sickness and whether or not he could treat it himself. If the case seemed serious, he reported it to the master, who sent for a doctor. Some planters with large holdings, like Jared E. Groce, had a doctor who lived on the estate and was paid a yearly salary. Otherwise the planter arranged for a doctor in a nearby town to take care of his family and slaves and submit a yearly bill.

The doctors tended to congregate in the larger towns such as Houston and Galveston. And in East Texas, as in the lower Brazos area, many of them were planters first and physicians second. By the time of the Civil War, in Harrison County there were at least five doctors who owned twenty or more slaves.[9]

Medical fees varied from place to place and from the colonial period

6. Rebecca Adams to Dr. Robert Adams, Oct. 21, 1863, Woods, comp., *Hicks-Adams-Bass-Floyd-Pattillo*, p. 329.

7. Rutherford B. Hayes, "Texas Diary," Jan. 27, 1849, Barker Texas History Center.

8. Leonard Waller Groce, "Personal Recollection of Leonard Waller Groce, as Related to His Son, William Wharton Groce," transcript, Barker Texas History Center.

9. Randolph B. Campbell, *A Southern Community in Crisis: Harrison County, Texas 1850–1880*, p. 100.

until the Civil War. Houston physicians seem to have charged the highest fees. Dr. Anson Jones of Brazoria submitted a bill to James Perry for $236.50 for visits, medicine, and treatments for whites and blacks from February, 1835, to October, 1836.[10] Ten years later the Perrys became exasperated with Dr. Jones over what they considered to be his opposition to annexation. But by that time Jones, who was serving as president of the Republic, was no longer practicing medicine. In August of 1848, Dr. William Beers visited Julien Devereux's plantation and remained to treat one of Devereux's sons for five days and nights, for which he charged one hundred dollars.[11] The fee schedule published by Dr. W. B. Wallace of Washington was fairly typical of the charges made by Texas doctors in the mid-1800s:

> Visit to the country by day per mile 50
> Visit to the country by night per mile 1.50
> Midwifery by day 10.00
> Midwifery by night 15.00
> Medicines & prescriptions, either written or verbal . . . . 1.50[12]

Other typical fees were: bleeding, one to two dollars; cupping (drawing blood by placing a glass to the skin), two to five dollars; medicines, twenty-five to fifty cents per dose; use of syringe, one dollar; extracting teeth, fifty cents to one dollar; and surgical operations, five to twenty-five dollars.[13]

The training of doctors in Texas varied. Some were outright quacks, who simply bestowed the title of doctor upon themselves, many had had brief apprenticeships with older doctors, and a few were highly trained physicians like Ashbel Smith. With a medical degree from Yale, a year's training in surgery in Paris under the outstanding surgeons of the day, and experience in cholera and yellow fever epidemics, Smith achieved a reputation that caused him to be called upon for his medical services even after he officially gave up his practice to devote his time to planting and to political and educational interests.

Nevertheless, no matter how well intentioned and well trained, the nineteenth-century physician was handicapped by the limitations of medical knowledge at that time. Treatment by amateurs and professionals alike was often heroic and potentially more dangerous to the patient than the disease. Harsh emetics, purgatives, and bloodletting (known as the "puke, purge, and bleed" regimen) were the order of the day. Quinine, calomel, blue mass pills (a mercury preparation), epsom salts, and castor oil were the doctors' favorite weapons against disease. Blistering with hot poultices and plasters was also a common treatment.

10. Bill from Dr. Anson Jones to James F. Perry, Oct. 13, 1836, in ibid.
11. Bill from Dr. William Beers to Julien Devereux, 1848, Devereux (Julien Sidney) Papers, Barker Texas History Center.
12. Pat Ireland Nixon, *The Medical Story of Early Texas, 1528–1853*, pp. 463–64.
13. Ibid.

The doctors' chief instrument of torture was the scarificator, used by the physician for "therapeutic vampirism." The scarificator was a small box containing ten to twelve lancets or blades cocked with a spring. When the spring was tripped, the blades punctured the skin and pierced a vein, usually just above the bend of the elbow. A glass cup with a bulb was used to suck out the blood.

In dry cupping a heated glass was placed on the patient's skin to create a vacuum and draw blood to the surface. Leeches were also used for bleeding. After the patient's skin was moistened with a little milk, the leech was placed on the skin until it attached itself. When the leech had sucked the desired amount of blood, it was removed and a bandage applied to stop the bleeding.[14]

Mrs. Houstoun noted in 1844 that almost any ship coming into Galveston brought "leeches by thousands, quinine by hogshead, and calomel by lots; to say nothing of demijohns of castor oil."[15]

Opium, laudanum, and whiskey were prescribed freely as part of many treatments and perhaps made the other parts more bearable. It is not surprising that slaves often preferred to conceal illnesses as long as possible to postpone undergoing the torment of being treated.

Texas newspapers advertised patent medicines promising to cure everything from baldness to cancer. Druggist Benjamin Franklin Rucker in Washington was famous for his tonics, especially his "Brazos Tonic and Alternative," which he advertised as a "certain cure for chronic ague, associated with enlargements of spleen and liver and digestive ills."[16] More extravagant claims were made for other medications. Vanderveer's Medicated Gin was billed as a "revivifyer of the constitution" and "a general remedy for all the ills of life." Radway's R.R.R. ("Ready Relief, Regulating Pills, and Renovating Resolvent") promised that there was no disease, plague or pestilence, pain or ache, however malignant, violent, or destructive that would not be "arrested and exterminated" by its use. J. Wright & Co. offered a catalogue of "Genuine and Popular Family Medicines" to those who preferred the convenience of mail-order shopping.[17]

Eye specialists advertised in newspapers and in the *Texas Almanac.* A Dr. Beard's Eye-Infirmary in New Orleans advertised that it had wards devoted to the treatment of slaves with eye afflictions, and it listed its fees as: "Whites, from $2 to $5 per day; Negroes, $1 per day. Operations charged extra."[18]

The popularity that some patent medicines attained, it must be sus-

14. *Washington-on-the-Brazos*, summer, 1983; Jonnie Lockhart Wallis and Laurance L. Hill, eds., *Sixty Years on the Brazos: The Life and Letters of Dr. John Washington Lockhart, 1824–1900*, pp. 174–75.

15. Matilda Charlotte Houstoun, *Texas and the Gulf of Mexico, or Yachting in the New World*, pp. 126–27.

16. *Texas Ranger and Lone Star* (Washington), Nov. 10, 1855.

17. *Texas Almanac*, 1857–1861, advertising section.

18. Ibid.

pected, was because they contained generous amounts of alcohol or opium. They were rather expensive and of questionable medicinal value. Most plantation residents put more faith in the home remedies prepared by their own white mistresses and black mammies from herbs, barks, roots, leaves, berries, weeds, and other natural ingredients. Mary Austin Holley noticed that Texas abounded in "valuable medicinal herbs and roots." Medicinal teas were made from many substances. Watermelon tea and catnip tea were given to babies to soothe them. Sage tea was used for fevers and chills, as was sassafras tea, which was also drunk to "purify" the blood. Butterfly-weed tea was used for pleurisy. Pepper tea (pepper in boiled milk) and corn-shuck tea were favorite home remedies for various ailments. Peppermint tea was used for the relief of indigestion.

Cold remedies included eating boiled or raw onions; drinking concoctions of whiskey, honey, and butter; and applying mustard plasters. Children with colds were frequently given a few drops of coal oil (kerosene) in a teaspoon of sugar. One recipe for a homemade cough syrup called for two tablespoons each of honey, whiskey, and lemon juice. The mixture was bottled and sipped as needed.

In East Texas turpentine (from pine trees) was readily available, and it was mixed with kerosene alone or with additional ingredients to cure indigestion, prevent pregnancy, or relieve toothache or rheumatism. Turpentine was mixed with honey and onions to make a syrup for coughs and colds. Pepper grass or pokeberries were stewed to make a laxative, as were senna leaves and the inner bark of the ash tree. Clay was used as a poultice to draw out aches and pains.

Moist, chewed tobacco was easily obtainable on plantations and was used in a variety of "cures." It was plastered on insect stings or bites, and applied as a poultice to snakebites. Tobacco was also used as an earache or toothache remedy. Powdered cloves or oil of cloves also relieved toothaches.

Cookbooks, whether bought or more commonly, homemade, contained sections on treatment of common ailments. And many households had such information in "commonplace books," which were little books containing maxims, household hints, records of events, and medical remedies. In the Julien Sidney Devereux commonplace book are medical memoranda such as applying scraped turnips to a sore leg, treating scalds and burns with clarified honey in a linen rag, and taking the juice of cockleburs internally with sweet milk and binding mashed cocklebur leaves on the bite of a rattlesnake.[19]

Since rattlesnake bites were fairly common among the outdoor workers on plantations, numerous "cures" were known. The copious use of whiskey, internally and externally, was popular. In addition to tobacco, mix-

19. Julien Devereux scrapbook, Devereux Papers, Barker Texas History Center.

tures of clay, soot, and vinegar and poultices from common plants such as milkweed were used. When he was bitten by a rattlesnake, Dr. Ashbel Smith treated himself entirely with iodine, drinking it diluted over a period of hours and applying it liberally to the wound. He survived to publish an article about his method of treatment. A more common treatment was to kill a chicken, other fowl, or rabbit, tear it open, and place it while still warm over the wound. When the flesh of the animal turned green, it was discarded and fresh meat applied.

Kerosene was used for cuts. Often when an accident severed a finger or toe, saturating the wound with kerosene and wrapping it in rags was the only treatment given. A common method to stop bleeding was to apply spiderwebs and soot.

Both black and white children went to their mammies to be rubbed with a salve made from elderberry flowers stewed in hog lard for relief from the red bugs and ticks they frequently picked up. And in the spring both groups held their noses as white mistresses poured spring tonics consisting of sulfur and molasses down the children's throats to "purify the blood."

For the adults most medicine chests contained a mixture called bitters, which was an all-purpose cure for various miseries. This well-named brew was made according to the mixer's taste and the ingredients at hand. A popular and particularly nasty version was a mix of tree bark, rust from iron nails, and whiskey. The threat of a dose of bitters was frequently enough to cause an ailing slave to suddenly recover his good health.

The habit of eating dirt or clay, a practice called "geophagy," was a phenomenon on many plantations. Those who became addicted were believed to ingest intestinal worms. In severe cases the victim became bloated and unable to eat regular food; some became seriously ill and died. A New Orleans drug company offered planters a medicine called "Diggers' Specific or Dirt-Eaters' Cure" at five dollars a bottle as a "certain and infallible cure" for this obsession.[20]

The prevention and treatment of illnesses in livestock was important to the planters, who might own hundreds of cattle, sheep, swine, and fowl in addition to work, carriage, and saddle horses. Professionally trained veterinarians were rare in the United States before the Civil War. Men who shod and treated horses might call themselves "farriers," but in reality this kind of work was most often done on Texas plantations by a resident blacksmith.[21] Aside from these blacksmiths, in general the owner, his overseer, or the slaves designated as stablemen were in charge of the health care of the animals.

A few books such as *The Anatomy of the Horse* and the monumental *Hippopathology* by the eminent English veterinarian William Percivall were available. Also widely reprinted in America were the books of English vet-

20. Affleck, *Southern Rural Almanac*, 1860, advertisement, Rosenberg Library.
21. The versatile blacksmiths often pulled teeth for humans.

erinarian William Youatt. Together Percivall and Youatt founded and published the *Veterinarian*, a periodical that furnished practical information about animal care and published reports on the latest findings in the veterinary science.[22]

In the nineteenth century medical treatments for animals were as harsh as those for humans and often had the same distressing outcome. Animals were frequently bled, blistered, and purged to death. One of the first American advocates of reforming the practice of veterinary medicine was George Dadd, a physician who turned to animal practice. He preached against the common practices of "pouring down the throats of the poor brutes salts by the pound, castor oil by the quart; aloes, lard and a host of kindred trash . . . converting the stomach into a sort of apothecary's shop." He was violently opposed to bleeding and pointed out the "absurdity of bleeding an animal to death, with a view to saving its life." He begged, "*No more bloodletting!*" and advised animal doctors to "use your poisons on yourselves."[23] Dadd's books, *Modern Horse Doctor* and *American Cattle Doctor*, were written not for doctors but for farmers, whom he called "the lords of creation."

Although Texas planters could have owned and read some of the literature available to them on veterinary practices, undoubtedly most of their animal medical lore was handed down or learned by observation or through trial and error. Many of the home remedies for animals were the same as those for humans. Spiderwebs and soot were applied to stop bleeding. Horse liniments of turpentine, vinegar, and raw eggs were applied to animals as well as to humans suffering from rheumatism. Mixtures of kerosene, castor oil, whiskey, calomel, tobacco, and opium were forced down the throats of ailing beasts. Poultices for snakebites, saddle sores, and other wounds were made from whatever was available: chewed tobacco, mud, clay, lard, buffalo or cow manure, pounded prickly-pear leaves, or mashed leaves of the creosote bush. A common treatment for sweeny (atrophy of the shoulder muscles) in horses was to cut a slit in the skin and insert a coin.[24] William Bollaert found the "Jimpsum [jimson] weed" growing luxuriously in Texas and noted it was used in salves or in poultices to cure sores on horses' backs.[25] Cattle and mules might be stabbed with sharp knives or ice picks to relieve bloating, and sheep were dipped in strong tobacco decoctions to relieve ticks and scabies.

Years before veterinarians were established—and accepted—as professionals in Texas, the plantation system had vanished in the aftermath of the Civil War.

22. J. F. Smithcors, *Evolution of the Veterinary Art*, pp. 359–68.
23. Ibid., pp. 375–77.
24. J. Frank Dobie, ed., *Man, Bird, and Beast*, pp. 30–49.
25. William Bollaert, *William Bollaert's Texas*, ed. William Eugene Hollon and Ruth Lapham Butler, p. 310.

Medicine was (and is) an inexact science, with every individual reacting to treatment in a different way. For the slaves on plantations, the line between medicine and magic was a thin one, and where preventive measures were concerned, it disappeared completely. Children wore asafetida,[26] sometimes mixed with spices, in small bags around their necks to ward off contagious diseases such as whooping cough, mumps, measles, and chicken pox. No doubt the evil-smelling bags did tend to keep others at a distance. Carrying a red onion in a pocket was thought to be good for keeping disease away. Slaves wore pennies on a string to prevent indigestion and rabbits' feet around their necks to escape chills and fever. Carried in a pocket or worn around the neck, the rabbit's foot was thought to bring good luck in general until it was lost, and then there was no escaping terrible consequences. To soothe arthritic pain, the sufferer wore copper bracelets or anklets around the affected joints. Some of the more unappealing remedies called for the use of cow manure, fresh or pulverized.

The most respected and feared blacks on plantations were the conjure men and women, who were the custodians of ancient rites handed down from voodoo practices of African ancestors. These "hoodoo" men and women mixed secret charms and uttered incantations. They were credited with the ability to cast spells, for either good or evil, and the wise slave tried to keep on the conjurer's good side. Usually, their identities and activities were kept secret from the white family.

Many slaves believed that conjurers could cause disease, accidents, blindness, minor annoyances such as boils, and major catastrophes such as bad luck and death. On the other hand, they believed that the conjurer could create charms to keep the master in a good humor, could make strong love potions, and knew magic ways to preserve good health. A number of slaves wore charm bags made by conjurers to protect them from their enemies. These little red-flannel bags typically contained small animal bones, powdered snakeskin, horse hairs, ashes, blood, and dirt from a graveyard.

If a person believed in conjurers' spells, he or she had to believe also that there was magic to break the spells. One way was to eat May butter. This butter, made on the first day of May and mixed with egg yolk and saltpeter, was powerful because presumably the cow had bitten off the top and bottom of every herb that grew in spring as they came out of the ground. Therefore the butter contained the best strength of every plant, and no conjurer could make stronger medicine than that.

One common practice to charm the master into kindness was to hang a horseshoe over a doorway where he would pass in and out without noticing

26. Asafetida is a brownish-yellow bitter resinous material obtained from the roots of several plants. It has a strong, offensive odor.

it. Another was to secretly hammer a green stick into the ground under the master's front gallery, and every night to slip in and drive it down another notch. The master's good humor was supposed to last as long as the stick stayed put.

A darker kind of voodoo was to make a straw or clay man of the cruel master or overseer, with some of his fingernail or toenail clippings or hair combings mixed in. The conjurer stuck pins or thorns into the figure as he uttered incantations. If the magic worked, the final jab into the heart should prove fatal to the human model. The consequences would of course have been dire if the magician were caught. But apparently the slaves considered their knowledge of the conjurer's activities a sacred trust.

Some of the slaves' superstitions, especially those that pertained to work methods, were shared by or learned from their white owners. The phases of the moon had great influence on many aspects of plantation life if the owner believed the old saws or even if he didn't fully believe in them but "liked to have them on his side." Root crops like potatoes were planted in the dark of the new moon, but crops that grew on top of the ground like corn, peas, and beans were planted in the light of the full moon. Soap was made and hogs killed on the full moon, and some planters were careful to "graft and prune on the wane of the moon." Planters who were not superstitious made their workers do their tasks by whatever timetable they preferred. But whether the masters knew it or not, conjures were set in the light of the moon to cause things to grow and in the dark of the moon to cause things to waste.

Before almanacs, the weather signs were as good a way as any of predicting the essentially unpredictable Texas weather. So the farmers looked at the tilted-up new moon as an indication it would hold water and there would be a dry spell. But if the moon was tilted downward so the water could pour out, they looked for rain. They counted the stars within a halo around the moon to see how many days before it would rain. They forecast winter by the activities of animals, insects, and plants as well as by heavenly signs. There would be a bad winter if the squirrels began gathering nuts early, or if the fur on the rabbit's foot or on the "woolly worm" was unusually thick, or if the bark on the trees grew thicker, or if the sweet potatoes had tougher skins.

Ghost stories fascinated all the plantation children and were passed down from the older to the younger ones. Slaves were more apt to retain their beliefs in ghosts and spirits since many of their parents did, while the parents of the white children in general did not.

One colorful early planter was featured in ghost stories that are still told in Brazoria County. James Briton (Brit) Bailey was settled on Bailey's Prairie when Stephen F. Austin arrived. After some negotiating, Bailey's squatter's claim was made legal by his admission as one of Austin's Old Three Hundred. He was a successful planter who became known for his love of drinking and fighting and for his eccentric behavior. He fought in the Battle of Velasco in 1832 and died the next year. At his request he was buried standing up, facing west. It is said he was buried with his rifle in one hand, his lantern in the other, and his whiskey jug at his feet. Soon after his death there were reports of strange lights being seen on Bailey's Prairie, and when Ann Raney Thomas (Coleman) and her husband moved into the Bailey house in 1836, they both had experiences in which they were sure they were visited by Bailey's ghost. To this day there are periodic reports of people who have seen and tried to follow "Bailey's light," a ball of fire that seems to rise out of the ground and wander over the country.[27]

RELIGION

Before the Texas Revolution, there was little formal Protestant worship in Texas. Until 1834, under Mexican law Catholicism was the official religion, but the law was very relaxed. The Mexican government did not try to make true converts of the colonists, so most Protestants quietly continued to practice their own religion—if they practiced any at all. In 1829, Stephen F. Austin wrote to Josiah H. Bell, "I am of the opinion that no evil will arise from [Protestant] family or neighborhood worship, provided it is not done in a way to make noise about public preaching. . . ."[28]

When Texas became a republic, there was an influx of Protestant preachers into the country. The Methodists, who sent hardworking circuit riders and organized camp meetings, were the most successful. By the time Texas became a state, they claimed more than half of all church members. In numerical strength the Baptists were next, followed by the Presbyterian and Episcopal denominations.[29]

Many plantation owners who were descendants of old southern families were Episcopalians, but there were also many Methodists and Baptists among them. The amount of religious freedom they gave their slaves depended on their dispositions: some forced religious training on them, some encouraged it, and some discouraged or forbade any overt religious expression.

The Right Reverend Alexander Gregg, first Episcopal bishop of the diocese of Texas, had been brought up on a plantation in South Carolina. He often expressed his opinion that the church had a deep responsibility for the spiritual welfare of the blacks in Texas and said, "The Christian master is

27. Ann Raney Coleman, *Victorian Lady on the Texas Frontier: The Journal of Ann Raney Coleman*, ed. C. Richard King, pp. 74–81.

28. Stephen F. Austin to Josiah H. Bell, Austin (Moses and Stephen F.) Papers, Barker Texas History Center.

29. William Ransom Hogan, *The Texas Republic: A Social and Economic History*, pp. 194–95.

Bernado—first Texas home of
Jared Groce, built south of Hempstead in 1822.

Moving into Texas

Bernardo, built in 1822, was the first Texas home of Jared Groce, an early Texas patriot (preceding page). Groce built Liendo, shown on the dust jacket, in 1858. Bernardo no longer exists; this rendition is based on a drawing by E.M. "Buck" Schiwetz. The planters moved into Texas with all their slaves, family & livestock (above) in caravans that sometimes stretched a mile long. The slave quarters during the day (left) were populated with the few women not needed in the fields or elsewhere & old-timers & children who entertained one another.

Down in "the quarters"

Reading the Emancipation Proclamation

Christmas on the Plantation

Summer was a time for the planter & his friends to play. A favorite activity was fox hunting (preceding pages), where the fox wasn't always caught. Christmas (above) was a time for extended visiting. Planters & their guests celebrated for the last two weeks of the year. The slaves worked in shifts so all had some time off. The end of the Civil War marked the death of the plantations. Planters were required to free all slaves (left), though some slave holders, notably Civil War widows, postponed freedom until the crops were gathered. Today, several plantation houses remain in a restored state. Freeman Plantation (overleaf) is a good example of these bits of the past.

Freeman Plantation~ Jefferson

bound by every motive of duty, to provide for the spiritual interests of his slaves."[30]

The Perrys of Peach Point were among the Episcopal planters who shared the bishop's conviction. As often as possible they got a minister to come to the plantation on Sundays to preach in the building set aside for a church and school. Otherwise, they packed a picnic lunch and went into Brazoria to attend church and Sunday school. If muddy roads or bad weather made the trip impractical, Emily Perry led religious services herself. Like Mrs. Holcomb of Wyalucing in East Texas, Emily Perry held Sunday school classes for her slaves. Grace was said at every meal, and evening worship was attended by all members of the white family and the house slaves. In July of 1849, twenty-one slave children between the ages of a few months to thirteen years were christened at Peach Point by a visiting minister.

Rutherford B. Hayes noted while at Peach Point that the Episcopal bishop arrived with three attendant clergymen and preached in the "church schoolhouse" to "thirteen gentlemen, six ladies, and five children." The bishop traveled from place to place over the primitive roads in a "stout cart covered by canvas, drawn by a pair of large mules, driven by a negro who cooks, etc."[31]

Methodist circuit riders traveled in considerably less comfort. They had little besides a horse and saddlebags containing a change of clothes and a Bible, and they were dependent on their far-flung congregation for food and lodging. Their stays on plantations must have been pleasant compared with some of the rough fare and poor lodgings that often were their lot. The Methodists, along with the Baptists, encouraged black membership in white churches. One slave, "Uncle Mark," in Washington County, was such a remarkable preacher that he was sought after by all-white Methodist congregations, as well as by mixed and black congregations.[32]

The Baptists gave special attention to missions among the slaves and appointed some of their ministers to devote themselves especially to their religious training. Many slaves joined the Baptist church, and after they were freed, black membership in Baptist churches grew, until by 1945 there were 400,000 black Baptists in Texas.[33]

Because of the scarcity of preaching facilities and of ministers, the different religious denominations often showed a remarkable ability to cooperate in the early days of settlement. Ministers shared whatever meeting place could be secured and were welcomed by plantation families and their slaves who were eager for preaching but unable to obtain their own brand. This

30. DuBose Murphy, "Early Days of the Protestant Episcopal Church in Texas," Southwestern Historical Quarterly 34 (Apr., 1931): 291–316.
31. Jones, Peach Point Plantation, p. 53.
32. Hogan, The Texas Republic, p. 197.
33. Handbook of Texas I, 109.

The spiritual life of the plantation was in the hands of the planter & his family, & most of them held regular religious services for blacks & whites. Circuit riding preachers passed by from time to time & found ample hospitality & an eager congregation regardless of their denomination. Two or three times a year, at a small settlement church or school house or, as shown here, at a

brush arbor built on a central campground, Baptist, Methodist, & Presbyterian preachers would gather for a revival. Families would bring their slaves, tents & cooking gear from as far away as fifty miles for a gathering that would last four to ten days. There would be preaching at eight, eleven & three o'clock. The remaining time was spent socializing & picnicking.

Spurred on by the
passionate exhortations of
the preachers & the throbbing, plaintive
pull of the music, sinners flocked to the mourners'
bench (some individuals several times a day for days in
a row) to repent their sins & be converted.
  In the
  light of day,
  they lined the banks
  of a nearby pond to have their
   souls washed clean.

cooperation extended to camp meetings, which might include Methodist, Baptist, and Presbyterian clergy.

Camp meetings were the most popular religious activities on the Texas frontier and for many years after the frontier disappeared. They offered a chance for a vacation from work, an opportunity to visit with old friends and to make new ones, singing, and picnicking as well as worship with a strong emotional current. Plantation families traveled as much as fifty miles to reach a campsite, bringing along slaves, tents, and cooking equipment. Meetings usually lasted four days, starting on Thursday and ending on Sunday night with an all-out, frenzied session that panicked overwrought participants into "professing" religion. Some meetings extended for ten days until the next Sunday.

Traditionally a ram's horn summoned the worshipers to assemble at 8:00 A.M., 11:00 A.M., and 3:00 P.M. From a pulpit erected under a brush arbor, preachers exhorted their listeners, who sat in the clearing on log benches. Before and after the sermons, there was singing. Hymns were lined out (read two lines at a time) by the preacher, and someone with a strong voice would give the pitch and lead the congregation. The revival hymns had repetitive choruses, which helped the singers learn them quickly.

The dramatic conclusion to the day was the evening meeting held after supper. Under the huge, starry Texas sky, with torches, lamps, and bonfires creating flickering shadows, sinners were summoned with words, music, and gestures to come to the mourners' bench. Under the influence of the beautifully moving surroundings, the urgent pleading of the preachers, and the plaintive, throbbing pull of the music, many of the whites and blacks were drawn to the mourners' bench to repent their sins and be converted.

In East Texas, planter William T. Scott built the first church in the community of Scottsville near Marshall. Named the Rock Springs Church because of the clear, cold springs nearby, the church membership included some of the wealthiest planters in the county, such as William J. Blocker. Planter John Webster, owner of more than fifty slaves, was a member of the Baptist church of Marshall. Marshall's Episcopal church was supported by wealthy planter Beverly Holcombe, while several other large planters in the area belonged to the Cumberland Presbyterian church.[34]

The finest church in Brazoria County was said to be the brick church Morgan L. Smith built for his slaves at Waldeck plantation. Over the door of this church was the inscription "Ethiopian Baptist Church—erected 1856." A white minister from Columbia came out to preach on Sundays to the slaves, who were required to be neatly dressed for the services.[35]

On some plantations services were arranged so there was one on Sunday morning for the white residents and one in the afternoon for the blacks.

34. Campbell, *A Southern Community in Crisis*, p. 103.
35. Adriance (John) Papers, Barker Texas History Center; Abigail Curlee, "A Study of Texas Slave Plantations, 1822–1865," Ph.D. diss., University of Texas, 1932, pp. 284–85.

On other plantations the slaves sat in the balcony or at the back of the church at the same service as the whites.

Some especially eloquent slaves were designated as preachers. Both white and black preachers were frequently reminded by plantation owners to leave certain topics such as "all men are created equal" alone and to bear down on the themes of honesty, patience, duty, humility, and obedience. One of the black exhorters threatened his slave audience with going to hell for stealing their master's chickens and watermelons. "Do you think the god of Shadrack, Maysack, and A-bad-Negro will save you?" he demanded.[36]

Baptizings were important events for both groups on the plantations. When a minister was available, all the candidates lined up on the banks of the nearest creek or water hole. The whites were baptized first with servants assisting their masters and mistresses into the water and other participants shouting and singing on the banks. Then the black candidates were immersed while everyone sang such hymns as "There Is a Fountain Filled with Blood." There might be more than a hundred people baptized on one day if several plantations joined in the ritual.[37]

Religious activities for slaves were carefully restricted on many plantations by planters who had uneasy feelings that religious freedom might lead to other kinds of freedom. Spontaneous praying, hymn singing, and unauthorized prayer meetings were considered dangerous and often forbidden. As one slave remembered, "We warnt allowed to pray cause the Lord might hear us and free us."[38]

With the passing of each generation of slaves in America, African tribal religious practices became more submerged in Christian practices and beliefs until only remnants of African tradition remained. Still, their ancestral traditions of poetry, rhythm, and harmony survived and mingled with the Anglo-Saxon teachings absorbed in their masters' churches. The black preachers' sermons often ended with chants in which the audience participated with voices, hands, and feet, as their responses became shouting, clapping, and stamping. On the whole, the services in the white churches were too restrictive to satisfy the slaves' desire to express themselves through religion. In the blacks' music, a drumlike syncopation of clapping and stamping replaced the white singers' common meter.[39]

Ring shouts, jump-up jigs, and improvised outbursts of song in their own services allowed the slaves to release pent-up feelings of repression, anger, sorrow and hope. Since they felt they had to pray aloud for God to hear them, they often resorted to "pot praying" for their unauthorized prayers. This was simply praying into one of the large kettles or washpots to keep the

---

36. George P. Rawick, ed., *The American Slave: A Composite Autobiography*, series 2, *Texas Narratives*, Wayman Williams, p. 4152.

37. Rawick, ed., *Texas Narratives*, pp. 2466, 4264.

38. Ibid., Sarah Benjamin, p. 256.

39. William A. Owens, *Tell Me a Story, Sing Me a Song: A Texas Chronicle*, pp. 290–91.

sound from being overheard by human listeners. Or they might post a guard and gather in one cabin to whisper prayers and softly hum hymns, ending with a gentle lament, "Someday, someday, someday."

When there was to be a secret prayer meeting at night, the field workers sang or hummed "Steal Away and Pray" to notify the others. That night in a creek bottom or thicket, they would gather to shout and sing and pray. For ring shouts they would form a circle, singing and dancing at first in a kind of slow shuffle. As they warmed up, the dance got faster and faster, accompanied by shouting and clapping. The ring tightened as exhausted individuals dropped out, and the feeling intensified until some of the participants reached a euphoric state. Sometimes the clandestine prayer meetings lasted until daybreak, when the slaves had to be back at their tasks.

All of the music the slaves knew they learned by ear. Many of the spirituals they sang were combinations of spirituals sung by the slaves in the eighteenth century and Anglo-American spirituals. A popular white spiritual, "Amazing Grace," became one of the favorites of slaves on Texas plantations, but probably none of them knew that it was composed by a reformed slave trader as an expression of his remorse and repentance.[40]

In the early pioneer days, Texans who wanted to marry solved the problem of not having a minister available by signing a marriage contract by which they agreed to have their union made official when a clergyman visited their area. After the country became more settled, weddings were often performed in connection with Christmas celebrations on plantations. Later, when ministers were more readily available, weddings were performed at any time of year.

Slaves were married in a variety of ways, depending on their owners' inclinations. No civil service was required or possible for them. Some masters who were religious insisted that their slaves be married by a minister. Some performed a kind of wedding ceremony themselves. Some asked the couple a few questions about their feelings for each other and their willingness to be mated. And some ordered unwilling couples to consider themselves married and to begin living together so they could produce children.

For favorite house servants a white family would often put on an elaborate ceremony and go to a great deal of trouble to provide clothes, food, and flowers, and sometimes a real minister or perhaps a member of the family to conduct the service. Jumping the broomstick, which probably began as a humorous part of the slave ceremony, came to be equated with marriage by some masters and slaves in Texas.[41] It simply amounted to stepping or hopping over a broom. When two slaves on different plantations married, the children of the marriage belonged to the owner of the mother.

40. The composer of "Amazing Grace" was John Newton, who became an Anglican priest in England.
41. John W. Blassingame, *The Slave Community: Plantation Life in the Antebellum South*, pp. 166–67.

When there was a death among the white family on a plantation, neighbors came from miles around, bringing food and staying to help the family make preparations for the funeral. If possible, a minister was summoned to hold the service. If none was available, someone else, using the prayer book or Bible, spoke appropriate words. Slaves participated in the preparations—digging the grave, making the coffin, and carrying it to the burial spot. If the deceased had been a kind master or mistress, he or she was sincerely mourned by the slaves, who knew their fates might now be uncertain.

When a slave died, he might be unceremoniously buried in the slave cemetery without an interruption of the daily work of the plantation. More commonly, the other slaves would be given time off, and the white family participated in the funeral, especially if it was a house servant who had died.

In the late 1840s the Sons of Temperance, a national organization, reached down into Texas and in a short time had three thousand members in the state. One of its most illustrious members was the reformed sinner Sam Houston, who had been a heavy drinker but then set out to help to spread the gospel of abstinence. The churches backed the temperance movement wholeheartedly. On Christmas Day of 1849, a "Temperance Celebration" at the Rock Springs Church in Scottsville began with a parade. Mrs. William T. Scott provided a bounteous feast, and Misses Elizabeth and Pennina Scott presented a Bible and a banner to the leaders in honor of the occasion. The *Texas Republican* (Marshall) called the affair a "grand celebration."[42] No doubt the pressure of the church and the temperance movement did modify the drinking habits of some Texans. However, whiskey, brandy, cognac, and fine wines appeared consistently on the invoices of planters as long as the plantation system operated.

42. *Texas Republican* (Marshall, Tex.), Jan. 3, 1850.

CHAPTER SIX

Mind & Spirit

*"The more opulent farmers and planters extend their hospitality
with an unsparing hand. . . ."*
—William Bollaert

EDUCATION

Educating their children was a major problem for parents on Texas
plantations. Although Mexico passed laws during the colonial period decree-
ing that schools should be established in the colonies, they were only paper
laws. Stephen F. Austin planned for all towns in the Republic of Texas to establish common schools in which reading, writing, and ciphering were to be
taught, as well as "catechism of the Christian religion, a short and simple
explanation of the constitution and the general one of the Republic; the rights
and duties of man in society and that which can conduce to the better education of youth."[1] However, a free public-school system in Texas did not actually begin until Gov. Elisha M. Pease established the school fund in 1854 and
provided for local districts. Educating the young children often became the
responsibility of the planter's wife, but a few private schools were established
in the territory before the Texas Revolution. And a number of individual
teachers moved to Texas to become private tutors and governesses.

When early pioneer planter Jared E. Groce moved to Texas, he had his
sons finish their college training before they moved permanently to his plantation, and his daughter, Sarah, graduated from fashionable finishing schools
in Nashville, Tennessee, and New York City.

Leonard W. Groce kept a live-in tutor at Eagle Island to teach his
young children and those of his neighbor planters at the "little white schoolhouse" on the plantation grounds. Then, like other planters who could afford to, he sent his children to schools in the United States to complete their
educations.[2]

1. Mary Austin Holley, *Texas*, p. 143.
2. Sarah Wharton Groce Berlet, *Autobiography of a Spoon, 1826–1856*, p. 42; Groce
(Jared E. and Leonard W.) Family Papers, Waller County Public Library.

One gentleman, H. M. Shaw, advertised for students for a school he planned to open in the courthouse in Brazoria. For a ten-week session the tuition was:

Spelling, Reading, & Writing	$15.00
All higher English Branches	$20.00
Latin and Greek Languages	$25.00[3]

In 1835 a courageous woman pioneer teacher from New England, Frances Judith Somes Trask, advertised the opening of a boarding school for "young ladies and misses" at Coles Settlement (Independence). On July 5 she wrote to her father back in Maine: ". . . my school is small, but profitable as tuition is high, from $6.00 to $10.00 per quarter. I have but 7 boarders at $2.00 wk but my housekeeping expenses are trifling, *Corn bread* and *Bacon* being the chief items of our diet." She boasted that her establishment of two one-room buildings ranked "second to none" in Texas, as one had two "glazed" windows on a side. The larger building served as schoolroom, parlor, bedchamber, and hall combined. The other building was the kitchen. The dining room was usually the open space under an oak tree. Lest her father should think her quarters cramped, she assured him that they were much better than "some planters have with their twenty or thirty negroes."[4] About 1839 Miss Trask sold her school to Henry F. Gillette, who operated it as Independence Male and Female Academy. In 1845 the academy was donated to the newly chartered Baylor University.[5]

After Texas achieved independence, the number of schools increased, although many of them were ephemeral. For a short time Brazoria had an academy that offered both male and female students "intellectual arithmetic, surveying and mensuration of conic sections, superficies and solids" as well as bookkeeping, and promised "every attention will be paid to the morals, conduct and deportment of the scholars."[6] Such schools were obviously trying to attract the attention and patronage of wealthy planters. Another was the Velasco Institute, which flourished briefly. When it closed, its former principal opened a "Classical School" with boarding accommodations for instruction in "all the English Branches and the Elements of Greek and Latin."[7]

There were many plantations scattered in the Rutersville area, and in 1843 William Bollaert observed that it boasted "a University and a very respectable female Academy."[8] Affluent Texans had no excuse for not educating

3. *Texas Republican* (Brazoria, Tex.), Apr. 28, 1840.
4. Frances J. Trask to Israel Trask, July 5, 1835, quoted in William Ransom Hogan, *The Texas Republic: A Social and Economic History*, pp. 143–44.
5. *Handbook of Texas* I, 876, II, 773–74.
6. *Texas Republican* (Brazoria), Apr. 28, 1840.
7. Ibid., July 4, 1840.
8. William Bollaert, *William Bollaert's Texas*, ed. William Eugene Hollon and Ruth Lapham Butler, p. 184.

their daughters. Although the "female seminaries" were separate schools and offered a different curriculum, there were many that at least professed to teach profound courses. The regular curricula at most seminaries included traditional academic subjects, and, for extra fees, French and Italian, drawing and painting, music, and ornamental needlework could be studied. In Velasco the "Misses Warner's (late of New York)" opened the Velasco Female Academy for "Young *Ladies* and *boys* under 12." Their course offerings included the three R's plus "natural philosophy, Chronology, and geography (with globes)."[9]

McKenzie College, a Methodist institution, was organized in a log cabin three miles southwest of Clarksville. Before the Civil War it had an administration building and three dorms, two for boys and one for girls. It drew an enrollment of three hundred students from the entire state plus Louisiana and Arkansas, and boasted a library of between two thousand and three

9. *Texas Republican* (Brazoria), Jan. 2, 1838.

thousand books. Tuition, room, board, and laundry cost $180 for ten months, with private piano lessons $60 extra per term.[10]

For the fall term in 1849 at Baylor University, Mary Coles, wife of plantation owner John P. Coles, paid a total of twenty-nine dollars in tuition for her two daughters and one son.[11]

Private schools with boarding accommodations were more numerous after annexation, and Thomas Blackshear, who had nine children, sent them to various schools convenient to his plantation near Navasota. Some went to Washington, some to Chappell Hill, some to a "Miss Seely's" school, and others to a "Mr. Markey's" school.[12]

Many planters were Masons and as such were involved in organizing schools throughout Texas. Brenham Masonic Academy and Washington Masonic School in Central Texas and the Masonic Institute of San Augustine and the Masonic Female Institute in Marshall are examples of this kind of educational institution. Asa Hoxey, a Masonic planter of Washington County, contributed to the support of Baylor University and other educational institutions.

The annual examinations at schools were important occasions. Plantation families that had children in the schools would come from miles to attend them. Dr. John Lockhart has given us a description of how these events were conducted:

> A platform was built the full width of the church. . . . Homes were thrown open to entertain the families of students. Three pianos would be on the stage at one time. Oral examinations would be held during the day, and concerts at night. One day would be given to Chappell Hill Female College, the next to Soule University. On the last day there would be a soiree. Long tables would be set for a banquet. Cakes of seven and eight layers would appear. Colonel Browning [a planter] furnished roasted peacock one year.[13]

However, these educational "shows" had their critics. E. H. Cushing, a well-known Houston editor, called public oral examinations "humbuggery" and branded calling secondary schools "universities" as ridiculous.[14] Apparently many planters agreed with Cushing, for although schools calling themselves universities or colleges proliferated in Texas during the "golden" decade of plantations, many planters sent their children back to established schools in other states. The Perry children went to Kenyon College in Ohio and Trinity College in Connecticut among other schools. Mordello and William Munson were sent from Oakland plantation to colleges in Illinois

10. *Handbook of Texas* II, 115.

11. Probate Minutes, Docket 190, County Courthouse, Washington County, 1849.

12. Journal, Blackshear (Thomas Edward) Family Papers, Barker Texas History Center.

13. Jonnie Lockhart Wallis and Laurance L. Hill, eds., *Sixty Years on the Brazos: The Life and Letters of Dr. John Washington Lockhart, 1824–1900*, pp. 20–21.

14. Earl Wesley Fornell, *The Galveston Era: The Texas Crescent on the Eve of Secession*, pp. 72–74.

and Alabama. And Jared Groce's grandson, John Austin Wharton, attended the University of South Carolina. Maj. Abner Jackson, owner of Lake Jackson plantation, sent two sons to schools in Vermont, one to Kentucky, one to Georgia, and his only daughter to Tennessee. His theory was that by going to different schools they would get "different ideas and views of life."[15]

A number of planters preferred to entrust their younger children's education to governesses and tutors rather than to the private schools.

Thomas J. Pilgrim, a noted Baptist preacher and teacher, taught privately at different plantations in Austin's colony. In 1833 he signed an agreement with two planters, Henry Munson and James Perry, to teach "as many scholars as shall be sent to him" if they would construct a "comfortable schoolhouse, dig a well, and furnish him with board and washing and guarantee him five hundred dollars in tuition a year."[16]

In East Texas, John Pelham Border hired private tutors to instruct his children on his plantation near San Augustine in academic subjects and in music. His daughter Emma studied voice, guitar, piano, and harp, and all of his sons and daughters were trained in piano and voice. On his business trips Colonel Border bought music for his wife and children. In Harrison County, William T. Scott built a schoolhouse and hired a governess for his large brood of children.[17]

In 1850 Laura J. Clarke found a teaching position for herself in Brazoria County on the Cedar Lake plantation of Charles K. Reese. She wrote to her father in New England that her circumstances were "very pleasant." Her schoolhouse, built expressly for her, was finished inside with red cedar. She had ten pupils—the sons, daughters, nieces, and nephews of the Reeses. She received her board plus $250 and her traveling expenses home if she wished to leave after a year. "There is danger of my getting too indolent to live in 'Yankee Land,'" she warned: "They allow me to do anything I please without any questioning or fault-finding, and out of school my time is my own. I do not even have to take care of my own room. The black servants do everything. I can ride, walk, read, sew or do nothing."[18]

The children under Miss Clarke's care must have enjoyed the situation too. Other young children, plucked from the warm cocoon of life on a Texas plantation, sometimes felt a wretched homesickness. William Garrett, an East Texas planter, must have been moved by a letter he received from his daughter Mary, who had been sent to a school in New Jersey:

15. Ironically, Major Jackson's children had such "different" ideas that one of the brothers publicly horsewhipped another, who later killed his sibling attacker. Abner J. Strobel, "Lake Jackson Plantation," *The Old Plantations and Their Owners of Brazoria County, Texas*, n.p.

16. Marie Beth Jones, *Peach Point Plantation: The First 150 Years*, p. 70.

17. Border (John Pelham) Papers, privately held, Elisabeth Bates Nisbet, Houston, Tex.; William T. Scott Papers, Harrison County Museum.

18. Letter to "my dear father," Jan. 28, 1851, Carpenter (Laura Clarke) Papers, Barker Texas History Center.

. . . I beg you to let me come home. . . . I tell you it is so cold we do not know what to do. . . . The ice is frozen in the mornings thick and the water that we have to wash in so cold that it makes our fingers ache so that we can scarcely make our bed up. . . . This is a very lonesum place. . . . I cannot keep from crying to think of the many happy days I have spent at *home*. And then to think that I will have to stay here. I could not think such a thing. I know I would die. Just to think of *home* that sweet place home pa you do not know how much we suffer here.[19]

Although educating slaves was illegal in some states, small white children on some Texas plantations "held school" for the small black children and taught them the ABCs. As the children grew up, sometimes the lessons went on through the blue-back spellers and *McGuffey's Reader*. On plantations where the masters discouraged the slaves from becoming literate and even punished them for trying, lessons were held in secret places.

On the other hand, there were masters like brothers-in-law Dr. Hugh Barton, Jr., and George Warren of Bastrop County, who on Sundays took it upon themselves to teach their slaves to read and write.[20] Others, like Ashbel Smith, encouraged their slaves to learn all they could; he would often correspond with them while on trips.

For their owners' convenience, some of the black drivers or foremen were taught to do simple arithmetic so they could keep records. And mistresses sometimes tried to teach house workers basic reading and writing skills. Their efforts, however, were not always welcome. Learning was uphill work, and many slaves realized that there was no advantage in it for them. Fannie Robinson, who lived on a plantation near Brenham, said, "My Missus's young daughter, she try to teach cullud chillun to read 'n' write. I wouldn' let 'em teach me."[21]

On the other hand, Jeptha (Doc) Choice, one of the many slaves who kept his master's surname after freedom, told his interviewer: "Yes, suh, my whitefolks was pretty good to me and sort a picked me out. You see if a nigger was smart and showed promise, he was taught how to read and write, and I went to school with the white children on the plantation."[22] And Mat Fowler, whose daughter finished college and became a teacher, had eagerly accepted the tutoring of the white children on his master's plantation. "The Reddings [his owners] didn't care how much their darkies knowed," he said.[23] However, Millie Ann Smith reported that her master "didn't 'low no nigger on the place that could read and write if he knowed it."[24] And Jack Maddox

19. Mary Garrett to William Garrett, Dec. 31, 1854, Cartwright (Matthew) Papers, Barker Texas History Center.

20. George P. Rawick, ed., *The American Slave: A Composite Autobiography*, series 2, *Texas Narratives*, p. 3192.

21. Ibid., Fannie Robinson, p. 3345.

22. Ibid., Jeptha ("Doc") Choice, p. 707.

23. Ibid., Mat Fowler, p. 1398.

24. Ibid., Millie Ann Smith, p. 3653.

remembered that if a slave was caught with a book, "he got whipped like he was a thief."[25]

RECREATION

Like log rollings and corn shuckings, hunting and fishing were recreation with a useful purpose. At least in the early years of settlement there was a real need for the fat, meat, and hides obtained from bear, deer, or buffalo. And the presence of wild hogs, cattle, and mustangs was of vital importance to the early Anglo-American arrivals in Texas.

Texas pioneers used dogs and rifles to hunt the black bear, which was often found in dense canebrakes. Averaging six hundred to seven hundred pounds, these bears provided a great deal of valuable oil. Their skins were useful, too, and their hams were considered good food by hungry pioneers.

Deer were hunted in various ways. By day the hunter stalked the deer or made a salt lick near their drinking places to entice them within range of his rifle. By night he killed them by fire hunting. Deerskin was valuable both for making durable garments and as a product for export. Their flesh was also a welcome food.

Texans hunted two types of wild hogs. Javelina, peccary, or Mexican hog were all names given to the small hogs that roamed the woods and hid in the hollows of trees. At times they roamed in small bands. Ann Raney Thomas (Coleman) described being chased by a pack of seven. She at first thought they were tame hogs and stood looking at them, observing how small and short their legs were, when ". . . one or two bristled up at me, gnashed their tusks, which were very long & large, and came after me. I took to my heels and ran as fast as I could." The hogs pursued her, but she managed to outrun them.[26]

The second type of wild hogs, the razorbacks, were thin-bodied, long-legged descendants of better breeds originally introduced into the country by the Spanish. Noah Smithwick observed that "old man Varner had a lot of wild hogs running in the Brazos bottom lands on his place, and when he wanted pork, he simply went out and shot it."[27]

Buffalo, so easily killed and so wantonly hunted, were gradually eliminated as a source of meat and hides and for sport. The same was true for the panthers, whose screams had often caused gooseflesh on camping pioneer Texans.

Both masters and slaves trapped, hunted with dogs, and shot small

25. Ibid., Jack Maddox, p. 2526.
26. Ann Raney Coleman, *Victorian Lady on the Texas Frontier: The Journal of Ann Raney Coleman*, ed. C. Richard King, pp. 64–65.
27. Noah Smithwick, *The Evolution of a State or Recollections of Old Texas Days*, p. 51.

game such as wild turkeys, ducks, opossums, raccoons, rabbits, beavers, squirrels, and gray foxes.

The Anglo-Americans found large herds of wild cattle and wild horses called mustangs, descendants of Spanish stock, roaming the prairies. Those animals were hunted for food, hides, and to provide transportation. Texans learned from the Mexicans the art of lassoing the mustangs. Another means of capturing them was to surround them and drive them into pens.

The early pioneers into Texas brought with them flintlock hunting guns primed by means of loose gunpowder. When the trigger was pulled, a spring-powered hammer holding a piece of flint was released to scrape the flint across a piece of steel, creating a shower of sparks on the priming charge. This flash set off the powder charge that fired the bullet. Percussion lock guns, which were more reliable because the priming charge was contained in a metal case that was exploded by the hammer, replaced flintlocks during the early part of the nineteenth century, and just before the Civil War the first successful breech-loading guns became available.

Every planter owned several guns. Among the items listed in Julien Devereux's estate were: "1 double barrel gun, 2 rifle guns, 2 pistols, 1 repeter & 1 durenger [derringer]."[28] A New Orleans store advertised in the *Texas Almanac* for 1857, offering Texans "Colt's pistols, American rifles, pistols and fire-arms of every variety." When traveling, both men and women went armed with Bowie knives and pistols. Mary Austin Holley noted that the women's visiting was done on horseback. "They will go 50 miles to a ball in their silk dresses. Women ride mustangs & hunt with their husbands & they also go to the seashore for fish & oysters."[29]

After the necessity for hunting passed, plantation hosts organized hunts for the amusement of themselves and their guests. Every plantation had its pack of hunting hounds. At Eagle Island plantation John Wharton liked to organize hunts, supplying his guests with his best horses, hounds, and servants, on an almost daily basis. At Mimosa Hall in East Texas, each Sunday morning slaves served guests a drink called a "Mimosa Scald" just before they set out on horseback. Like the English "hunt cup," the Mimosa Scald became a ritual.[30]

Slaves who were skillful and useful in the hunts were allowed to go along. When work permitted, many masters allowed their slaves to fish or hunt for opossums, rabbits, or squirrels. The slaves enjoyed the activity and the meat, which gave them a welcome change from corn bread and bacon.

Nineteenth-century Texans had much the same attitude toward their horses that twentieth-century Texans have toward their cars. For some, horses

28. Dorman H. Winfrey, *Julien Sidney Devereux and His Monte Verdi Plantation*, p. 126.
29. Holley, *Texas*, pp. 138–45.
30. Mimosa Scald: half bourbon, half pineapple juice, one egg white beaten together. Douglas Blocker, interview with Frank Tolbert, Marshall, Tex., quoted in *Dallas Morning News*, Mar. 31, 1974.

were merely a means of transportation, but for others they were status symbols and objects of devotion. Horse trading was an art in which the caveat "Let the buyer beware" was as important as it is today in buying a used car.

One of the virtues cultivated by southern aristocrats was the ability to judge fine horseflesh. After empresario Sterling C. Robertson had served as senator in the First and Second Congresses of the Republic (1836–38), he retired to breed thoroughbred race horses at his home three miles northeast of Nashville on the Brazos River in Robertson County. He named his horses after characters in Sir Walter Scott's novels and had an especially fine stallion named Black Douglas, which was the foundation for Arabian horse breeding in Texas.[31]

Every white child and most of the black children on Texas plantations learned to ride well. Ladies did not ride astride but on sidesaddles, right leg resting in a cradle-like pommel. These saddles had a single stirrup and a lower (leaping) pommel, against which the left leg could push upward for a better grip. A long riding skirt gracefully and completely covered the rider's "limbs."

Manufacturers in the eastern United States made fortunes turning out bridles and bits, saddles and saddle blankets, harnesses and whips, cowhide-covered traveling trunks, and horse clothing to meet the demands of the carriage trade to which the planters belonged.

Horse racing, a popular pastime in early nineteenth-century America, became a passion among Texans. William Bollaert found a good racecourse with a stand and stables at Galveston and one at Houston.[32] Most plantations had racetracks laid out, some of them quite elaborate, and many planters took pride in owning fine thoroughbred horses and in racing them. At Ellersly plantation, J. Greenville McNeel had a stallion said to be valued at six thousand dollars.[33] Betting was heavy at the private courses as well as at the public ones.[34] Josiah Bell, prominent Brazoria County planter, was the proprietor of the Columbia Jockey Club, which was in operation before the Texas Revolution. The *Telegraph & Texas Register* (Houston) carried a notice on November 9, 1836, that the turf would be open for any horse, mare, or gelding to run on November 21, 22, and 23 for the following fees:

1st Day, for 2 miles and repeat	$150
2nd Day, for 1 mile and repeat	200
3rd Day, for 1 mile and repeat	150
4th Day, single dash of 1 mile	100

Planters in East Texas could attend races at San Augustine, Nacogdoches, and Douglass. "Frolicking" was billed as a part of the races. Balls

31. Malcolm D. McLean, comp. and ed., *Papers Concerning Robertson's Colony in Texas* XI, 89–90.
32. Bollaert, *William Bollaert's Texas*, p. 280.
33. Strobel, "Ellersly Plantation," *Old Plantations and Their Owners*, n.p.
34. *Texas Republican* (Brazoria, Tex.), Oct. 25, 1834, May 9, 1835, June 6, 1835.

were held nightly, and everyone wore his or her finest costume. Those who did not dance promenaded and dined on the lavish buffets.

William H. Wharton, founder of Eagle Island, was the vice-president of the racing club at Velasco, which managed the famous New Market Course. Comfortable hotels at Velasco and its sister town, Quintana, accommodated the wealthy planters who came for the spring and fall races. Many planters, like Col. John H. Herndon, owner of Calvit plantation in Brazoria County, had spacious frame residences at Velasco or Quintana. There, in addition to attending horse races and balls, they enjoyed visiting, bathing in the Gulf, and riding on the beach.

Newspapers, politicians, and private citizens frequently cursed the condition and the scarcity of roads in Texas. Mud, huge tree stumps, and dust made it difficult, if not impossible, to travel safely in carriages and buggies. Too, before the coming of the railroad, it was quite difficult to import carriages. And yet, in addition to their high-wheeled work carts, most plantations had one or more pleasure carriages. The most practical carriage for traveling through Texas mud had large wheels to raise the body high and had the same size wheels in front as in back. Staggering the wheels on either side so as not to have two wheels moving in the same rut also helped.

Different manufacturers called the same carriages by different names. For example, the phaeton was a generic body type with the frame under the seat built higher than the floor. Phaetons, surreys, democrats, and road wagons were popular with Texas planters.[35] The *Texas Almanac* carried ads from New York carriage sellers who catered to the plantation market. William L. McDonald of Beekman Street invited planters to visit his Southern Carriage Repository, where he kept on hand a stock of vehicles "adapted in every feature to the particular wants of the South, with which he is thoroughly acquainted." Closer to home, J. M. Brown's Carriage Repository in Galveston kept on hand "Rockaways, Barouches, top and no-top buggies, slide-seat, Extension top & Jump-seat, Concord & all other styles of carriages." In Houston, A. A. Tucker announced that they carried "all the latest styles" of carriages made "especially for the Texas market," and they "respectfully solicited orders from the country."[36]

Early Texans learned to temper their luxury with practicality. The Whartons drove from their plantation to the grand Washington's Birthday Ball held at the opening of a new hotel in Velasco in 1838 in a barouche-and-four, with two plow horses in the lead to get them through the mud.[37]

Many early Texas planters and their wives were well educated and well read. All of them were eager for newspapers and journals. Usually they

---

35. Clarence P. Hornung, *Wheels across America*, pp. 455–59; Robert Strange, interview with the author, Gay Hill, Tex., Mar. 27, 1985.
36. *Texas Almanac* for 1857–1861, advertisements; *Galveston News* (Galveston, Tex.), n.d.
37. Berlet, *Autobiography of a Spoon*, pp. 29–30.

subscribed to several and devoured those sent them by relatives back in the States. Some planters had extensive libraries. At Peach Point, Stephen F. Austin kept his books in a special cabinet in his office, and the Perrys kept theirs on long shelves in the parlor, where they were convenient for frequent use.

Robert Mills, who with his brother owned four plantations, also owned a large library of history books. At Eagle Island, William H. Wharton and his wife had a library of several hundred volumes. Ashbel Smith was probably the most avid reader and book lover among Texas planters. He had a choice library to which he continually added until he was forced to construct a separate building to house his books.[38]

Ira Ingram, from his plantation on the San Bernard River, wrote to a cousin back in Vermont that reading was one of his principal "enjoyments." He and his brother owned between three hundred and four hundred books and a valuable collection of maps and atlases. Explaining his leisure to read, he said: "By removal here, I have removed also, from a thousand artificial wants."[39]

One young plantation belle purchased *The History of Texas* by Yoakum in two large volumes for six dollars and thought it almost as good as Prescott's *Conquest of Mexico*. She also read novels such as Oliver Goldsmith's *The Vicar of Wakefield* and stories in the *Saturday Evening Post* and *Harper's*. She and her friends exchanged magazines after they had read them. They were fascinated by Edgar Allan Poe and traded information about his mysterious life from facts they gleaned from magazines and newspapers. They found "The Raven" and "Annabel Lee" particularly exquisite and liked to read his poetry aloud. In their letters they often quoted from the Bible, Shakespeare, and Dickens.[40]

Wives and daughters of planters also enjoyed the sociability of quilting bees and sewing circles in which they practiced such exotic arts as hair crocheting and tatting.

Before the railroads came to Texas, traveling professional stock companies and circuses generally confined their appearances to towns such as Houston, Galveston, and Jefferson, which were accessible by water. From about 1838, families living on plantations near these settlements had an opportunity to enjoy this kind of entertainment. Amateur dramatic performances were popular also. San Augustine had an acting company called the "Thespian Corps," in which planter John Pelham Border was a sponsor and an actor. This company performed several plays written by the many-talented Texan, John S. (Rip) Ford.[41]

In addition to festive Fourth of July and Christmas celebrations, early Texans went all out to mark the anniversaries of the Battle of San Jacinto on

38. William Ransom Hogan, *The Texas Republic: A Social and Economic History*, p. 186; Elizabeth Silverthorne, *Ashbel Smith of Texas*, pp. 25, 195, 227.
39. Ingram (Ira) Papers, Manuscript Division, Library of Congress.
40. Neblett (Lizzie Scott) Papers, Barker Texas History Center.
41. Hogan, *Texas Republic*, pp. 119–28; Border (John Pelham) Papers, privately held, Elisabeth Bates Nisbet, Houston.

April 21 and the signing of the Declaration of Independence on March 2. These dates were celebrated with barbecues, banquets with numerous toasts, parades, orations, recognition of veterans of the Texas Revolution, singing by children, reading of patriotic documents, prayers, and all-night balls.

Dinners and dances were given at the slightest excuse—to honor a visitor, to celebrate a friend's return from a trip, to mark a birthday or a christening, and especially to promote political candidates. Planters, like other Texans, involved themselves enthusiastically in politics. Many of them held government offices and served in the legislatures of Texas. Consequently, they often gave and attended political barbecues.

In spite of the difficulty of travel before the Civil War, planters and their families made frequent trips to visit each other and also numerous trips to the States for various purposes. In 1837 Emily Perry made a lengthy visit to the States to "improve" her health, visit relations and friends, investigate schools for her children, and to shop. She accomplished all of her goals and returned to Peach Point in better health with purchases including fine linens, silver, china, crystal, and material for clothing. She also wrote her husband: "Thir is no place like [Texas] that I have seen; I shall return continted to spend the remainder of my Days in that delightful Climet."[42]

Ashbel Smith's constant traveling caused him trouble in running Evergreen plantation, as his series of overseers claimed difficulty in coping with his "spoiled" slaves.

Travel by steamboat could be wretched or it could be luxurious. Some had elegantly furnished cabins, well-stocked bars, and fancy dining rooms with bands for entertainment. Plantation families frequently used steamboats for part of their journeys to New Orleans for shopping and celebrating at Mardi Gras. Each year John Border left his plantation to take his music-loving wife, Kitty, to the opera in New Orleans. Attended by servants, they journeyed by horseback from San Augustine to Natchitoches, Louisiana. There they boarded a steamboat to travel down the Red River to the Mississippi and from there to New Orleans. The Border children were left in charge of slaves—Uncle Byrd, the overseer of the plantation, and his wife, Aunt Fanny. To entertain the children, Aunt Fanny would take them on her lap and tell them ghost stories. Screaming with fear, the children would clutch her around the neck and beg for more.[43]

Hospitality was a way of life for plantation families. While the planter made plans for constructing his house, he kept in mind the need to accommodate many guests at the same time. The strangers' rooms, which were a part of the house, but which did not open into it, protected their privacy when they gave shelter to chance travelers, as they were apt to do. Also, many plantations had separate guest quarters.

Visits were long, and house parties often lasted two or three weeks.

42. Jones, *Peach Point Plantation*, pp. 76–87.
43. Border (John Pelham) Papers, privately held, Elisabeth Bates Nisbet, Houston.

The women especially enjoyed making protracted visits to the plantations of kin and friends. When they could not visit in person, they visited by way of long, gossipy letters.

Like George Washington in the United States, Sam Houston was a great visitor in Texas. Plantations from Bernardo to Glen Eden could claim "Sam Houston slept here," and most could add "frequently." One of the plantations he visited often was Leonard Groce's Liendo, which was famous for its hospitality. In the huge kitchen, which was separate from the house, a whole ox could be roasted. A favorite item on the menu was whole roast pig.

Although it is hard to imagine the dignified David Burnet as "frolicking," he told Leonard Groce in a letter he wrote in March of 1852: "I have never forgotten the olden times in Texas or the three days of my pleasant frolic and amusement which I spent at your Father's hospitable mansion."

Rutherford B. Hayes was impressed by the fun and frolic he found in Texas in 1848. He enjoyed hunting and fishing, "music and flirting," and spending an afternoon with "three agreeable young ladies, singing and dancing." He reported there was "no end of entertainment": ". . . balls and parties rapidly followed one another, the guests riding ten, fifteen, and even twenty miles, arriving early in the afternoon, and remaining for nearly twenty-four hours, the great plantation house supplying room for all. An exceedingly agreeable, gay and polished company . . . merriment and dancing until 4:30 a.m.—like similar scenes elsewhere."[44]

At plantation balls ladies in hoopskirts and gentlemen in tailcoats performed dignified cotillions, minuets, reels, quadrilles, schottisches, and waltzes under lusters lit with hundreds of candles.[45] The musicians might be hired professionals playing accordions, pianos, violins, and flutes, or they might be some of the plantation's slaves who showed musical talent. Frequently, the callers for the square dances were slaves who had strong voices and good stage presence.

Slaves were often called on to amuse their owners. Various kinds of competitions such as races, wrestling matches, and jigging contests provided the white owner entertainment and sometimes a chance to make bets with neighbor planters. The slaves who could sing or play an instrument were a source of pleasure for the white families, who enjoyed their singing and dancing. In most cases the slaves were pleased by this recognition of their talents, but when they were forced to entertain against their wills, it caused deep resentment.

At all the whites' entertainments lavish refreshment tables were kept laden by slaves, who also served the guests champagne, juleps, brandy, and fine liqueurs. Stephen F. Austin tried hard to keep his colony free of those who had the "vice of intoxication," but when Martin Varner and his partner

44. Rutherford B. Hayes, "Texas Diary, 1848–49," Barker Texas History Center.
45. Not all parents allowed their daughters to dance the waltz; the "hugging" involved was considered somewhat risqué.

set up a rum distillery on the Varner plantation, Austin gave the "industry" his reluctant blessing.[46]

Other planters made their own beer, wine, and corn liquor and imported large quantities of whiskey, brandy, and fine wines. Certainly the planters drank a better quality of alcohol than less affluent Texans imbibed in the innumerable "groggeries" or "groceries" that sprang up in every town almost before it was laid out by the surveyors. And when they traveled, the planters were more apt to patronize hotel bars that served champagne, good wines, and cocktails in addition to whiskey.

It was a part of the southern gentleman's code to be able to drink without showing any outward effects. A real gentleman could "hold his liquor." So although many occasions called for liberal drinking, men of the planters' class would have felt it demeaning to appear drunken in public. There were, of course, a few exceptions, such as Brit Bailey. But even he always repented his sprees the next morning.

Masquerade balls and kissing games were popular among the young people in a society where opportunities for physical contact between the sexes were limited. Another game popular at the fashionable "watering places," or seaside resorts, was the "sale" of young men and women, with the ladies bidding for the gentlemen and the gentlemen bidding for the ladies. The successful bidders could then make their "slaves" do their bidding—within limits, of course.

Musical skills were considered important for young ladies whether they had any natural talent or not. If their schools did not offer musical instruction, professional music teachers were employed to come to the plantation, or the student was taken to the teacher's house in town. Sheet music purchases appear frequently on planters' bills. One order by Thomas Blackshear of music for his daughter Sally included four polkas, two marches, a waltz, a cotillion, and a serenade, among other pieces.[47]

Taffy pulls and contests were especially popular with young people. Sorghum molasses was boiled down until it was thick, and it was then poured out onto greased platters. The contestants pulled and folded the sticky substance until it became light in color and could be twisted into a slender rope. They worked in pairs or individually, and part of the fun was to try to snatch the well-pulled rope of an unwary contestant.

The most exciting social events on plantations were weddings of the white family members. The bride-to-be usually had a dower or "hope" chest filled with handmade linens and clothing items of fine needlework, which she and her female relatives had made over the years. Cleaning and cooking began weeks ahead of time. Guests came on horseback and in carriages or wagons from miles away, sometimes camping along the way. Cooks used all

46. Hogan, *Texas Republic*, pp. 39–40.
47. "Purchases for 1860," journal, Blackshear (Thomas) Papers, Barker Texas History Center.

their creative skill to make the towering cakes into works of art, adorned with thick icing shaped into fruits, flowers, and leaves. House servants helped with the preparations, and some cried to see the white children they had helped raise leave the plantation. The other slaves crowded onto the gallery and into the doorway and peered through the windows to see the young master or mistress take the vows and to get some of the wedding goodies. After a lavish wedding supper, the wedding party danced the night away. Infares, or housewarmings, given by the newlyweds or by the husband to celebrate bringing the wife to his home, were popular continuations of the festivities.

Although for some slaves the only marriage ceremony was the master's permission to live together, for others the white family put on a big production. One former slave remembered being married on a bright moonlit night with all the white and black folk watching. The preacher and the groom stood under a big elm tree waiting, and she recalled: "I come in with two little pickninnies for the flower girls a holding my train. I has on one of my Mistiss dresses with a long train, hit is a white dress and I wear a red sash and a big bow in the back, then I has on red stockings and a pair of bran new shoes, and a big wide brim hat."[48]

An elderly white woman who had grown up on a plantation remembered that the slaves' weddings were events of "supreme importance" to the white children. They talked of nothing else for weeks and saved their pennies to buy presents for the couple. They searched the house for stray bits of ribbon, lace, and artificial flowers for the bride to bedeck herself with. And they watched the supper preparations with great anticipation. Pine torches in the trees lighted the supper area where a long table was set up and covered with snowy linen from the big house. The table was loaded with all the good produce of field, garden, and orchard: "ham from the smoke-house, fowls . . . cooked in every way, enormous chicken pies, pumpkin pies and different kinds of fruit pies and a baked pig with an apple in its mouth." The children's particular delight was the butter witches—sculptures made from rich, yellow butter in the form of tall fairy-tale witches with arms akimbo and wide-spreading robes. Ginger cakes added color and aroma. The nicest preserves and jellies and a bowl of honey from the plantation hives completed the feast.[49] As with the white weddings, slave weddings usually ended with an all-night dance.

Slaves broke the monotony of their daily lives by telling ghost stories, animal folktales, tall tales of narrow escapes from snakes and wild animals, and by practicing magic to make or break charms. But the highlight of the week on many plantations was the Saturday-night breakdown dance. These dances were held in some large building such as the community dining hall or outside by the light of the moon. Instruments might be skillet lids, tin

48. Rawick, ed., *Texas Narratives*, p. 2096.
49. Amzina Wade, "Recollections of a Child's Life on a Pioneer Plantation," *Chronicles of Smith County, Texas* (Winter, 1980).

pans and spoons, bones, banjos made from sheep hides, guitars made from gourds, quill flutes made from reeds, drums made by stretching rawhide over a barrel, or a hoe scraped with a case knife. One popular instrument among the slaves was the clevis, played by striking it with a "pin," or small metal rod. The clevis itself was a U-shaped piece of metal used to fasten the tongue of a plow or wagon to the swinging bar to which the traces of a harness were fastened. Anything that could be shaken, plucked, blown, or thumped was used to make music. If nothing else was available, finger snapping and knee slapping provided the rhythm.

One of the most popular dances was the juba, a complex dance that involved rhythmic clapping and body movements. Probably of West African origin, the movements and the patting technique were handed down from generation to generation. The rough flooring of their meeting places was not suitable for smooth gliding steps, but this only made the dances more lively. Square dances, for which the caller made up words as he went along, were free and wild, with much vigorous swinging of partners. Round dances, pigeon wings, buck-and-wings, free-style gallops, stomping, and jumping freed the slaves' spirits for a few hours.

Jigging contests were popular at these entertainments. The dancers, on small raised platforms, began to shuffle their feet slowly and easily. As the tempo of the music increased, so did their movements, until their feet were slapping the boards with a rat-tat-tat like a snare drum. The other slaves crowded around, yelling and clapping to encourage their favorites, until one of the contestants dropped from exhaustion. Expert jiggers competed with cups of water on their heads to see who could dance the fastest without spilling any. The excitement and suspense mounted over who would slosh the first drop. The tension was even greater if some of the white men on the plantation dropped by to place bets on the outcome of the contest.

It would be hard to overestimate the importance of music in the lives of the slaves on Texas plantations. They sang as they toiled to make the work easier. The ax or grubbing hoe was swung up on "Hi" and down on "Ho," and the swinger grunted "UG" as the tool hit home. The rhythm of his song was:

> Hi, Ho, UG, Hi, Ho, UG
> The sharp bit, the strong arm
> Hi, Ho, UG, Hi, Ho, UG[50]

A mammy sang a lullaby to soothe a restless baby or a churning song to charm the butter into coming. A cook sang to forget her aches and pains and to comfort herself as she stooped and sweated, stirred and sifted. Field work was done to the rhythm of spirituals or secular songs as the mood indicated. Early in the morning the song might be "High-heel Shoes and Calico Stockings," but late in the evening the workers might hum:

50. Rawick, ed., *Texas Narratives*, Giles Smith, p. 3605.

My knee-bones am aching
My body's racking with pain
I really believe I'se a chile of God
This ain't my home
Cause heaven's my aim.[51]

Warning songs such as "Look-a long black man, look-a long; there's trouble coming sure" and "Hold up, hold up, American Spirit! Hold up, hold up, Hooooooooooooo!" told the lagging laborer to pick up his hoe and his pace before the master or overseer arrived on the scene.

Slaves sang the same songs differently to express different emotions. For example, "Swing Low, Sweet Chariot" was sung and shouted fast as a song of joy and praise, but at funerals it was sung slowly and mournfully until it became a dirge that dwindled to a low-pitched drone.

The slaves composed many of their songs on the spot to express the mood and feelings of the moment. They were good at satire, and their songs made fun of themselves and of their white owners.

Music expressed the slaves' pain and their joy, their deep religious feelings, their frustrations, and their hopes. It also expressed their expectations:

Massa sleeps in de feathah bed
Nigger sleeps on de flooah.
When weuns all git to Heaven,
Dey'll be no slaves no mo'.[52]

51. Ibid., Anderson Edwards, p. 1262.
52. Ibid., Millie Williams, p. 4113.

CHAPTER SEVEN

The End

> *"Hallelujah broke out!"*
> —Felix Haywood, Texas Slave Narratives

THE FREEDOM WAR

The U.S. Census for 1860 listed fifty-one planters in Texas who owned one hundred or more slaves. Of these, one, D. G. Mills, owned more than three hundred slaves, and two, Abner Jackson and J. D. Waters, were listed as owning more than two hundred each. All but three of these large landowners depended on cotton as their main cash crop. Of the ten largest sugar growers, eight also grew cotton, leaving only two who were devoting full attention to sugar production in 1859.[1]

By 1861 there were about 200,000 slaves in Texas. Since colonization, plantations had come and gone, but there were probably at least two thousand agricultural establishments in Texas that could be called plantations, by virtue of having at least 20 slaves when the Civil War began. Just before 1861 and during the next three years, planters from other states "refugeed" in droves to Texas with their equipment and their slaves. They came in the vain hope that somehow the impending war and the threatened emancipation of the slaves would not reach them in Texas.

In the 1850s the African slave trade into Texas (which had never completely stopped) showed renewed vigor. Newly arrived planters and established planters, who constantly acquired more land, created an ever-growing market for cheap labor. Northern capital fitted out and operated most of the slave-trading vessels, and by one estimate, a slave fleet, consisting of "about 40 vessels of various sizes, ranging from one hundred to five hundred tons, capable of carrying from four to six hundred slaves each" left New York, Boston, and other seaports every year.[2]

By the late 1850s some Southern capitalists were beginning to get in

---

1. Ralph A. Wooster, "Notes on Texas' Largest Slaveholders, 1860," *Southwestern Historical Quarterly* 65 (July, 1961): 72–79.
2. Earl Wesley Fornell, *The Galveston Era*, pp. 247–48.

on the quick riches to be made in importing "black diamonds." The U.S. consul at San Juan, Puerto Rico, estimated that an outlay of $35,000 "often brings in $500,000."[3] The long Gulf Coast, with many secluded spots along its beaches and islands, was favorable for the smuggling of slaves. But a number of ships boldly put in at Galveston, where the ambivalent feelings of the law-enforcement agents caused them to overlook the unloading of the contraband cargo, which they felt was vital to the economic growth of Texas. This growth was dramatic. During the pre-war decade, slave productivity increased at a rapid rate, enabling planters to produce more goods per slave and thereby realize more profit.[4]

The few Union sympathizers among Texas planters either fled to the North, accepted the secession decision and helped the Confederacy, or maintained an uncomfortable neutrality. Whatever the various and complicated causes of the "War for Separation," for most Texas plantation owners it became a fight to preserve their traditions and their livelihood. Like their counterparts in other states, they entered into the Confederate cause with enthusiasm and high expectations of a quick victory.

Plantation neighbors joined together to hold lavish barbecues and dinners to give their departing soldiers a rousing send-off. Brand-new Confederate flags waved defiantly, and the air was filled with martial music and oratory. The women labored by daylight and by lamplight to make uniforms of the best materials available for their men.

Behind their brave fronts, the women were under great emotional stress. Lizzie Neblett, whose main concerns had been how to get enough reading material and what to plant in her garden, told her cousin: "My husband is upon the eve of leaving me and his babies for the war to set himself up as a target for the abominable yankees (how my blood boils with hatred at the base mention of those creatures) to shoot at."[5]

A trusted body servant usually accompanied the master as he rode away to do his duty. Former slave John McAdams told his interviewer that his master had taken him to the war with him "so'es I could tend his horse and keep his guns cleaned up good for him." They went through terrible periods together when they didn't have anything to eat but green corn for weeks at a time and were without water to drink for three or four days. "And then," he said, "we would find water in some of them mud holes it would be plum bloody, but we would drink that water just like it was the best water in the world."[6]

3. Consul C. DeRonceray to Lewis Cass, August 22, 1860, U.S. House Executive Documents, 36th Cong., 2nd sess., IV, no. 7.
4. Randolph B. Campbell and Richard G. Lowe, "Some Economic Aspects of Antebellum Texas Agriculture," *Southwestern Historical Quarterly* 82 (Apr., 1979): 351–78.
5. Lizzie Neblett to "Dear Cousin," Mar. 23, 1862, Neblett (Lizzie Scott) Papers, Barker Texas History Center.
6. George P. Rawick, ed., *The American Slave: A Composite Autobiography*, series 2, *Texas Narratives*, John McAdams, p. 2473.

John Crawford, who was only ten when the war started, remembered seeing his father and grandfather go off to war with the young masters of their plantation. John begged to accompany his young master, "Mr. Tipsy Bill," but was denied permission because of his age. His master, however, promised to bring him back a Yankee sword.[7]

A slave called "Ole Alec" used to dream about his experiences in the war. Annie Little, another slave to whom he told his dream, said:

> He saw once more old Massa an hisself going to de war, Ole Massa on his white horse an in his new gray uniform what de wimmen made fur him and de band a playin' "Dixie." An all de foks in de country dar to see dem go to de war to whip de Yankees. Ole Alec could see hisself riding his little roan pony by old Massa's side. How happy he was 'n den he dreamed ob de days after de battle wen he looked for ole Massa until he found him an his hoss lyin side by side done gone to where de aint no more war. How he buried him an den went back to tell old Miss. . . .[8]

Just as they were leaders in other community affairs, planters took the lead in organizing and marching with their neighbors into battle. In East Texas, Col. John Border formed seven companies in the counties of San Augustine, Nacogdoches, Sabine, and Shelby. They were consolidated into a regiment that was eventually reorganized and called Border's Battalion.[9]

According to Confederate regulations, planters or overseers charged with the supervision of twenty or more slaves were exempt from the draft. Also, a man who could afford it could hire a substitute to go to war in his place. These exemptions caused less affluent Texans to grumble that it was "a rich man's war and a poor man's fight." However, many of the first volunteers were men who could have claimed exemption. One of these was fifty-six-year-old Ashbel Smith, who owned twenty-seven slaves. He chose to enter the Confederate army not as a physician but as an active soldier. At Galveston Bay he got up a company called the Bayland Guards which he drilled, trained, and then led at Shiloh and Vicksburg.[10]

Two sons of plantation owner Harry Foster of Fort Sullivan joined the Five Shooters, which later became a part of Hood's Texas Brigade. This group made its headquarters at the Foster plantation and later gained fame on eastern battlefields far from Texas.[11]

Benjamin Franklin Terry, a sugarcane planter in Fort Bend County, was married to Mary Bingham, daughter of Francis Bingham, one of Stephen F. Austin's Old Three Hundred. Terry participated in the First Battle of Manassas, then returned to Texas and organized the regiment of cavalry

7. Ibid., John Crawford, p. 980.
8. Ibid., Annie Little, p. 2392.
9. Border (John Pelham) Papers, privately held, Elisabeth Bates Nisbet, Houston.
10. Elizabeth Silverthorne, *Ashbel Smith of Texas*, pp. 134–59.
11. Foster (Harry A.) Family Documents, Log Cabin Village Museum, Fort Worth.

known as Terry's Texas Rangers, consisting of ten companies of one hundred men each. He was killed leading a charge near Woodsonville, Kentucky, on December 17, 1861.[12]

John Austin Wharton, son of William H. and Sarah Groce Wharton, entered the Confederate army as a captain in Terry's Texas Rangers. When Terry was killed, Wharton was elected colonel to take his place. After the Chickamauga campaign, John Wharton became a major general.[13]

Not every eligible Texas planter was eager to fight; in some cases, the slaves helped them hide from the conscripters. Jacob Branch remembered that one of his young masters, Shake Stevenson, had volunteered to go into the army and had been killed in Virginia. But "young Marster Tucker Stevenson" didn't believe the war was right, and refused to go, hiding in the woods to escape the army recruiters sent to bring him in. Finally Jacob and his "ol' Marster" took a load of supplies down to Galveston and exchanged it for Tucker Stevenson's exemption.[14]

Joe Barnes said his master "scouted [hid out in the woods] so he wouldn't hafter go to de war."[15] Tobe Zollicoffer reported that his master, Ed Zollicoffer, was not well enough to go to war, so Tobe hid him in a cave. Every day he took food and other comforts to his master and, as it was needed, cut fresh brush to cover the entrance to the cave.[16]

Andy Anderson, who lived on a plantation in Williamson County, recalled that his master had gone off to war leaving an overseer to help his son John run the place. But three months later, soldiers came to take John away. Andy and the other slaves crowded around the soldiers menacingly, determined they "warnt gwine to 'low dem to took him." They were only persuaded to desist when John told them the soldiers had a right to take him and ordered them to disperse before the soldiers hurt them.[17]

In addition to active military service, planters and their families made other contributions to the war effort. At Scottsville, near Marshall, the log house that had been the Scott family's first home was turned into a blacksmith shop to make weapons. The mistresses, in addition to supervising the operations of the plantation, worked at spinning wheels to make yards of much-needed cloth to outfit the fighting men with blankets, uniforms, tents, haversacks, and knapsacks. They gathered at sewing "bees" to make the work go faster. Some of the women raised funds; other raised poppies and extracted the juice for use in hospitals. Some of them packed gunpowder into paper cartridges.[18] Also near Marshall, Henry Ware had set up a small indus-

---

12. *Handbook of Texas* II, 889.
13. Ibid.
14. Rawick, ed., *Texas Narratives*, Jacob Branch, p. 413.
15. Ibid., Joe Barnes, p. 176.
16. Ibid., Tobe Zollicoffer, p. 4323.
17. Ibid., Andy Anderson, pp. 50–51.
18. Scott (William T.) Papers, Harrison County Museum.

trial complex on Cedar Grove plantation. With his slaves he operated factories that turned out material of various kinds, blankets, yarns, and shoes.[19]

At Liendo, a recruitment center named Camp Groce was established. Hundreds of boots and hooves trampled the manicured lawns and gardens of the plantation. Later in the war Camp Groce was converted to a prisoner-of-war camp and housed the Federal troops captured at the Battle of Galveston.[20]

Texans suffered the loss of one of their best-known heroes from the days of the Republic when Gen. Albert Sidney Johnston was killed in the Battle of Shiloh on April 6, 1862. Johnston, who had been one of the owners of China Grove plantation in Brazoria County, ironically had won the engagement in which he was killed. His death stirred the Texans to a renewed determination to win the war.

As time went on, more plantation mistresses found the full burden of managing plantations, with large numbers of slaves, on their shoulders. Although she was only in her mid-thirties, Sarah Devereux's hair turned gray as she struggled to manage Monte Verdi and rear her four young sons.[21] Inflation, ever-increasing demands of the Confederacy for plantation goods, and shortages of important items such as the cards needed to prepare wool for spinning were constant worries.

In 1864, Rebecca Adams wrote her husband from Fairfield plantation that she had traded one hundred bushels of corn for three pounds of sugar and had paid "$21 for coffee pot and 4 tin cups, $10 for a quire of paper, and $100 to Mrs. Garrett [a teacher] for three months." But Rebecca refused to pay one hundred dollars for a calico dress that she wanted.[22]

At the other end of the state, up on the Red River, the mistress of Glen Eden plantation performed a service for the Confederacy that earned her the title of "Paul Revere of the Civil War." One night a troop of Confederate soldiers under the command of Col. James Bourland came to Glen Eden. Coming from the south and headed for Fort Washita across the border, they were running just ahead of a troop of Union scouts.

Bourland and his men stopped only briefly at Glen Eden and then headed across the river to the fort. In a few minutes the Northern scouts came galloping into the yard and demanded lodging for the night. Sophia Butts (Porter), the widowed mistress of the plantation, pumped the officers for information, gave them the key to her famous wine cellar, and waited. When she judged that the men were sufficiently inebriated not to notice her absence, she slipped out to the log barn—only to find that all of the horses were in the pasture. Discovering an old mule in the lot, she saddled him and

19. Plantation file, Harrison County Museum.
20. Groce (Jared E. and Leonard W.) Family Papers, Waller County Public Library.
21. Dorman H. Winfrey, *Julien Sidney Devereux and His Monte Verdi Plantation*, pp. 134−35.
22. Rebecca Adams to Robert Adams, Jan. 28, 1864, Gary D. Woods, comp., *The Hicks-Adams-Bass-Floyd-Pattillo and Collateral Lines, Together with Family Letters, 1840−1868*, pp. 356−57.

prodded him along the river road to the ferry. The ferryman was fast asleep, and fearing he would make a noise and raise an alarm if she awakened him, she plunged the mule into the treacherous waters of the Red River. The mule, having no desire to be a hero, balked and tried to turn back. Sophia kicked and beat him till they reached the opposite bank. Soaked and almost frozen from the cold, she rode to the house of friends and got a quilt to wrap around her for the rest of her twenty-five-mile journey. Finally she reached the Confederate troops and relayed the valuable information concerning the Federal plans. Then, without resting, she turned the mule homeward and went back to Glen Eden, where the Union soldiers were in a drunken stupor, blissfully ignorant of her mission.[23]

As the war continued, the once elegantly dressed white women were forced to wear homespun dresses in their mansions; they had bonnets of corn shucks or wheat straw and homemade shoes and gloves. They ate plain food, had sweets only rarely, and experimented with grains, seeds, dandelion roots, and skins of fruits and vegetables trying to find a substitute for the sorely missed coffee. They burned corncobs and used the ashes for soda, and they endeavored to extract sugar from watermelons.

Luxuries and resort trips became only pleasant memories. Life came full circle as Texas plantations became almost as completely self-sustaining as they had been in the early days of settlement. When plantation owner Jon Winfield Scott Dancy of Fayette County was buried in February of 1865, his body was dressed in a fine wool suit from wool grown on his sheep, spun and woven by his slaves, cut out and sewed by his wife. The spinners and weavers on his plantation also made all the blankets, towels, slave clothing, hats, and shoes needed.[24]

One of the great frustrations of the Civil War for those back on the plantations was the scarcity of news and the slowness of the mail, which had never been speedy. In 1862 it took a month for a letter to travel from Rebecca Adams on a plantation in Fairfield to her father on his plantation near Columbia, a distance of just over two hundred miles. Letters from Texas soldiers on faraway battlefields might take many months to reach the addressee and often were lost or deliberately destroyed along the way.

Rumors, however, traveled on faster currents and caused much anxiety. After a battle was reported, there could be a delay of weeks before accurate lists of the survivors and the dead were received. Therefore, when anyone received a letter containing details of fighting and the names of acquaintances involved, these precious documents were widely shared. Reports of illnesses and deaths among Terry's Texas Rangers greatly worried the Perry and Wharton families until a letter from a friend reassured them. From this

23. *Handbook of Texas* II, 395; Mrs. J. W. Johnson, interview with Hazel B. Green, Woodville, Tex., n.d., transcript, Barker Texas History Center; Coffee (Holland) Papers, Barker Texas History Center.
24. Dancy (John Winfield Scott) Papers, Barker Texas History Center.

letter they learned that Perry Bryan (Emily Perry's grandson) was alive, although he had been wounded, and that John Wharton had survived the battles he had taken part in.[25]

All during the war, plantation owners whose land lay close to Texas' borders had to face the very real threat of invasion by the enemy. Many of the families along the Gulf Coast could hear Union guns bombarding coastal towns. Stephen Perry, who had inherited Peach Point when his parents died, went off to war as a volunteer, leaving his wife Sarah to manage the crops and the slaves and to care for their small children. The sound of the guns only a few miles away plus the wild behavior of some of the Confederate troops stationed in the area caused her to retreat temporarily with her children to the inland town of Independence. During her absence from Peach Point, Confederate troops stationed nearby kept their horses in her yard and broke down her trees and uprooted her shrubbery.

East Texas landowners also had to be constantly watchful of the long border in that area, with its many vulnerable spots. There were well-substantiated reports that Northern leaders had detailed plans to force Texas to supply beef to the Union armies. For this purpose, the Federals acquired extensive knowledge of the topography, weather, and feasible routes through the area. It seemed certain to the residents that it was only a matter of time before they were invaded by Federal troops.[26]

A severe drought in 1862 caused crop failures and short rations on Texas plantations, with periods of actual hunger on some. Even affluent planter Hamblin Bass, who reported owning 223 slaves in the 1860 census, suffered when the vegetable garden he had planted twice failed to come up, and his four hundred acres of corn only made two bushels an acre. He fed his slaves on his own pickled beef and on goats that he bought at a dollar apiece from a Mexican. "Never lived so poor in all my life," he told his son-in-law. These troubles were nothing, however, compared with the grief of losing his son, Eddie, who died of a fever in an army camp near Houston.[27]

By March of 1863, the government of the Confederate States of America was impressing slaves to work for the Confederacy. A notice dated November 9, 1863, appeared on the front page of the *Henderson Times* addressed to "the Slave-Holders of Rusk County," notifying them that the Confederate States required of them "one third of the ablebodied negro men between the ages of 18 and 50, to be employed immediately."[28] After General Magruder impressed thirty of Bass's slaves and took them to Galveston to

25. Marie Beth Jones, *Peach Point Plantation: The First 150 Years*, p. 136.

26. Ashbel Smith to Capt. Edmund P. Turner, Nov. 6, 1863, Confederate Southern Army Trans-Mississippi Dept. Correspondence, 1863–65, Smith (Ashbel) Papers, Barker Texas History Center.

27. Correspondence, Rebecca Adams, Dr. Robert Adams, Hamblin Bass, June 15, 1862, June 22, 1862, Aug. 2, 1862, June 13, 1864, Woods, comp., *Hicks-Adams-Bass-Floyd-Pattillo*, pp. 295–96, 297–98, 300–301, 371–72.

28. Winfrey, *Julien Sidney Devereux*, p. 132.

work on fortifications there, Bass heard they were not being cared for, and he immediately went to Galveston and got the slaves back. He reported to Rebecca that there was "great rejoicing" among his slaves.[29]

As the war effort depleted Confederate supplies, voluntary contributions by planters became insufficient. Everything was impressed by the military authorities—beef, corn, hogs—and in return the farmers got worthless IOUs. In March of 1863, Sarah Devereux furnished the Confederacy a hundred bushels of corn at two dollars per bushel and more than fifty-five hundred pounds of fodder at two cents a pound. The officer who received the produce noted, "I have not pd. this acct. for want of funds."[30] The quantity of the cotton crop taken by the Confederate States increased from a tithe to a fifth and then to a half.

As the Union blockade tightened around Texas, getting cotton to market became increasingly difficult. Running it through the Galveston blockade was dangerous, and for a time, almost the only route was through Mexico. Paper money steadily declined in value until most traders would accept only gold or silver. Since food could not be bought, it became imperative for plantations to produce as much food as possible. The women, children, and older men left on the plantations were more dependent than ever on the slaves to produce the food and grain necessary to feed livestock and humans, as well as to supply their share to the Confederacy. Even more plantations had trusted slaves acting as overseers during the war.

Many of Texas' plantation families had close relatives in the North. Ashbel Smith lamented being cut off from his mother in Connecticut. And Sarah Perry's brother, Hiram Brown, who had also come to Texas, commented on the cruelty of a war in which he and his brother-in-law, Stephen, might be fighting against their kinfolk: "Do they ever think that some of their dearly gotten victories may have been gained over some one of the family who is fighting for everything he holds dear on earth His home his family and his principles?"[31]

What did the slaves on Texas plantations think about the Civil War? On isolated farms a few slaves were not aware there was a war going on, but these were only a few. Most slaves were well aware of the conflict. They felt the mounting tension of the white people; heard the Confederate songs; helped with the preparations as the white men made ready to leave to join the army, taking some of their own people also. The slaves shared the grief of the people in the big house over the death of a kindly master or one of "their" white sons. And they suffered the shortages and hardships of war and performed the extra labor it called for.

29. Hamblin Bass to Rebecca Adams, Mar. 2, 1863, Woods, comp., *Hicks-Adams-Bass-Floyd-Pattillo*, pp. 319 21.

30. "Receipt for Requisitioned Goods," A. P. Corley, Captain, Asst. Quartermaster, C.S.A., Apr. 10, 1864, Devereux (Julien Sidney) Papers, Barker Texas History Center.

31. Jones, *Peach Point Plantation*, p. 150.

Among the white plantation residents there were frightening rumors of threatened uprisings among slaves. In general, whites avoided talking about how the war was going in front of their slaves. But the grapevine was well established among blacks. Bits and pieces of news were carried from plantation to plantation by messengers, carriage drivers, visiting husbands, and by hired-out workers. In front of their owners, slaves kept their eyes and ears open and their mouths shut. But when they were alone in their cabins at night they whispered to each other about the "Freedom War." As they smoked corncob pipes and stirred the ashes with a poker to rake out the roasted sweet potatoes, they talked in low tones about what they would do when Mr. Lincoln set them free. There were scary rumors to speculate on. The worst were that white Southerners would kill their slaves rather than free them or that all slaves would be put on ships and sent back to Africa.

During the war a small number of slaves ran away from Texas plantations to the North or to Mexico. But on the whole they continued to work and to wait—but with rising expectations.

The war came to an end in the spring, the crucial time for crops. Gov. Pendleton Murrah appointed W. P. Ballinger and Ashbel Smith as commissioners to make peace terms for Texas with the Union officials in New Orleans. In vain the commissioners argued with the Northern officials that slaves should be required to remain on their plantations until after the crops were made and gathered. But the Federal officials felt no sympathy for the planters, and told the commissioners that Texas planters would have to solve their own problems. A few planters tried to solve them by concealing the fact from their slaves that the war was over, but the Federal troops soon put an end to this practice. Most planters read the "freedom papers" to their slaves as soon as they received word that Gen. Gordon Granger had issued the emancipation proclamation for Texas on June 19, 1865.

AFTER THE WAR

No black ever forgot the emotion of that moment when he realized he was no longer a slave. Masters summoned slaves to the yard, read them the freedom order, and explained that they were as free as he to come and go, to work or not, and that no one owned them anymore—or would take the responsibility for their care any longer. Although most of them had expected this moment, the reality of it stunned many of them into silence. Others shouted "Hallelujah! Hallelujah!" and sang, danced, hugged each other, jumped fences, or performed whatever acrobatics they were capable of to express their joy, but some cried along with their former masters and mistresses.

After reading the freedom order to their former slaves, many plantation owners asked those who were willing if they would stay on and help make the crops in exchange for shelter, food, clothes, and a part of the crops.

Some planters who still had money offered a small wage. Many of the freed-men who had had kind masters recognized the security of remaining on the plantation, at least for a while. Others, euphoric at their first taste of freedom, could not escape the scene of their bondage fast enough and left with little more than the ragged clothes on their backs. Frequently they had no idea of where they would go or what they would do.

Perhaps the cruelest rumor that circulated among the blacks during the war was that along with freedom they would receive a portion of their master's estate, or at least a mule and forty acres of land as their own. Instead, they were turned loose with nothing but their freedom. Illiterate, ignorant of matters such as personal finances, and inexperienced in the ways of the world outside the tight little structure of the plantations where they had spent their lives, the freed slaves were the prey of unscrupulous individuals.

Hostile feelings harbored by some blacks spewed forth in acts of retaliation for past injustices. Their resentment toward white Southerners was encouraged by opportunistic Northerners called "carpetbaggers," who had come to Texas ostensibly to help the blacks adjust to freedom but found their way into lucrative or powerful positions over the defeated Southerners. Angry, frustrated whites organized the Ku Klux Klan in opposition to the carpetbaggers and their activities, which often involved courting and patronizing black voters. The Klan was soon committing atrocities that came to represent for the blacks a sinister counterpart to the dreaded "patter rollers" of slavery days. Some whites formed, in addition to the Klan, local vigilante groups, some of which had the sanction of the state government.

Scores of Texas freedmen supplied their needs by stealing and spent their time roaming and reveling in the freedom to do nothing at all, which they felt they deserved. Other freedmen survived the first phase of Reconstruction by remaining on the plantations and working under contract to their former owners. A contract between Leonard Groce of Liendo, and Lewis, a freedman, provided ". . . for himself [Lewis] and wife, Frances for the present year $100.00 and 20 acres of land: food, lodging, cloth for two suits, and medicine, they bind themselves to be polite." Groce noted on the back of the document, "settled in full—perfectly satisfactory. LWG Jan. 7, 1867."[32]

But the adjustment was not easy or complete for either former master or former slave. In almost every case the plantation had become rundown during the hard war years and had accumulated debts (some for slaves now freed). Those who had Confederate money could find nothing better to do with it than to give it to their children to play with. One plantation family made a fire screen out of their useless Confederate bonds. Treasury agents took possession of everything they could find that had belonged to the Confederacy, especially the cotton. The planters were naturally not eager to point out which cotton should have gone to the Confederate states. Confusion

32. Groce (Jared E. and Leonard W.) Family Papers, Waller County Public Library.

over cotton ownership led to bitterness and charges of fraud and cheating on both sides.

In addition, much of the planters' stock and supplies had fallen victim to the military of one side or the other. As one former slave described it: "First the 'Federate soldiers came and took some of the mules and coach-horses, then some more came for the corn. After while, 'twas the Yankee soldiers that came and took some more. When they got through tookin' there warn't much more tookin' to be done."[33]

As the horrors of Reconstruction grew, some planters conceived the idea of uprooting their families and going to South America to begin anew. In East Texas, John Pelham Border sold all his real estate in Texas and invested the money in outfitting a ship to carry his family and others to Brazil as colonists. Unhappily, before it sailed, the ship was pirated by the captain with all its supplies and never heard of again.[34]

In 1866 Leonard Groce tried to sell Liendo out of frustration and financial necessity. He noted in his diary, "May I never forget the impudence and ungrateful conduct of free negroes. The cause of my selling out and leaving my old home." He, too, planned to get a fresh start in Brazil until he discovered that the slaves there were going to be freed. The following year he was forced to take back his plantation when the purchasers could not make it pay for itself. In 1868 Leonard Groce was declared bankrupt, and five years later he died at Liendo. His sister, Sarah (Groce) Wharton, once the pampered "princess" of Bernardo and the former mistress of the splendid Eagle Island plantation, died poverty stricken in Houston in 1870.[35] Jared Groce's original big house at Bernardo was destroyed by the flood in 1870, and in 1882, the family offered the remaining buildings and land there for sale.

Stephen Perry and his wife Sarah received much patronizing advice from their Northern relatives about how they should manage Peach Point after the war. A cousin told Stephen Austin that the situation could be easily handled by making an agreement with the former slaves for "monthly cash wages with a patch of land for Garden and a House to live in." He added: "Gen Gidion W. Pellow writes the chief of the Freedmans Bureau that he has employed all the force he wanted (400 freedmen on his 3 plantations) and found no difficulty in obtaining them also that his Bro had obtained sufficient force for his 3 plantations and could have obtained 1000 more than they wanted and every thing was working like a charm."[36]

Another relative, Robert Baldwin, after accusing the South of collu-

33. Rawick, ed., *Texas Narratives*, Pauline Grice, p. 1603.

34. Border (John Pelham) Papers, privately held, Elisabeth Bates Nisbet, Houston.

35. In 1874 Leonard W. Groce, Jr. sold Elisabet Ney and Dr. Edmund Montgomery eleven hundred acres, "the homestead tract of the late Leonard W. Groce, Sr.," for $10,000, Groce (Jared E. and Leonard W.) Family Papers, Waller County Public Library.

36. Jones, *Peach Point Plantation*, p. 153.

sion and treachery, said, "Now you will see the advantage the South had in the beginning Laying a side the important and beloved advantage that one Southern Man could cope with five of the Mudsills of the Nation I presume You are all satisfied on this last Subject." He went on to express doubt that Southerners were "a law abiding people," giving as proof the fact that on his visits he had found them "armed with sword cane pistol & Dirk." Then he offered his advice:

> My desire is that you . . . should make the best of your present condition and advise you to Employ all your old Servants allowing them monthly wages Sanctioned by the Freedman officiall of your district and should not have the Money to pay make a sacrifice to obtain it. pay cash Monthly and you will always have reliable Help use no coertion when a Freedman refuses to work discharge and settle his a/c in presence of the official of the Freedman Bureau All persons in Mississippi Tennessee & Louisiana who pursue this course are making splended crops and will be highly renumorated.[37]

If Stephen and Sarah were able to laugh at this gratuitous advice, it must have been with bitterness for the idea of their being able to pay cash wages was indeed laughable. For five years, the plantation had barely fed the family and slaves, and the Confederate money they did have was worthless. However, the Perrys did keep the plantation in the family by selling some land to their own and their neighbors' former slaves on credit.[38]

Charles William Tait, who ran his large plantation near Columbus so efficiently by his well-planned rules, was able to pass his acres on to his descendants. Sixty years after his death in 1878, cotton, corn, and cattle were being raised by some of the descendants of his sixty-three slaves, who owned small portions of the six-thousand-acre plantation.[39]

Thomas Affleck, the mentor of his fellow planters, felt compelled to express his disgust and frustration at his freedman tenants in a letter to the *Galveston News*:

> For my part, I will endure as patiently as I can, until better can be done. But, not one hour longer will I endure the impudent leer and lounging movement; the drawling, disrespectful manner; the neglect of duties; the want of care of stock, gates left open, fences laid down and left down; horses and mules ridden off at night; the stealing of anything upon which they can lay their hands—the slighting or dodging of orders to be obeyed; the quarreling and fighting among themselves; the infamous debauching of mere children; the brutal language used, even in the hearing of white females and children, and other like conduct, which is of every day occurrence, where fear of immediate consequence does not even yet afford some check.[40]

37. Robert Baldwin to Stephen and Sarah Perry, Nov. 9, 1865, Perry (James F. and Stephen S.) Family Papers, Barker Texas History Center.
38. Jones, *Peach Point Plantation*, p. 154.
39. Tait (Charles William) Papers, Barker Texas History Center.
40. Thomas Affleck, letter to the editor of the *Galveston News* (Galveston, Tex.), Oct. 9, 1865.

Affleck, like others, tried to solve the problem by importing white laborers. He planned to hire cotters from England and Scotland, but a shortage of funds frustrated this venture. He then gave up the idea of being a planter, and at the time of his death he had turned his energies to setting up a meatpacking plant.

William T. Scott, who had owned more than a hundred slaves at the end of the war, refused to meet the demands of his former bondsmen, who offered to farm his land on halves. He tried importing laborers from Georgia but never recovered his former station after the devastating war and its effects.[41]

Ashbel Smith held on to Evergreen and maintained his interest in improving farming methods and stock raising. He wrote numerous articles encouraging other planters to invest in modern machinery that would eliminate the need for a great many laborers.

Hamblin Bass wrote to his son-in-law that his first impulse after the defeat of the South was to leave Waldeck, but he thought better of it. He hired one hundred of his former slaves to work his extensive fields and got 1,000 acres planted in cotton, and 150 in corn, but he told Rebecca gloomily that he had "little hope of cultivating . . . for they will not work more than seven hours in the day nor more than 5 days in the week," which in the nineteenth century was less than the usual ten- or twelve-hour days, six days a week.

In July, 1866, Robert Adams went to Waldeck to visit his father-in-law, and wrote to Rebecca that Hamblin Bass's freedmen had quit work about July 1 and that "the army worm (catterpillar) has attacked his cotton." The blacks respected her father, Robert reported, "but do not always obey him." The picture Robert painted of Waldeck was not encouraging: ". . . weeds and grass are luxuriating in the sick soil and all look as if this place was deserted. Weeds and cuckle burrs are all over the plantation higher than corn and cotton; roads unkept; houses falling down & this is the common picture of the country." What the worms left of Bass's cotton crop was destroyed by torrential rains in September. He told Robert that his "destruction" was complete. "I am ruined—I have lived longer than life is worth living for." Bass did, however, rally for one last effort. He hired Scottish laborers—twenty men, one teenage boy, four women, and two small children. After eleven weeks at short rations at sea, they were ravenous. When they continued to eat an astonishing amount, Bass finally made an agreement with them to confine their rations to the same amounts that were issued by the army to its soldiers. He was pleased with their deportment toward him, their working habits (ten hours a day), and their good care of the livestock. But the following year

41. An article in the *Austin Daily Statesman* on Oct. 3, 1880, reported on a story in the *Marshall News Messenger* that said two of W. T. Scott's former slaves had gone to Liberia with their children. When they found the promised paradise to be more of a hell, they wrote to their former master, asking him to help them return to Texas. They promised to work hard to repay Scott, but the newspaper speculated that they would have to remain in Liberia as Scott would probably again refuse his former slaves' offer, given the sixteen-hundred-dollar per person cost for a return trip.

some of the Scots left for higher-paying jobs, and when the cotton worm again attacked his crop, he was unable to meet his mortgage payments. Waldeck then passed into the control of a New York company.[42]

The story of Henry Ware's Oak Grove plantation near Elysian Fields in East Texas has a happier ending. Ware was one of the few planters who prospered after the war. An enterprising and foresighted man, he had sent a large shipment of cotton to England before the war started. Consequently, there was $250,000 waiting for him in England at the end of the war. He had also built an industrial complex on his plantation and operated a thriving manufacturing business during the war. In the late 1860s he gave Oak Grove to his daughter and bought a still more stately mansion, Belle Grove, on the Mississippi River. This marble-and-brick edifice was said to be the most expensive house on the Mississippi.[43]

The Mills brothers, the owners of four plantations, had been the largest slaveholders in Texas, freeing about eight hundred slaves in 1865. The Millses struggled to plant with hired labor, but by 1873 they were bankrupt.[44]

Former planters like the Munsons and Binghams of Brazoria, who converted their operations to cattle raising, succeeded better than those who tried to cling to the old way of life in the turmoil of Reconstruction. In a matter of years, many of the former plantation holdings, like Waldeck, passed into the control of commission houses in New York, Galveston, and Houston. Today, thousands of acres that once were extensive cotton or cane fields are again woodlands or have become a part of ranches.

Some former slaves maintained their old relationships with their white families to some degree all of their lives. Some planters gave their former bondsmen a start in their new lives: a few acres of land, a team of mules, hogs, and chickens. Others gave them advice about going into business for themselves. A few white owners left land or livestock to their liberated slaves in their wills. A number of blacks kept in touch with their former masters and received an annual "pension" from them.

During the early years of freedom, most of the freed slaves worked on plantations or farms or as domestic servants. There was a gradual drift to other occupations as more of them were able to acquire training and education in other fields. But in 1910, when the first comprehensive data on black employment was published, 60 percent were still working in agriculture.[45]

"I expected different from what I got out of freedom I can tell you," John McAdams told his interviewer. "I was not expecting to be turned loose like a bunch of stray cattle, but that is exactly what they done to us." He was not one of those who expected to be given some of his master's land, but he

---

42. Robert Adams to Rebecca Adams, Feb. 11, 1867, and Feb. 25, 1867, Woods, comp., *Hicks-Adams-Bass-Floyd-Pattillo*, pp. 415–18.
43. John Blocker Ware, "The Ware House," typescript, Harrison County Museum.
44. *Handbook of Texas* II, 200.
45. *Handbook of Texas* III, 644.

had not expected to have so much difficulty in earning enough to live on. He had farmed, cleared land and done whatever other jobs he could find, often for "cents a day." Some of his employers had not paid him "because they knew they did not have to pay us and we could not make them pay us. Sometimes they would give us their old cast off clothes and that we could not eat, so that made us have steal lots so'es we could feed our kids."[46]

Sarah Wilson explained to her interviewer how share cropping worked:

> De w'ite man say he gwine see dat de sharecropper git somefin' eat an' some close ter wear up to a 'specified 'mount. An' de cropper he promise ter wukk de land lak de w'ite man want hit done, an' w'en de crop am gadered, de share-cropper he gotta pay half ob de corn and de cotton dat he make on de land as rent; an' he gotta pay fer all de groceries, close an' medecine an' doctor bills dat he had w'ile he makin' de crop.
>
> No ma'am, de w'ite man he don't gib de nigger no sho' nuff money, he jes' gib him a doodlum book an' in dis here book dar's little pieces all printed an' fixed up, an' de share-cropper he trades dese here little scraps ob paper down at de plantation sto' fer what he gwine git. But he can't go no whar else ter trade, only jes' on de plantation whar he makin' de crop. Dat er way de nigger man he can't go git drunk an' sech but de ole woman an' de kids dey git somefin' dey needs.[47]

It is easy to see how an unscrupulous landowner could cheat the workers under this system.

Eli Coleman told his interviewer:

> I was share cropper, and Mr. White Man, that was really when slavery begins for when we got our crop made he took every bit of it to pay our debts and had nothing left to buy winter clothes or pay Dr. bills and Maser he never owned us anymore. He didn't care what become of us as he wouldn't loose anything then if we got sick or died and it never mattered cause he could get another negro without it costing him anything.[48]

For some of the slaves changing locations was as difficult psychologically as it was physically, and they preferred to endure the evils they were familiar with rather than face others they did not know. Katie Darling, for example, remained with her former owners for six years, although she reported, "Mistress whip me after the war just like she did before."[49]

Among the former slaves who praised their master's kindness after freedom was Mary Glover. "Jedge Harper give every one of his slaves a sow apiece; he give 'em seeds, and saw to it dat dey had a staht."[50]

46. Rawick, ed., *Texas Narratives*, John McAdams, pp. 2474–75.
47. Ibid., Sarah Wilson, pp. 4221–22.
48. Ibid., Eli Colman, p. 851.
49. Ibid., Katie Darling, p. 1051.
50. Ibid., Mary Glover, pp. 1513, 1519.

Jeptha (Doc) Choice, who had attended the plantation school with the white children, was eager for more education after the war. His former master paid twenty-five cents weekly tuition for him at a nearby school. He got a job teaching in a school that ran for six months, and between terms he farmed and took other jobs. Eventually he learned barbering and in 1888 opened a barbershop in Houston.[51]

Although some southerners hoped to keep the blacks illiterate, those who considered the problems of the former slaves' futures with intelligence and compassion realized that educating the freedmen was the only solution. Ashbel Smith wrote an article entitled "Education of the Negro" for the *Texas Christian Advocate* in which he pointed out that whether the southerners liked it or not, their former slaves would exercise their rights at the ballot box. Educating them, he said, was the only way their power and influence could be made to harmonize with the "common good" of both races.[52]

Smith railed against the "stupid prejudice" that kept Texans from acting in their own best interests as well as those of their former slaves. The fates of two plantations display the efforts to educate blacks in Texas as well as the prejudice that led to the destruction of one of the most beautiful of the antebellum mansions.

In Marshall, Texas, there once stood a spacious, white-columned mansion called Wyalucing, an Indian name said to mean "home of the friendless." The lovely young belle of the family was Lucy Holcombe, who married Col. Francis Pickens in the mansion a few years before the war started. When her husband was appointed U.S. ambassador to Russia by President Buchanan, the newlyweds went there to live. Lucy Holcombe Pickens became a favorite of Czarina Catherine II, who was godmother to the Pickenses' daughter. In 1860 Pickens was elected governor of South Carolina, and Lucy reigned during the war years as first lady of that state and as "Lady Lucy, Queen of the Confederacy." Her picture was on Confederate money, and she sold the jewelry given her by Czar Alexander II to outfit an army unit for the Confederacy, which became known as the Lucy Holcombe Legion.

During the Civil War, Wyalucing plantation served as the headquarters of the Trans-Mississippi Agency of the Confederate Post Office Department. In 1880 former slaves of Harrison County purchased Wyalucing for a school to be known as Bishop College. The school began with just the one building, and by 1945 there were twelve buildings, and Wyalucing had become the music building.

In 1961 the school was greatly expanded and moved to Dallas. A decision had to be made about what to do with the historic old music building. Some of those entrusted with the decision wanted to preserve it. But there were others who disliked the idea of its having been a part of a black college so much that they wanted it destroyed. In 1962 wreckers began work. They

51. Ibid., Jeptha ("Doc") Choice, pp. 705, 712.
52. Silverthorne, *Ashbel Smith*, pp. 194–95.

had great difficulty in tearing down the solid walls and beautiful columns. Within a few weeks, however, Wyalucing was demolished.[53]

In Waller County, a few miles from Hempstead, Col. Jared Ellison Kirby, a cousin of Leonard Groce, owned a plantation named Alta Vista, a Spanish name meaning "high view," because of its elevation. When Colonel Kirby died soon after the Civil War, his widow turned Alta Vista into a fashionable school for young ladies. But the school was not successful, and Mrs. Kirby offered the plantation to a group of commissioners headed by Ashbel Smith, who were searching for a site for the Agricultural and Mechanical College of Texas for the Benefit of Colored Youth, which had been authorized by the Fifteenth Legislature of Texas. The Kirby plantation was purchased by the state and renamed Prairie View, instead of Alta Vista. The manor house was called Kirby Hall until it was torn down. But the school remained and grew over the years, and thousands of its black graduates became leaders in their occupations and professions and in their communities. In 1963 Prairie View A&M became integrated.[54]

53. Holcombe Family Papers, Harrison County Museum; Elizabeth Brooks, *Prominent Women of Texas*, pp. 166–68; "Only Texas Girl Ever Pictured on Money," *Dallas Morning News*, May 19, 1929; *Handbook of Texas* I, 166, II, 374, 939, III, 84, 1133.

54. Silverthorne, *Ashbel Smith*, pp. 194–95; *Handbook of Texas* II, 406; III, 752–53.

For almost half a century the plantation owners were of major importance in influencing the destiny of Texas. Predominantly southern, Protestant, educated, wealthy, slaveholding gentry, they assumed leadership roles in colonizing, gaining independence, establishing schools and churches, developing river transportation, and bringing the railroads to Texas. They set standards for social behavior in their communities and held political positions at every level of government. And they were leaders in influencing Texas to join the Confederacy. They fought battles, wounded and were wounded, killed and were killed trying to preserve their way of life. In the end, the costs of the war and the freeing of the slaves, who embodied the planters' chief asset along with the land, bankrupted the plantation system. When the confusion of Reconstruction had passed, former masters and freedmen had to find new ways to coexist in a world that would never be the same.

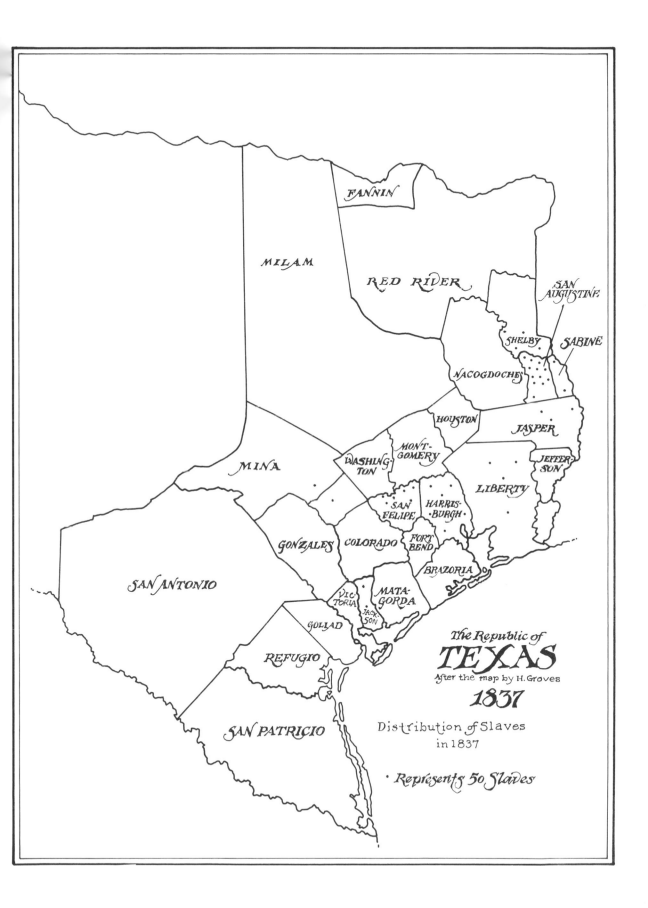

FANNIN

MILAM

RED RIVER

SAN AUGUSTINE

SHELBY

SABINE

NACOGDOCHES

HOUSTON

JASPER

MONT-GOMERY

WASHING-TON

MINA

LIBERTY

JEFFER-SON

SAN FELIPE

HARRIS-BURGH

GONZALES

COLORADO

FORT BEND

BRAZORIA

SAN ANTONIO

VIC-TORIA

MATA-GORDA

JACK-SON

GOLIAD

The Republic of
TEXAS
After the map by H. Groves
1837
Distribution of Slaves
in 1837

REFUGIO

· Represents 50 Slaves

SAN PATRICIO

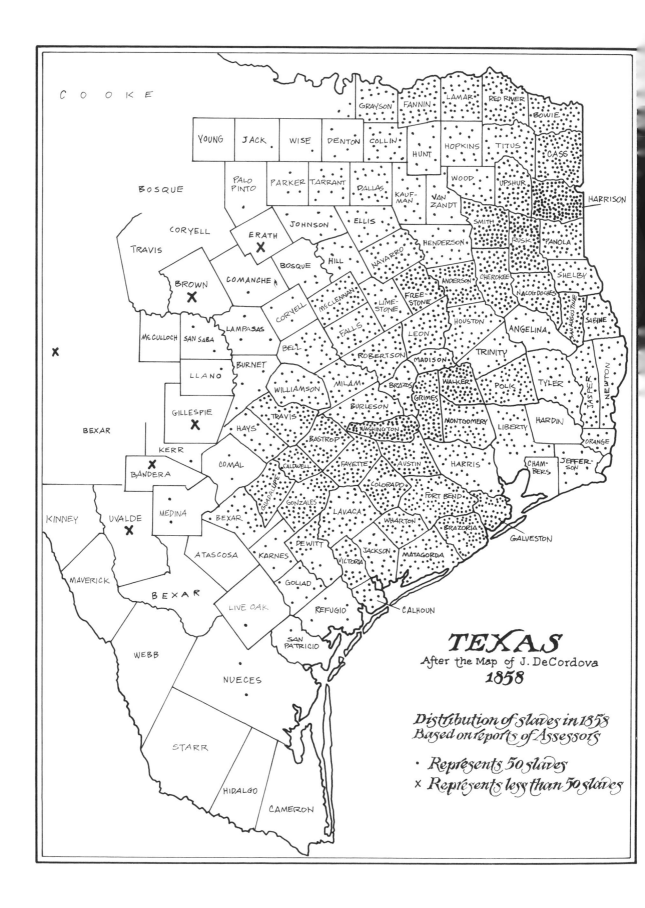

TEXAS
After the Map of J. DeCordova
1858

*Distribution of slaves in 1858
Based on reports of Assessors*

· *Represents 50 slaves*
× *Represents less than 50 slaves*

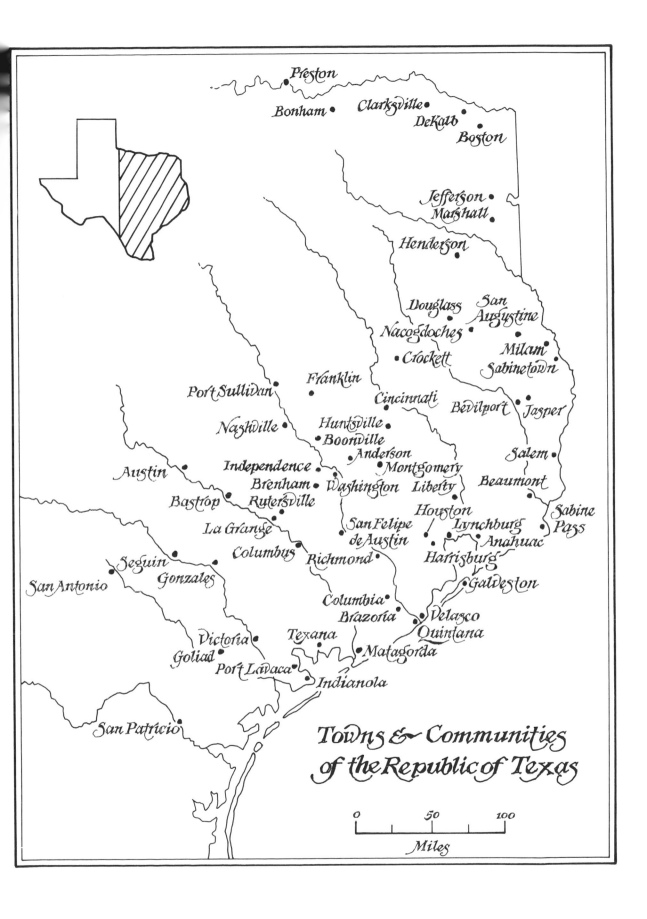

Preston

Bonham   Clarksville
DeKalb
Boston

Jefferson
Marshall

Henderson

Douglass   San
Augustine
Nacogdoches
Milam
Crockett   Sabinetown

Franklin
Cincinnati   Bevilport   Jasper
Port Sullivan
Nashville   Huntsville
Boonville   Salem
Anderson
Independence   Montgomery   Beaumont
Brenham   Washington   Liberty
Austin   Rutersville
Bastrop   Sabine
Houston   Lynchburg   Pass
La Grange   San Felipe   Anahuac
de Austin
Columbus   Richmond   Harrisburg
Seguin   Galveston
San Antonio   Gonzales
Columbia
Brazoria   Velasco
Quintana
Victoria   Texana
Goliad   Matagorda
Port Lavaca
Indianola

San Patricio   Towns & Communities
of the Republic of Texas

0   50   100

Miles

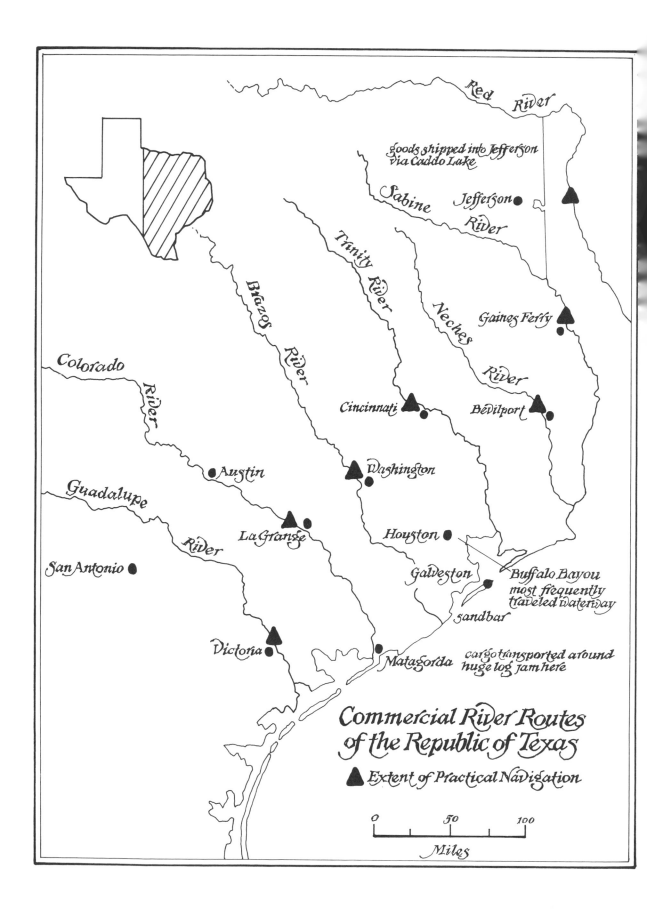

Red River

goods shipped into Jefferson
via Caddo Lake

Sabine

Jefferson ●

River

Trinity River

Neches

Gaines Ferry ▲
●

Brazos River

River

Colorado

Cincinnati ▲
●

Bevilport ▲
●

River

Washington ▲
●

Guadalupe

Austin ●

La Grange ▲ ▲

Houston ●

River

San Antonio ●

Galveston
●

Buffalo Bayou
most frequently
traveled waterway

sandbar

Victoria ▲
●

Matagorda
●

cargo transported around
huge log jam here

Commercial River Routes
of the Republic of Texas

▲ Extent of Practical Navigation

0   50   100

Miles

BIBLIOGRAPHY

MANUSCRIPTS AND DOCUMENTS

Adriance (John) Papers, 1822–1903. Barker Texas History Center, University of Texas at Austin.

Affleck (Thomas) Papers, 1830–1866. Rosenberg Library, Galveston.

Affleck's (Thomas) Scrapbook. Texas State Library Archives, Austin.

Armstrong, James Curtis. "The History of Harrison County, Texas." M.A. thesis, Stephen F. Austin State Teachers College, 1926.

Ashbury (Samuel E.) Collection. Texas State Library Archives, Austin.

Austin (Moses and Stephen F.) Papers, 1785–1836. Barker Texas History Center, University of Texas at Austin.

Bell, Josiah H. Will no. 26, Brazoria County Courthouse, Angleton.

Black, Sarah H., Diary. Privately held, Ruth Munson Smith, Angleton.

Black (William W.) Papers, 1845–1870. Barker Texas History Center, University of Texas at Austin.

Black History Collection, 1826–1867. Barker Texas History Center, University of Texas at Austin.

Blackshear (Thomas Edward) Papers, 1830–1889. Barker Texas History Center, University of Texas at Austin.

Bollaert (William) Papers, 1837–1849. Barker Texas History Center, University of Texas at Austin.

Border (John Pelham) Papers. Privately held, Elisabeth Bates Nisbet, Houston.

Brazoria County Deed Records. County Clerk's Office, Angleton.

Brazoria County Probate Files. County Clerk's Office, Angleton.

Brazoria County Records, vol. J. (Nov. 16, 1859). Brazoria County Historical Museum, Angleton.

Brazoria County Scrapbook. Barker Texas History Center, University of Texas at Austin.

Brockman, John Martin. "Port Sullivan: Ghost Town." M.A. thesis, Texas A&M University, 1968.

Bryan (Guy M.) Papers, 1821–1880. Barker Texas History Center, University of Texas at Austin.

Bryan (James Perry) Papers. Texas State Library Archives, Austin.

Bryan (James Perry) Papers, 1820–1870. Barker Texas History Center, University of Texas at Austin.

Bullard, Lucille Blackburn, ed. 1860 Federal Census, Marion County, Texas. Jefferson Historical Museum, Jefferson.

Canebrake Plantation Records, 1856–1858. Barker Texas History Center, University of Texas at Austin.

Carpenter (Laura Clarke) Papers, 1850–1860. Barker Texas History Center, University of Texas at Austin.

Cartwright (Matthew) Papers, 1830–1859. Barker Texas History Center, University of Texas at Austin.

Chambers (Thomas W.) Papers, 1805–1880. Barker Texas History Center, University of Texas at Austin.

Coffee (Holland) Papers, 1837–1871. Barker Texas History Center, University of Texas at Austin.

Colorado County Scrapbook. Barker Texas History Center, University of Texas at Austin.

Corbin, Harriet T. (Porter). "A History and Genealogy of Chief William McIntosh, Jr. and His Known Descendants." Typescript. Jefferson Historical Museum, Jefferson.

Curlee, Abigail. "A Study of Texas Slave Plantations, 1822–1865." Ph.D. dissertation, University of Texas, 1932.

Dancy (Jon Winfield Scott) Papers, 1836–1856. Barker Texas History Center, University of Texas at Austin.

Devereux (Julien Sidney) Papers, 1835–1856. Barker Texas History Center, University of Texas at Austin.

Dienst (Alexander) Papers, 1826–1870. Barker Texas History Center, University of Texas at Austin.

Duncan (Green C.) Papers, 1853–1880. Barker Texas History Center, University of Texas at Austin.

Fitch, Rebecca Fortson. "The Use of Native Materials in the Ante Bellum Buildings of Harrison County, Texas." M.A. thesis, North Texas State College, 1952.

Foster (Harry A.) Family Documents. Log Cabin Village Museum, Fort Worth.

Foster (Harry A.) Papers. Privately held, J. W. Foster, Jr., Calvert.

Freeman (Williamson) Collection. Privately held, Jesse M. DeWare IV, Jefferson.

Groce (Jared E. and Leonard W.) Family Papers. Waller County Public Library, Hempstead, Texas.

Groce, Leonard Waller. "Diary of Leonard Waller Groce, 1866–1867." Transcript. Barker Texas History Center, University of Texas at Austin.

Groce, Leonard Waller. "Personal Recollection of Leonard Waller Groce, as Related to his Son, William Wharton Groce." Transcript. Barker Texas History Center, University of Texas at Austin.

Hagerty (Rebecca McIntosh Hawkins) Papers, 1823–1880. Barker Texas History Center, University of Texas at Austin.

Hagerty (Rebecca McIntosh Hawkins) Papers. Jefferson Historical Museum, Jefferson.

Haley (T. P.) Collection, 1838–1898. Texas State Library Archives, Austin.

Hanke, Frank O. "Reminiscences of Bastrop County," August, 1931. Typescript. Texas State Library Archives, Austin.

Hanrick (Edward) Papers, 1840–1865. Barker Texas History Center, University of Texas at Austin.

Hayes, Rutherford B. Texas Diary, 1848–1849. Galley proofs. Barker Texas History Center, University of Texas at Austin.

Holcombe (Beverly Lafayette) Papers. Harrison County Museum, Marshall.

Holley (Mary Austin) Letters, 1808–1832. Texas State Library Archives, Austin.

Holley (Mary Austin) Papers, 1829–1846. Barker Texas History Center, University of Texas at Austin.

Hughes, Inez H. "Landmarks of Harrison County: Plantation Homes." Typescript of speech, November 5, 1970. Harrison County Museum, Marshall.

Ingram (Ira) Papers. Manuscript Division, Library of Congress, Washington, D.C.

Johnson, Mrs. J. W. Interview with Hazel B. Greene, Woodville, Tex., n.d. Transcript. Barker Texas History Center, University of Texas at Austin.

Jones (Anson) Papers, 1838–1858. Texas State Library Archives, Austin.

Kemp (Louis W.) Papers, 1819–1836. "Fannin Notes." Barker Texas History Center, University of Texas at Austin.

Lale, Max S. "Edgemont." (July 6, 1981) Typescript. Harrison County Museum, Marshall.

Ledbetter (Lena Dancy) Papers, 1830–1890. Barker Texas History Center, University of Texas at Austin.

"Liendo Plantation." Waller County Historical Commission. Texas State Library Archives, Austin.

Lincecum (Gideon) Papers, 1829–1860. Barker Texas History Center, University of Texas at Austin.

Mills (Robert) Papers. Barker Texas History Center, University of Texas at Austin.

Moseley (Samuel F.) Journal. Jefferson Historical Museum, Jefferson.

Neblett (Lizzie Scott) Papers, 1849–1870. Barker Texas History Center, University of Texas at Austin.

Perry, Hally Bryan. "Family Notes by Request." Typescript. Texas State Library Archives, Austin.

Perry (James F. and Stephen S.) Papers, 1831–1863. Barker Texas History Center, University of Texas at Austin.

Plantation file. Harrison County Museum, Marshall.

Platter, Allen Andrew. "Educational, Social, and Economic Characteristics of the Plantation Culture of Brazoria County, Texas." Ed.D. dissertation, University of Houston, 1961.

Puryear, Pamela Ashworth. Personal files, Navasota.

Rochelle, Levonne Durham, comp. "Notes on Early Residents of Brazoria County." Texas State Library Archives, Austin.

Rose (Preston R.) Papers, 1837–1875. Barker Texas History Center, University of Texas at Austin.

Scott (William T.) Papers. Harrison County Museum, Marshall.

Smith (Ashbel) Papers, 1823–1886. Barker Texas History Center, University of Texas at Austin.

Smith, T. L. "Plantations and Their Owners of Brazoria County, Texas." Texas State Library Archives, Austin.

Solms-Braunfels Archives, 1842–1862. Barker Texas History Center, University of Texas at Austin.

Stuart (Ben C.) Papers. Rosenberg Library, Galveston.

Sweeny (John) Family Papers. Privately held, John Bannister, Old Ocean.

Sweeny (John) Papers. Brazoria County Historical Museum, Angleton.

Tait (Charles William) Papers, 1844–1855. Barker Texas History Center, University of Texas at Austin.

Texas State Census for 1847. Texas State Library Archives, Austin.

U.S. Census for 1850, 1860. Texas State Library Archives, Austin.

U.S. House Executive Documents. Consul C. DeRonceray to Lewis Cass, August 22, 1860. 36th Cong., 2nd sess., IV, no. 7. Washington, D.C.: Government Printing Office, 1860.

Ware (Henry) Papers. Harrison County Museum, Marshall.

Ware, John Blocker. "The Ware House." Typescript. Harrison County Museum, Marshall.

Washington County Deed Records, Probate Minutes, Records of Final Estates, Washington County Courthouse, Brenham.

Webster (John) Plantation Journal. East Texas Baptist College Library, Marshall.

White (R. G.) Papers. Barker Texas History Center, University of Texas at Austin.

Works Progress Administration Records: Slave Stories. Barker Texas History Center, University of Texas at Austin.

Abshier, Mildred. *A History of Waller County, Texas*. Waco: Texian Press, 1973.

Affleck, Thomas. *Southern Rural Almanac and Plantation and Garden Calendar*. New Orleans: Office of the *Picayune*, 1852, 1860.

Alexander, Drury Blakeley. *Texas Homes of the Nineteenth Century*. Austin: University of Texas Press, 1966.

Almonte, Juan N. "Statistical Report on Texas," translated by C. E. Castañeda. *Southwestern Historical Quarterly* 28 (January, 1925): 177–91.

Anderson, John Q., ed. *Texas Folk Medicine*. Austin: Encino Press, 1970.

Ashburn, Karl E. "Slavery and Cotton Production in Texas." *Southwestern Social Science Quarterly* 14 (December, 1933): 257–71.

Baker, D. W. C., comp. *A Texas Scrap Book*. Facsimile reproduction of original. Austin: Steck, 1935.

Baker, J. W. *A History of Robertson County, Texas*. Waco: Texian Press, 1970.

Barker, Eugene C. "The African Slave Trade in Texas." *Quarterly of the Texas State Historical Association* 6 (October, 1902): 145–58.

———. "The Influence of Slavery in the Colonization of Texas." *Southwestern Historical Quarterly* 28 (July, 1924): 1–33.

———. *The Life of Stephen F. Austin, Founder of Texas, 1793–1836*. Nashville: Cokesbury Press, 1925.

Barker, Eugene C., ed. *The Austin Papers*, vols. 1 and 2, Washington, D.C.: American Historical Association, 1919–22; vol. 3, Austin: University of Texas, 1927.

Barr, Alwyn. *Black Texans: A History of Negroes in Texas, 1528–1971*. Austin: Pemberton Press, 1973.

Berlet, Sarah Wharton Groce. *Autobiography of A Spoon, 1828–1856*. Beaumont, Texas: LaBelle Printing Co., 1971.

Bertleth, Rosa Groce. "Jared Ellison Groce." *Southwestern Historical Quarterly* 20 (April, 1917): 358–68.

Blassingame, John W. *The Slave Community: Plantation Life in the Antebellum South*. New York: Oxford University Press, 1972.

Boatright, M. C., Wilson M. Hudson, and Allen Maxwell, eds. *Texas Folk and Folklore*. Dallas: Southern Methodist University Press, 1954.

Bollaert, William. *William Bollaert's Texas*. Edited by William Eugene Hollon and Ruth Lapham Butler. Norman: University of Oklahoma Press, 1956.

Bowers, Eugene W., and Evelyn Oppenheimer. *Red River Dust*. Waco: Word Books, 1968.

Bracken, Dorothy Kendall, and Maurine Whorton Redway. *Early Texas Homes*. Dallas: Southern Methodist University Press, 1956.

Brewer, J. Mason. *Dog Ghosts: The Word on the Brazos*. Austin: University of Texas Press, 1976.

Brooks, Elizabeth. *Prominent Women of Texas*. Akron, Ohio: Werner, 1896.

Brooks, Eugene Clyde. *The Story of Cotton and the Development of the Cotton States*. Chicago: Rand McNally and Company, 1911.

Brown, Lawrence L. *The Episcopal Church in Texas, 1838–1874*. Austin: The Church Historical Society, 1963.

Bugbee, Lester G. "The Old Three Hundred." *Quarterly of the Texas State Historical Association* 1 (October, 1897): 108–17.

———. "Slavery in Early Texas." *Political Science Quarterly* 13 (September, 1898): 389–412, 648–68.

Calvert, Robert A. "Nineteenth-Century Farmers, Cotton and Prosperity." *Southwestern Historical Quarterly* 73 (April, 1970): 509–21.

Campbell, Randolph B. *A Southern Community in Crisis: Harrison County, Texas, 1850–1880*. Austin: Texas State Historical Association, 1983.

Campbell, Randolph B., and Richard G. Lowe. "Some Economic Aspects of Antebellum Texas Agriculture." *Southwestern Historical Quarterly* 82 (April, 1979): 351–78.

———. *Wealth and Power in Antebellum Texas*. College Station: Texas A&M University Press, 1977.

Carter, James David. *Education and Masonry in Texas, 1846 to 1861*. Waco: Committee on Masonic Education and Service for The Grand Lodge of Texas, 1964.

Clark, Anne, comp. *Historic Homes of San Augustine*. Austin: Encino Press, 1972.

Coleman, Ann Raney. *Victorian Lady on the Texas Frontier: The Journal of Ann Raney Coleman*. Edited by C. Richard King. Norman: University of Oklahoma Press, 1971.

Commerce. (Pamphlet) Washington, Tex.: Star of the Republic Museum, 1983.

The Complete Encyclopedia of Arms and Weapons. Edited by Leonid Tarassuk and Claude Blair. New York: Simon and Schuster, 1979.

Connor, Seymour V. *Texas: A History*. Arlington Heights, Ill.: AHM Publishing, 1971.

"Cotton Gins of Waller County, 1825–1976." Brenham: Waller County Historical Commission, 1981.

Creighton, James A. *A Narrative History of Brazoria County*. Waco: Texian Press, 1975.

Crocket, George Louis. *Two Centuries in East Texas: A History of San Augustine County and Surrounding Territory from 1685*. Dallas: Southwest Press, 1932. Facsimile reproduction for the Christ Episcopal Church, San Augustine, 1982.

Curlee, Abigail. The History of a Texas Slave Plantation, 1831–1863." *Southwestern Historical Quarterly* 26 (October, 1922): 79–127.

Dobie, Bertha McKee. "Tales and Rhymes of a Texas Household." *Texas and Southwestern Lore*. Austin: Texas Folk-Lore Society, 1927.

Dobie, J. Frank. *The Longhorns*. Boston: Little, Brown, 1941.

————. *Man, Bird and Beast*. Austin: Texas Folk-Lore Society, 1930.

————. *The Mustangs*. Austin: University of Texas Press, 1952.

Eaton, Clement. *A History of the Old South*. New York: Macmillan, 1949.

Exley, Jo Ella Powell, ed. *Texas Tears and Texas Sunshine: Voices of Frontier Women*. College Station: Texas A&M University Press, 1985.

Fehrenbach, T. R. *Lone Star: A History of Texas and the Texans*. New York: Macmillan, 1968.

————. *Seven Keys to Texas*. El Paso: Texas Western Press, 1983.

Fisher, Orceneth. *Texas in 1840*. Reprint. Waco: Texian Press, 1964.

[Fiske?] *A Visit to Texas*. Reprint. Austin: Steck, 1952.

Foote, Henry Stuart. *Texas and the Texans*. 2 vols. Philadelphia: Thomas Cowperthwait and Company, 1841.

Fornell, Earl Wesley. *The Galveston Era: The Texas Crescent on the Eve of Secession*. Austin: University of Texas Press, 1961.

Friend, Llerena B. "The Texan of 1860." *Southwestern Historical Quarterly* 62 (July, 1958): 1–17.

Gambrell, Herbert Pickens. *Anson Jones, the Last President of Texas*. Austin: University of Texas Press, 1964.

Gammel, H. P. N., comp. *The Laws of Texas, 1822–1897*. 4 vols. Austin: Gammel Book Company, 1898.

Greer, Jack Thorndyke. *Leaves from a Family Album*. Edited by Jane Judge Greer. Waco: Texian Press, 1975.

Groce, William Wharton. "Major General John A. Wharton." *Southwestern Historical Quarterly* 19 (January, 1916): 271–78.

The Handbook of Texas, vols. 1 and 2. Austin: Texas State Historical Association, 1952; vol. 3. Austin: Texas State Historical Association, 1976.

Hansom, Otho Anne. *Parade of the Pioneers*. Dallas: Tandy Publishing, 1935.

Harris, Dilue Rose. "The Reminiscences of Mrs. Dilue Harris." *Quarterly of the Texas State Historical Association* 4 (October, 1900): 85–127; 4 (January, 1901): 155–89; 7 (January, 1904): 214–22.

Hilliard, Sam Bowers. *Hog Meat and Hoecake: Food Supply in the Old South*. Carbondale: Southern Illinois University Press, 1972.

History of Texas: Together with a Biographical History of Milam, Williamson, Bastrop, Travis, Lee, and Burleson Counties. Chicago: Lewis Publishing, 1893.

Hodge, Floy Crandall. *A History of Fannin County*. Hereford, Tex.: Pioneer Publishers, 1966.

Hogan, William Ransom. *The Texas Republic: A Social and Economic History*. Austin: University of Texas Press, 1969.

Holbrook, Abigail Curlee. "Cotton Marketing in Antebellum Texas." *Southwestern Historical Quarterly* 73 (April, 1970): 431–55.

————. "A Glimpse of Life on Antebellum Slave Plantations in Texas." *Southwestern Historical Quarterly* 76 (April, 1973): 361–83.

Holley, Mary Austin. *Texas*. Reprint. Austin: Steck, 1935.

Hornung, Clarence P. *Wheels across America*. New York: A. S. Barnes and Company, 1959.

Houstoun, Matilda Charlotte. *Texas and the Gulf of Mexico, or Yachting in the New World*. 2 vols. London: John Murray, 1844.

Jones, Marie Beth. *Peach Point Plantation: The First 150 Years*. Waco: Texian Press, 1982.

Jordan, Terry G. *Texas Log Buildings: A Folk Architecture*. Austin: University of Texas Press, 1978.

Kennedy, William. *Texas: The Rise, Progress and Prospects of the Republic of Texas*. Reprint. Fort Worth: The Molyneaux Craftsmen, 1925.

Kenney, M. M. "Recollections of Early Schools." *Quarterly of the Texas State Historical Association* (April, 1898): 285–96.

Kirkland, Elithe Hamilton. *Love Is a Wild Assault*. New York: Doubleday, 1959.

Kybalová, Ludmila, Olga Herbenoóá, and Milena Lamarová. *The Pictorial Encyclopedia of Fashion*. New York: Crown Publishers, 1968.

Lale, Max S., and Randolph B. Campbell, eds. "The Plantation Journal of John B. Webster, February 17, 1858–November 5, 1859." *Southwestern Historical Quarterly* 84 (July, 1980): 49–79.

Little, Carol Morris. *Historic Harrison County: As Preserved through Official Texas Historical Markers*. Longview: Hudson Printing, 1984.

Lomax, John A., and Alan Lomax. *Our Singing Country: A Second Volume of American Ballads and Folk Songs*. New York: Macmillan, 1941.

Looscan, Adela B. "Harris County, 1822–1845." *Southwestern Historical Quarterly* 19 (July, 1915): 37–64.

McClinton, Katharine M. *The Complete Book of American Country Antiques*. New York: Coward, McCann, 1967.

McCormick, Andrew Phelps. *Scotch-Irish in Ireland and in America, as Shown in Sketches of the Pioneer Scotch-Irish Families McCormick, Stevenson, McKenzie, and Bell in North Carolina, Kentucky, Missouri, and Texas*. N.p.: privately printed, 1897.

McLean, John H. *Reminiscences of Rev. Jno. H. McLean, A.M., D.P.* Nashville: Smith and Lamar, 1918.

McLean, Malcolm D., comp. and ed. *Papers Concerning Robertson's Colony in Texas*. vol. 11. Arlington: University of Texas at Arlington Press, 1984.

Malone, Ann Patton. *Women on the Texas Frontier: A Cross-Cultural Perspective*. El Paso: Texas Western Press, 1983.

Matthews, Sallie Reynolds. *Interwoven: A Pioneer Chronicle*. Reprint. College Station: Texas A&M University Press, 1982.

Merk, Frederick. *Slavery and the Annexation of Texas*. New York: Alfred A. Knopf, 1972.

Middlebrooks, Andy J., and Glenna Middlebrooks. "Holland Coffee of Red River." *Southwestern Historical Quarterly* 69 (October, 1965): 145–61.

Miller, Robert Finney. "Early Presbyterianism in Texas as Seen by Rev. James Weston Miller, D.D." *Southwestern Historical Quarterly* 19 (October, 1915): 159–83.

Moore, Francis, Jr. *Map and Description of Texas, Containing Sketches of Its History, Geology, Geography and Statistics, with Concise Statements Relative to the Soil, Climate, Productions, Facilities of Transportation, Population of the Country; and Some Brief Remarks upon the Character and Customs of Its Inhabitants.* 1840. Reprint. Waco: Texian Press, 1965.

Muir, Andrew Forest, ed. *Texas in 1837: An Anonymous, Contemporary Narrative.* Austin: University of Texas Press, 1958.

Murphy, DuBose. "Early Days of the Protestant Episcopal Church in Texas." *Southwestern Historical Quarterly* 34 (April, 1931): 291–316.

Murry, Ellen N. *The Code of Honor: Dueling in America.* Washington, Tex.: Star of the Republic Museum, 1984.

Neville, A. W. *The Red River Valley Then and Now.* Paris, Tex.: North Texas Publishing, 1948.

Newcomb, W. W., Jr. *The Indians of Texas: From Prehistoric to Modern Times.* Austin: University of Texas Press, 1961.

Nixon, Pat Ireland. *The Medical Story of Early Texas, 1528–1853.* San Antonio: Mollie Bennett Lupe Memorial Fund, 1946.

Olmsted, Frederick Law. *Journey through Texas: A Saddletrip on the Southwestern Frontier.* Austin: von Boeckmann-Jones Press, 1962.

Owens, William A. *Tell Me a Story, Sing Me a Song: A Texas Chronicle.* Austin: University of Texas Press, 1983.

Partridge, Michael. *Farm Tools through the Ages.* Boston: New York Graphic Society, 1973.

Pearson, P. E. "Reminiscences of Judge Edwin Waller." *Quarterly of the Texas State Historical Association* 4 (July, 1900): 33–53.

Plummer, Betty. *Historic Homes of Washington County, 1821–1860.* San Marcos, Tex.: Rio Fresco Books, 1971.

Puryear, Pamela Ashworth, and Nath Winfield, Jr. *Sandbars and Sternwheelers: Steam Navigation on the Brazos.* College Station: Texas A&M University Press, 1976.

Ramsdell, Charles William. *Reconstruction in Texas.* Austin: University of Texas Press, 1970.

———. "Texas from the Fall of the Confederacy to the Beginning of Reconstruction." *Quarterly of the Texas State Historical Association* 11 (January, 1908): 199–219.

Rankin, Melinda. *Texas in 1850.* Boston: Damrell and Moore, 1850.

Rawick, George P., ed. *The American Slave: A Composite Autobiography.* Series 1 (vols. 4 and 5). Series 2 (vols. 2–10) *Texas Narratives.* Westport, Conn.: Greenwood Publishing Co., 1972–73.

———. *From Sundown to Sunup: The Making of the Black Community.* Westport, Conn.: Greenwood Publishing, 1972.

Red, William Stuart. *A History of the Presbyterian Church in Texas*. Austin: Steck, 1936.

Richardson, Rupert Norval, Ernest Wallace and Adrian N. Anderson. *Texas: The Lone Star State*. Englewood Cliffs, N.J.: Prentice-Hall, 1970.

Roemer, Ferdinand. *Texas: With Particular Reference to German Immigration*. Translated from the German by Oswald Mueller. San Antonio: Standard Printing, 1935.

Russell, Traylor. *Carpetbaggers, Scalawags and Others*. Waco: Texian Press, 1973.

Schmitz, Joseph William. *Thus They Lived: Social Life in the Republic of Texas*. San Antonio: Naylor, 1935.

Shuffler, R. Henderson. "Winedale Inn at Texas' Cultural Crossroad," *Texas Quarterly* 8 (Summer, 1965): 129–44.

Sibley, Marilyn McAdams. *Lone Stars and State Gazettes: Texas Newspapers before the Civil War*. College Station: Texas A&M University Press, 1983.

———. *Travelers in Texas, 1761–1860*. Austin: University of Texas Press, 1967.

Silverthorne, Elizabeth. *Ashbel Smith of Texas: Pioneer, Patriot, Statesman, 1805–1886*. College Station: Texas A&M University Press, 1982.

———. "Once Right in the Eyes of God." *Civil War Times Illustrated* 19 (December, 1980): 18–25.

Simkins, Francis Butler, and Charles Pierce Roland. *A History of the Old South*. New York: Alfred A. Knopf, 1972.

Sloane, Eric. *A Museum of Early American Tools*. New York: Ballantine Books, 1964.

———. *The Seasons of America Past*. New York: Funk and Wagnalls, 1958.

Smith, Ashbel. "A Brief Description of the Climate, Soil and Productions of Texas." Appendix to Henry Stuart Foote's *Texas and the Texans*. Philadelphia: Thomas Cowperthwait and Company, 1841.

Smithcors, J. F. *Evolution of the Veterinary Art*. Kansas City, Mo.: Veterinary Medicine Publishing, 1957.

———. *The Veterinarian in America, 1625–1975*. Santa Barbara, Calif.: American Veterinary Publications, 1975.

Smithwick, Noah. *The Evolution of a State or Recollections of Old Texas Days*. Compiled by Nanna Smithwick Donaldson. Austin: Steck, 1935. Reprint. Austin: University of Texas Press, 1983.

Stampp, Kenneth M. *The Peculiar Institution: Slavery in the Antebellum South*. New York: Vintage Books, 1956.

Streeter, Thomas Winthrop. *Bibliography of Texas, 1795–1845*. 5 vols. Cambridge: Harvard University Press, 1955–1960.

Strobel, Abner J. *The Old Plantations and Their Owners of Brazoria County, Texas*. Houston: The Union National Bank, 1926.

Taylor, Joe Gray. *Eating, Drinking and Visiting in the South: An Informal History*. Baton Rouge: Louisiana State University Press, 1982.

Taylor, Lonn. "The McGregor-Grimm House at Winedale, Texas." *The Magazine Antiques* 108 (September, 1975): 515–21.

Texas Almanac. Galveston: Richardson and Company, 1857, 1858, 1859, 1860, 1861.

Thrall, Homer S. *A History of Texas, from the Earliest Settlements to the Year 1885*. New York: University Publishing, 1885.

"Tour Guide through Varner-Hogg Plantation House Museum." (Leaflet) Texas Parks and Wildlife Department, July, 1984.

Tyler, Ronnie C., and Lawrence R. Murphy, eds. *The Slave Narratives of Texas*. Selected extracts. Austin: Encino Press, 1974.

Vigness, David M. *The Revolutionary Decades: The Saga of Texas, 1810–1836*. Austin: Steck-Vaughn, 1965.

Volz, Candace, ed. *Texana II: Cultural Heritage of the Plantation South*. Austin: Texas Historical Commission, 1982.

Wade, Amzina. "Recollections of a Child's Life on a Pioneer Plantation." *Chronicles of Smith County, Texas* (Winter, 1980).

Wallis, Jonnie Lockhart, and Laurance L. Hill, eds. *Sixty Years on the Brazos; the Life and Letters of Dr. John Washington Lockhart, 1824–1900*. Reprint. Waco: Texian Press, 1967.

Warwick, Edward, Henry C. Pitz, and Alexander Wyckoff. *Early American Dress*. New York: Bonanza Books, 1965.

Webb, Walter Prescott. "Christmas and New Year in Texas." Texas Collection. *Southwestern Historical Quarterly* 44 (January, 1941): 357–78.

White, Gifford. *The 1840 Census of the Republic of Texas*. Austin: Pemberton Press, 1966.

White, Raymond E. "Cotton Ginning in Texas to 1861." *Southwestern Historical Quarterly* 61 (October, 1957): 257–69.

White, William W. "The Texas Slave Insurrection of 1860." *Southwestern Historical Quarterly* 52 (January, 1949): 259–85.

Willett, C., and Phillis Cunnington. *The History of Underclothes*. London: Faber & Faber, 1951.

Williams, Annie Lee. *A History of Wharton County, 1846–1961*. Austin: von Boeckmann-Jones Co., 1964.

Williams, Jack K. *Dueling in the Old South: Vignettes of Social History*. College Station: Texas A&M University Press, 1980.

Williams, Robert W. "Thomas Affleck: Missionary to the Planter, the Farmer, and the Gardener." *Agricultural History* 31, no. 3 (1957): 40–48.

Winfield (Mr. and Mrs. Nath), comp. *All Our Yesterdays: A Brief History of Chappell Hill*. Waco: Texian Press, 1969.

Winfrey, Dorman H. *Julien Sidney Devereux and His Monte Verdi Plantation*. Waco: Texian Press, 1964.

Winkler, E. W., ed. "The Bryan-Hayes Correspondence." *Southwestern Historical Quarterly* 25, no. 2 (October, 1921): 98–120; no. 3 (January, 1922): 121–36; no. 4 (April, 1922): 274–99.

Woods, Gary D. comp. *The Hicks-Adams-Bass-Floyd-Pattillo and Collateral Lines, Together with Family Letters, 1840–1868*. Salado, Tex.: Anson Jones Press, 1963.

Wooster, Ralph A. "Life in Civil War East Texas." *East Texas Historical Journal* 3 (October, 1965): 93–102.

———. "Notes on Texas' Largest Slaveholders, 1860." *Southwestern Historical Quarterly* 65 (July, 1961): 72–79.

———. "Wealthy Texans, 1860." *Southwestern Historical Quarterly* 71 (October, 1967): 171.

Wooten, Dudley G., ed. *A Comprehensive History of Texas, 1685–1897*. 2 vols. Dallas: William G. Scarff, 1898.

NEWSPAPERS AND PERIODICALS

Austin Daily Statesman (Austin)
Brazos Courier (Brazoria)
Brazosport Facts (Freeport)
Civilian and Galveston Gazette (Galveston)
Dallas Morning News (Dallas)
Galvestonian (Galveston)
Gazette (Matagorda)
Houston Chronicle (Houston)
Houston Post (Houston)
Illustrated London News (London, England)
Longview Morning Journal (Longview)
Marshall News Messenger (Marshall)
Planter (Columbia)
Standard (Clarksville)
Telegraph and Texas Register (Columbia)
Telegraph & Texas Register (Houston)
Telegraph and Texas Register (San Felipe)
Texas Ranger and Lone Star (Washington)
Texas Republican (Brazoria)
Texas Republican (Marshall)
Texas State Gazette (Austin)
Washington-on-the-Brazos (Washington)

INTERVIEWS

Through two and a half years of research many people have kindly shared with me their knowledge of various facets of plantation life in Texas through informal conversations, by telephone and in person, and through letters. This list represents some of those whom I have interviewed extensively about specific plantations or specific artifacts or activities connected with plantations.

Anderson, Richard. (Edgemont plantation). Marshall, Texas, August 31, 1984.

Bannister, John. (Sweeny plantation). Old Ocean, Texas, November 12, 1984.

Bauman, Richard. (plantation music). Salado, Texas, October 28, 1984.

Blocker, Douglas. (Mimosa plantation). Telephone conversation, August 30, 1984.

Bullard, Lucille. (Marion County plantations). Jefferson, Texas, September 2, 3, 1984.

Bullock, Thomas A., and Jane Bullock. (Hutchinson-Korth Homestead and log cabin). Washington County, January 29, 1985.

Caldwell, Jim. (Edgemont and other Harrison County plantations). Marshall, Texas, August 31, 1984.

Cotton, Dorothy. (Levi Jordan plantation). Brazoria County, Texas, November 10, 1984.

Dorsey, Mrs. C. T. (Garrett plantation house). San Augustine, Texas, August 28, 1984.

Detering, Carl, Sr. (Liendo plantation). Hempstead, Texas, January 30, 1985.

DeWare IV, Jesse. (Freeman plantation). Jefferson, Texas, September 3, 1984.

Easterwood, Ed. (crops, food preparation). Salado, Texas, February 17, 1985, and numerous conversations.

Foster, Catherine. (Brazoria County plantations). Telephone conversation, November 12, 1984.

Foster, Mildred, and Joe Bill Foster. (Foster plantation). Calvert, Texas, December 27, 1984.

Goldberg, Mary Love Scott. (Harrison County plantations). Marshall, Texas, August 30, 1984.

Hughes, Inez. (Harrison County plantations). Telephone conversation, August 31, 1984.

Jones, Jerry E. (Lady Bird Johnson plantation home). Karnack, Texas, August 31, 1984.

Jones, Marie Beth. (Brazoria County plantations). Angleton, Texas, November 12, 1984.

Munson, Betty Bingham. (Bingham plantation). Telephone conversation, November 10, 1984.

Nisbet, Elisabeth Bates. (John Border plantation). Numerous telephone conversations, 1984–85.

Puryear, Pamela Ashworth. (central Texas plantations). Navasota, Texas, November 3, 4, 1984; January 28, 29, 1985.

Robertson, Lucille. (Robertson plantation). Salado, Texas. Numerous conversations.

Scott, John Thomas. (William T. Scott and William Pinckney Rose plantations). Bonham, Texas. March 10, 1985, and numerous conversations.

Smith, Ruth Munson. (Munson plantations). Angleton, Texas, November 9, 10, 11, 12, 1984.

Strange, Robert. (plantation carriages). Telephone conversation, February 22, and March 27, 1985.

Wallace, Carson. (guns and arms). Wallace Gun Works, Rosebud, Texas, February 20, 1985.

Winfrey, Dorman. (Monte Verdi plantation). Austin, Texas, September 12, 1984.

INDEX

Plantation Life in Texas was composed into type on the Linotron 202 digital phototypesetter in eleven point Bembo with two points of spacing between the lines. The calligraphic display was rendered by the book's illustrator, Charles Shaw. The book was designed by Jim Billingsley, composed by G & S Typesetters, Inc., printed offset by Thomson-Shore, Inc., and bound by John H. Dekker & Sons. The paper on which the book is printed bears acid-free characteristics for an effective life of at least three hundred years.

TEXAS A&M UNIVERSITY PRESS : COLLEGE STATION